**A Gestalt Institute
of Cleveland Publication**

ADOLESCENCE

Mark McConville

ADOLESCENCE

Psychotherapy and the Emergent Self

Jossey-Bass Publishers · San Francisco

A Gestalt Institute of Cleveland publication.

Substantial discounts on bulk quantities of Jossey-Bass books are available to corporations, professional associations, and other organizations. For details and discount information, contact the special sales department at Jossey-Bass Inc., Publishers (415) 433-1740; Fax (415) 433-0499.

For sales outside the United States, please contact your local Paramount Publishing International office.

 Manufactured in the United States of America on Lyons Falls Pathfinder Tradebook. This paper is acid-free and 100 percent totally chlorine-free.

Produced by *Publishing Professionals*, Eugene, Oregon.

Library of Congress Cataloging-in-Publication Data

McConville, Mark.
   Adolescence : psychotherapy and the emergent self / Mark McConville.
      p.   cm. — (Jossey Bass social and behavioral sciences series)
   Includes bibliographical references and index.
   ISBN 0-7879-0124-5
   1. Adolescent psychotherapy.   2. Adolescent psychology.
3. Gestalt psychology.   I. Title.   II. Series.
RJ503.M36   1995
616.89′ 14′ 0835—dc20   95-16964
                                                                          CIP

HB Printing   10 9 8 7 6 5 4 3 2 1   FIRST EDITION

For Jo

Contents

Preface

Years ago, when I was freshly out of graduate school, I had the good fortune of falling almost by accident into the field of adolescent psychotherapy. I was on the consultation and education staff of a large community mental health center at the time, in a job that required me to do a large amount of public speaking. But I was very nearly phobic about public speaking back then, and when a position opened up for a therapist to work with adolescents, I jumped at the chance—out of the frying pan and into the fire. It seemed like a good move to me.

I also thought it was something of an honor to be awarded the position, for which I was certain there must have been heavy competition. Several months later, a colleague confided to me that there had been no competition at all, and that the director had been relieved when I took the job. "Why," I asked. "Who wants to work with adolescents?" my colleague replied.

And so I learned quickly, in my little corner of the mental health world, that adolescents are the bane of many therapists' professional existence. Other staffers would offer encouragement when I came to them with my clinical questions and dilemmas, assuring me that I was doing fine, which meant that they were grateful to have their own caseloads thinned of teenagers. I also learned that mental health culture had its jokes about adolescents, at least in the mid-1970s. These expressed, beneath the humor, genuine perplexity and befuddlement about clinical work with this age group: "How do you treat adolescents?" began one standard quip. "Diagnose them as temporarily insane, put them on the waiting list, and get back to them in three years."

There were times when the wisdom of this clever (if unkind) riddle did not escape me, for my clients' behavior often did betray a certain degree of craziness, a style of decision making that often defied good sense. In spite of the best efforts of parents, teachers, youth ministers, and youth officers, to say nothing of the efforts of therapists like myself, adolescent clients chose to do things that seemed patently to violate their own self-interest. What I remember most clearly from those early years is my own deep frustration, which came from caring too much and not knowing enough. For example, I wanted to know why it was that when neutral, well-intentioned adults offered bits of perspective about life's path, about the probable outcome of dropping out of school, having unprotected sex, or indiscriminately inhaling toxic chemical substances, this wisdom was frequently met with a total lack of interest, even annoyance. I was told at the time by my older colleagues (that is, by nearly all my colleagues) that my relative youth was an asset to my work, and I think I believed it myself at the time. I no longer agree (at least where my own work is concerned), but I think this common belief—that adolescents will connect better with someone closer to their own age—reflects just how unconnected and alien most adults feel to kids who are in trouble.

In spite of my bewilderment (or perhaps because of it), I devoted those early years to the practical business of learning to form constructive connections—what John Meeks (1971) calls "fragile alliances"—with adolescent clients. I tried everything. I was straightforward. I was gentle and nonthreatening. I was confrontational. I was strategic. Once, when a fourteen-year-old girl steadfastly refused to leave the waiting room and come to my office, I sat down next to her and matter-of-factly congratulated her for being the best resistant client I had seen all month. I then slipped a folded dollar bill into the edge of her shoe, stood up, briefly sympathized with her mother for having such a strong-willed daughter, and left the waiting room. A phone call from the mother, later in the day, informed me (to my barely concealed delight) that the daughter was now willing to come back and meet with me. My success was short-lived, however: two weeks later she again refused to come, this time for good.

In general, the business of making truly therapeutic connections retained for me its mysterious and unpredictable character, its apparently hit-or-miss nature. I recall many times when I formed what felt like a useful relationship with a teenage client, with little discernible therapeutic effect when all was said and done. The presenting patterns of symptoms sometimes changed, but all too often they did not—in spite of what felt (for a while, at least) like good therapy.

Several years ago, I received a phone call from a twenty-four-year-old woman. She informed me that she had been a client of mine ten years before. Our work together, she announced with conviction, had saved her life. Before our scheduled appointment, and with much curiosity, I rooted through my old files and dug out my therapy notes, eager to read the record of my evident wizardry. What I found astonished me. I had seen her for a total of four visits. My notes from our four sessions merely told a story of mild frustration on my part. I had recorded not a single impression of anything therapeutic and had closed the case as a failure to engage my client. I wondered what she had found so helpful that she now regarded it as having saved her life.

"You told me that I wasn't crazy," she said. "You took me seriously when I said I thought my mother was crazy. It turned out that she was."

My client's brief contact with a neutral adult who took her seriously had left her feeling supported enough to trust her own perceptions of her mother's untreated mental illness. And, with that sliver of trust in herself, she had been able to pull herself out of the family orbit and begin to direct her own life. As an adult, it seemed to me, she had been doing an impressively competent job of it. And such, in short, were the mysteries of psychotherapy with adolescents: sometimes good therapy got next to nowhere, and sometimes minimal contact had profound effects.

My struggles and frustrations as I groped to establish therapeutic alliances with troubled and often uninterested adolescents led me, still early in my career, to turn to family therapy, whose working model was quite different from the one in which I had been trained, and which in the late 1970s was making a dramatic impact on treatment practices with symptomatic children and teenagers. What this new work made clear to me was the interconnectedness of adolescent behavior and family process. I learned, by reading Salvador Minuchin (1974), about the importance of maintaining hierarchical boundaries within families, and about how adolescent impulsivity sometimes becomes the directing force in families where the parents are unable to take charge. From Virginia Satir (1967) I learned how the process of marital communication becomes the axis around which family process organizes itself. And from Jay Haley (1973) I learned how the family, like the individual, evolves, well or badly, through discernibly different developmental stages as its children turn into adolescents. What became increasingly clear to me, as it did to many other therapists at the time, was that transactions among family members provide a powerful organizing context, or *ground,* for much of adolescent experience and behavior, and that if one is to make a consistent therapeutic difference with teenagers, this context must somehow be addressed. This seems elementary now, but at the time this idea was a revelation.

If the functional relationships between symptomatic adolescent behavior and the family environment became clearer to me through the work of family therapy researchers, the *phenomenology*—that is, the *sense and meaning*—of adolescent experience remained something of a mystery. Family therapy, after all, was and is not particularly interested in the subjective whys and wherefores of adolescent experience. This domain has received more careful attention from psychoanalytic writers, particularly in the brilliant work of Peter Blos (1979). According to Blos, changes in the adolescent's outward behavior—distancing from adults, intense ambivalence about dependency, changing relationships with both parents—are triggered primarily by the explosion of "libidinal energy" that marks the beginning of the second decade of life. The real business of adolescent development, from this point of view, is internal, or *intrapsychic,* and ultimately involves what Blos labels a "second individuation," wherein the child gains "independence from the internalized infantile objects" (p. 483). Its completion is marked by the intrapsychic harmonizing of primitive drives and ego functioning.

Blos's discussions of adolescent development offered me, with the aid of phenomenological extrapolation, extremely penetrating and valuable insights into the inner workings of adolescent experience and behavior. But his descriptions, like those found in most other traditional psychoanalytic writing, ultimately reduce the business of adolescent development to the contingencies of psy-chosexual maturation, losing much of the descriptive richness of adolescent culture, experience, and behavior.

Psychoanalytic writing on adolescence—perhaps *all* clinically inspired writing on adolescence—is also marked by a decidedly pathological slant. Adolescents as a group invite this, to be sure, by virtue of the patent irrationality of so much of their behavior and decision making. But this kind of judgment always operates implicitly from the standpoint of adult culture and common sense, both of which tend to overvalue conventional logic and conform-ity. This sort of mainstream thinking is always accentuated where children and adolescents are concerned. It often causes us, I be-lieve, to miss the hidden logic of the adolescent's creative if some-times "irrational" adjustment to the existential dilemmas of growing up. Most structured treatment programs, for example, judge the success of treatment by the adolescent client's acclimation to the "reality" of the treatment program and milieu (that is, by his or her ability to operate within its rules, accept consequences, and so on). And while this kind of adaptation is certainly important, especially for adolescents from understructured life circumstances, it seems to me that the genuine growth of my clients has always been more directly a function of *my* gradual acclimation to and understanding of *their particular* illogic. Time and again in therapy I have noted the beginnings of constructive behavioral change pre-cisely when an adolescent client's "temporary insanity" was begin-ning to seem not so crazy after all.

For ten years or so, my associate Marlene Blumenthal and I have given a workshop for professionals who work with adolescents. One of our activities in this workshop has been to ask the partici-pants to recollect, as concretely as possible, their own adolescent-era struggles. We have heard—from solid, stable, mature, successful, productive, committed people—many retrospective accounts of "in-sanity": stories of impulsive behavior, irrational decisions, alien-ation, loneliness, victimizing, and victimization. I have heard the same stories in my consulting room, from my clients and their parents—with one important difference, of course. We can see our workshop participants' struggles and troubles within the context of the outcomes, and so we can chart them as part of larger life his-tories, seen in perspective.

I have most often been left with the impression that the stories of our participants are not, for the most part, tales of pathology but instead stories of attempted and achieved development. I have come to the conclusion that in the fabric of troublesome, even dangerous, symptomatic behavior, what we witness is an individual's best effort at adjusting to the developmental imperative that, somehow, childhood be left behind and a sense of viable selfhood be attained. Where preparation for this challenge is insufficient, or where environmental support has been unavailable, a best effort can be frightening indeed, involving choices that may include criminal behavior, chemical anesthesia, and even suicide. But our adult anxiety about these possibilities leads us, I think, to lose our capacity, or our willingness, to consider phenomenology—that is, to enter the adolescent's experience and find out for ourselves how it actually does make a certain kind of developmental sense.

When then is adolescence? Is it a period? a phase? a kind of "temporary insanity"? Is it a necessary developmental stage, with tasks and processes of its own? Or is it just something in between the more important life phases of childhood and adulthood? How are we to describe and discuss it? Do we approach it largely in terms of what it is not, neither childhood nor adulthood? in terms of its own sequences and processes? What are its processes and tasks and their sequence? How do we turn any kind of developmental lens on a period that seems characterized first and foremost by change, that sometimes borders on chaos? How do we avoid the common pitfalls of models, which impose theoretical grids so neat and rigidly sequential that they seem neither to fit nor even to clarify any actual, messy, real-life case?

It seems to me that adolescence represents something broader, more comprehensive, than what I have found described in most developmental and family therapy literature. It is something more than sexual development, changing societal role expectations, or cognitive maturation. It is more than family patterns that change (or fail to change). But it certainly is all these things, and that is precisely the point I wish to make: adolescence involves something akin to a *paradigm change*, a bedrock alteration of existential status, a reorganization of the whole, which subsumes all these individual manifestations. And so it is not, in my opinion, just one of a series of equally transformative developmental stages. It is a literal recollecting of childhood, a radical reorganization of the psychological self for the journey that lies ahead.

Cultural traditions support me in my perspective, particularly traditions from primitive cultures, which almost universally single out adolescence as a special time, a time of transformation profound enough to warrant special rites and rituals that confirm the singular importance and irrevocable nature of the changes taking place.

The clinician who works with adolescents and their families can attest that this age group presents clinically like no other. Problems are seldom well defined, and clearly delineated *symptoms* are more the exception than the rule. More often, the therapist is confronted with a *situation*, an unfolding drama with a cast of characters on the family stage, and he or she is often struck by the knowledge that the playing out of this drama, the resolution of this situation, may affect the course of at least several lives, possibly for years to come. Typically, the therapist is handed a single thread protruding from a tangled knot. It may be a call from a colleague, from a school official, or even from a court or probation officer. Usually it is from a distraught parent. Something has happened. A fifteen-year-old boy has stormed out of the house in a rage and now refuses to come home. School officials have noticed a fourteen-year-old's abrupt change in peer associates, and the adolescent's grades have recently tumbled; substance use and abuse, even criminal behavior, may be manifested or suspected. A sixteen-year-old has withdrawn deeply from her family and shorn off most of her hair; now she writes desolate poetry about the pointlessness of living, having broken off any steadying contact with extrafamilial adults and rejected their influence the way the body rejects foreign tissue. The parents are left with the acutely painful feeling that their child—in soul if not in body, and for the time being, at least—is beyond their reach.

There are invariably supporting characters in the drama, too. A divorced father proves unreliable in his interest in and support of his children. One or both parents may be entirely absent, or abusive, or caught up in the personal chaos of life. A troubled, needy girlfriend or boyfriend has recently entered the picture and become the object of what is almost an obsession. An old partner in crime has recently returned from the detention center. A father or a mother has been promoted. A mother or a father has become depressed, relapsed into drinking or taking drugs, and so on and so on.

Nor does any of this happen in a developmental vacuum. There is always a history that asserts its relevance to the present situation: sometimes by virtue of its continuity, as when the present appears to grow naturally from childhood conditioning, and sometimes by virtue of its discontinuity, as when the present appears to break abruptly with the past. Parents may describe a child, difficult all along, who only now, in adolescence, has exceeded their capacity for control. Or they may describe a child who seems to have changed overnight, before their eyes, into someone they do not know. The problems of the parents themselves, other siblings, and the wider social field may also be long standing or recent. Custody of the adolescent may have moved from one parent to another, or to a grandparent, or to someone else entirely; and, again, these changes may be radically new or part of a long-standing pattern of chaotic caretaking arrangements and relationships.

For the clinician, there are always immediate decisions to be made. Is safety an issue? Is the child in danger? Should parents or other caretakers step up and assert control? Should they all adopt a palpably respectful posture of listening and dialogue, or something in between? Is the professional to insinuate himself or herself into this situation primarily as a *case manager*, one who offers guidance designed to gain access to resources and provide direction to the other adults involved? Is the situation one that calls for a *family therapeutic* response, one that addresses the process and dysfunction of the family system? Or would the situation best be served by the professional in the guise of an *individual therapist*, one who reaches out and establishes an adult lifeline with the alienated adolescent (which is not to say that the other modalities would not also come into play from time to time)? And if this third option is chosen (as it eventually is at some point with most referrals), how will this encounter between two individuals of vastly different age, life experience, and (in a very real sense) *cultures* be managed so that something useful can result? The initial objectives may be straightforward—to assess mental status, insight, and accessibility—but conversation may be remarkably difficult. "How do I explain myself to someone who can't possibly understand?" a fifteen-year-old may be thinking. "How do I connect with someone so angry, so withdrawn, so untrusting?" the therapist may be thinking. And if the clinician is successful in making a connection and initiating a working relationship, what can actually be done with the adolescent, in fifty or sixty minutes a week, that will make a difference in the life history unfolding in this drama?

These are the issues for which a new model of development and therapy is needed. The situation that presents itself is highly complex, often intrinsically ambiguous, and in evolution over time. It involves not just one psyche but rather a cast of characters. It is heading *from* somewhere *to* somewhere, and it is not infrequently confusing, even overwhelming, to the so-called experts who are asked to make sense of it and then do something. Thus the model that is needed is one that would be simple and clear enough to orient clinicians to a rapidly changing social field and, at the same time, flexible and open enough, sufficiently lifelike, to have some relevance to the actual lives of our real patients and their world.

Searching for a Model

Clinicians need models. Confronted daily with complex and delicate human situations, and accepting the responsibility to sort through the tangle of information and observations, we need frameworks that organize our inquiry and orient us toward interventions and outcomes. As a therapist working with adolescents and their families, and dissatisfied with existing psychotherapeutic models, I continually found myself forced to improvise. From psychoanalytic writers on the mysteries of adolescence I learned a tremendous amount, but relatively little that guided me through the practical exigencies of the clinical situation. Peter Blos seemed able to get his patients to lie down and tell him, rather openly, what was on their minds. I was not. As I have said, family therapists offered much that was useful for affecting the adolescent's family system, and their literature was packed with case histories that exuded common sense about childrearing and development. But, much as psychoanalysis confined itself to the hidden workings of the adolescent's inner world and neglected the systemic context of that experience, family therapy did just the opposite.

What was needed, it seemed to me, was a model that could bridge this theoretical and clinical gap, one that could be a guide

through the constantly shifting complexities of the adolescent's social and family worlds, while orienting the therapist to the inner
subjective world of the particular adolescent client. I knew, too,
that such an integrative model did exist, at least for adult clients
and adult psychotherapy: the model of Gestalt therapy. By focusing
our attention on the construction of experience, this model serves
to clarify both the inner world of the person and the ever-changing
relationship of the person to the social field.

Because of its capacity to address the integration of the whole
field of experience, both inner and outer, the Gestalt model had
long since become my preferred model for understanding and working with adult clients. Yet somehow this useful model seemed to
lose its vibrant relevance when I viewed my adolescent clients
from its perspective. For one thing, Gestalt therapy had not articulated a clear developmental theory, although implications for
such a theory were plainly contained (undeveloped themselves) in
the model. For another, I found most of my adolescent clients skittish and anxious when I engaged them in the manner that had
become familiar to me with my adult clients: concentrating on
immediate here-and-now experience, heightening awareness (often
of bodily states and other quite private aspects of experience), at
times proposing relational experiments and fantasy explorations
that from time to time only increased my adolescent clients' sense
of emergency.

And yet, throughout my career of working with people in this
age group, I found myself time and again returning to Gestalt therapy as a theoretical and attitudinal home. As one who ardently
believes that any adequate model of adolescent development and
therapy must take account of the adolescent's first-person experience, I found myself continually drawn back to Gestalt therapy
because of its insistence on phenomenology as the foundation for
theory. I found myself drawn back again and again because of
Gestalt therapy's unshakably positive view of human nature, which
supports us in seeing the person and the social environment as
"made for each other" at some fundamental level, rather than opposed to each other (as Freud and many other theorists implicitly
or explicitly assume). Likewise, I found myself drawing on the
Gestalt faith in *experimental creativity*, which supports us in seeing,
even in the most objectionable behavior, the human organism's

struggle to adjust creatively to its circumstances and make some-thing of them to support life and growth. Indeed, I feared that any working model of adolescent therapy that did not incorporate such a view would not only fail to grasp the essentially creative and growth-oriented spirit of adolescence but also would dishearten and defeat the therapist.

In my opinion, Gestalt theory has an enormous amount to offer the clinician who works with adolescents and who seeks to understand the intrinsic, unfolding meaning of adolescent devel-opment. Gestalt theory honors the integrity of the adolescent's per-sonal experience while situating it within its immediate interpersonal context. The Gestalt model allows the clinician to organize the many facets of change into a comprehensive whole and thus map out, in an integrated fashion, the multiple possibilities of clinical intervention. Finally, with its emphasis on wholes of experience—created anew in each successive moment, yet tending always to-ward ongoing meaning and cohesion—Gestalt theory gives us the basis of a developmental model that is not linear but recursive, drawing on recurrent themes and issues and integrating them in increasingly satisfying ways. Thus Gestalt theory may begin to pro-vide the outlines, at least, of a model that can make sense of the confusion of tasks and issues in the adolescent world while remain-ing open enough to help us see how those tasks and issues are resolved again and again, in recursive rather than linear fashion, in the real lives and development of real adolescents. To imply, as many developmental models do, that adolescent development is linear is to move so far from the real subjective world of adolescent experience as to lose our relational moorings with the client, and thus much of our potential for understanding and effectiveness.

Overview of This Book

This book is divided into two parts. Part I presents the Develop-mental Tasks Model of adolescence and adolescent experience, drawing on the themes and precepts of Gestalt theory to support a new conceptual framework for clinical work. Part II turns to the clinical work itself: the practical issues and challenges of working with adolescents in psychotherapy.

In Chapter One, the stage is set with the presentation of some essential constructs of Gestalt theory, in the interest of supporting the development of a model that can help us clarify the necessary developmental tasks of adolescence (these tasks are not necessarily lived through and resolved in a rigidly linear fashion). In the words of the Gestaltist Kurt Lewin, there is nothing so practical as a good theory. In this spirit, we can expect to return from this excursion into theory all the better equipped for the practical tasks of understanding the adolescent and intervening therapeutically.

In the remaining five chapters of Part One, my objective will be to describe the creative reorganization of the self during adolescence. This project begins in Chapter Two, with a look at the preadolescent child's *embeddedness* within the world of the family. From that platform, we will explore the adolescent's *emergence* from the family, and from childhood generally, and the reorganization of self that accompanies this movement. In Chapter Three, by exploring the changes that take place in the adolescent's relationships with peers, parents, and the adult world in general, we will look specifically at how this developmental task shapes the adolescent's interpersonal boundaries and processes. And in Chapters Four and Five, we will shift our focus to the intrapsychic dimension of adolescent experience, paying special attention to issues of ownership and to the emergence of polarities as important aspects of adolescent experience. Finally, in Chapter Six we will track the *interplay* of intrapsychic and interpersonal boundary development and see how this interplay is manifested in relationships and evolves over the course of adolescence. Here, we will find that the developmental process is (for the clinician, at least) most usefully understood as a creative reworking of the processes that Gestalt theory emphasizes as central to the survival and growth of the human organism at every stage: the functioning of the *contact boundary*.

Part Two consists of five chapters, each devoted to a different aspect of clinical work with adolescent clients. Chapter Seven takes up the development of the therapeutic process itself, conceiving the project of adolescent psychotherapy as a series or set of nested tasks, each one supporting and underlying the others. Chapter Eight addresses the assessment of the family context and shows that adolescent clients are best understood when their symptoms and struggles are viewed against the backdrop of the family's contact style. In Chapter Nine, we delve straight into the pragmatics of initiating therapy and creating a therapeutic milieu, particularly with adolescents who are still very much engaged in the disembedding process (that is, not yet ready to do the self-reflective, exploratory work that is often associated with psychotherapy). Chapter Ten deepens our exploration and discussion of the disembedding stage of adolescence, a stage that we may think of as early, or as preceding the other stages outlined in the model (but, again, the tasks of adolescent development come up anew for consideration at each developmental stage). Finally, in Chapter Eleven, we will explore the therapeutic project of engaging and cultivating the adolescent's interiority—that is, of contacting, heightening, and supporting the adolescent's emerging inner world—and turn our attention to the developmental stage of integration. In the process we will integrate the Developmental Tasks Model, the applications, and the overall discussion and argument of this book.

The intent of this book, beyond any specific idea or method, is to convey a *way of seeing* and a *way of thinking about* adolescents, their struggles, their "temporary insanity," and their triumphs of development. Adolescents can be understood only as part of the larger fields in which they live, and only when we see and appreciate their very personal, subjective struggles to renegotiate their status within those fields, find meaning and a place for themselves, and, at the heart of that struggle, give birth to an existential self.

Acknowledgments

Writing this book has been, itself, an emergence and a passage. Like all developmental journeys, it reflects the generous support of many individuals. I wish to acknowledge some of them here.

I am indebted to Robert McCarty, S.J., D.H. Richardson, and Amedeo Giorgi, for their assistance in the earlier stages of this project.

I also offer my heartfelt gratitude to Sonia Nevis, for introducing me to Gestalt therapy and, in many ways, to myself. Much the same is true of John Margrett, in whose debt I remain. Without his Gandolfian guidance and extraordinary generosity of spirit, I would certainly never have begun this work.

I would also like to thank my long-time associate, Marlene Blumenthal, for her encouragement and support over the years. Her work, particularly with adolescent females, has been an invaluable source of learning and inspiration.

I wish to acknowledge Anne Ferguson, Bill Christ, and the faculty and staff of Hathaway Brown School, for their inspirational dedication to child development and superlative education. I also wish to thank my colleague, Margaret Mason of University School, for her faith in my work.

Patricia Papernow, Penny Backman, Edwin Nevis, Beverly Relfman, Jean-Marie Robine, Joseph Melnick, Gloria Melnick, and Lynne Jacobs, as participants in Gestalt Institute of Cleveland (GIC) Press Writers' Conference, read portions of the manuscript and offered invaluable, constructive criticism. Mary Ann Kraus thoroughly and thoughtfully read the manuscript; her encouragement over the years has been a greater support than she knows in helping me formulate my ideas.

Paul McConville, Maury Kittle, Barbara Fields, Robert Antall, Michael McConville, Peter Mulbury, Mary E. McConville, Dorothy Siminovich, John McConville, and Cynthia Jenne, dear friends all, gave their encouragement and support at different points along the journey.

Thanks to Gordon Wheeler, for his competency as an editor, and for his clarification and reformulation of certain aspects of Gestalt theory. Thanks also to James Isiah Kepner, who has generously availed his friendship and presence, his keen and always provocative intellect, and his encouragement and inspiration to write.

I would also like to acknowledge my nephew, David McConville, who has the head, the heart, and the humor to become a first-rate adolescent therapist.

And, finally, I want to thank my family. Mary and Louis Kaucic have been there in every way with their unconditional love and support. I am deeply grateful. My children, Luke and Meghan McConville, have blessed me with their love, their tolerance, their friendship, and their infectious spirit for living. I have dedicated this book to my wife, Joanne Kaucic McConville, I am grateful for her unflagging encouragement, boundless support, willingness from time to time to set me straight, and her faith and confirmation. But most of all, I am grateful for the effortless integrity and uncompromising grace with which she lives her life.

The Author

Mark McConville was born and grew up in Rochester, New York. At seventeen, and still very much an adolescent, he enrolled at Duquesne University. As an undergraduate, he captained the golf team and was awarded the J. H. Burns Memorial Scholar-Athlete Prize. More important, he encountered existential psychology and received his B.A. in 1968. He went on to obtain an M.A. degree in psychology from the University of Windsor, Ontario, and returned to Duquesne University in 1970 for his Ph.D. studies.

At Duquesne, he developed interests that contributed to the writing of the present volume. The first of these was in the phenomenology of perceptual experience, which led him to the philosophy of Maurice Merleau-Ponty and to the seminal writings of the early Gestalt psychologists. The second was in developmental and adolescent psychology, which became a focus of his duties as a teaching fellow. He earned his degree in existential-phenomenological clinical psychology in 1974. His academic interests, braided together with Gestalt therapy, grew into the developmental field theory presented in this volume.

After his graduation from Duquesne he joined the staff of Marymount Hospital, in Cleveland, Ohio, serving there from 1974 to 1978. During this period, his clinical duties led him to organize and participate in intensive study and practice groups in family therapy and Eriksonian hypnosis. In 1978, he began his involvement with the Gestalt Institute of Cleveland. He received four years of clinical supervision from Sonia Nevis and three years from

Joseph Zinker. His postgraduate training in Gestalt therapy was taken at the Gestalt Institute of Cleveland from 1980 to 1984. He joined the Institute's faculty in 1989.

Since 1978, McConville has been in private practice in Cleveland, specializing in adolescent and family psychotherapy. He also serves as clinical consultant for the Shaker Heights Youth Center and is an affiliated consultant for Hathaway Brown School and University School. In 1991, he developed and wrote an innovative computer program for interpreting the results of the High School Personality Questionnaire directly with adolescent respondents. This program has been adopted by the Institute for Personality and Ability Testing, the test's publisher, for national distribution.

The author's current interests include the elaboration of Gestalt developmental field theory and the applications of phenomenological psychology to clinical practice. In addition to his professional activities, he pursues an active interest in the outdoors and in wilderness camping and is a founding member of the Wood Nymph Golfing Society. He and his wife, Joanne, are the parents of two adult children.

ADOLESCENCE

PART I

Adolescent Development: A Tasks Model

CHAPTER ONE

A Framework for Adolescent Development

In adolescence, modes of interpersonal relatedness undergo dramatic change. Friendships are more personally and intensely invested so that peers are no longer playmates but become self-mates. Friendships, romances, and rivalries all play a major role in shaping and defining the adolescent's experience of self and sense of worthiness, attractiveness, viability, acceptability, and so forth.

Relationships with parents change, in many instances dramatically, and these changes are certainly instrumental in redefining the adolescent's existential posture in the world, toward the past, and toward the future. These relationships may become more distant, more subject to challenge, and more characterized by conflict and disaffection. Entirely new themes—rejection, rebellion, abandonment, the struggle for emancipation—may emerge. But, by the same token, a new capacity for closeness and connecting may also emerge, a heightened interest in the other precisely *as* an Other. Adolescents by and large, in spite of their sometimes intense denials, care much more desperately about what their parents think of them, and about whether their parents accept their newly evolving differences, than younger children do. In general, relationships between teenagers and their parents undergo a gradual transformation in the direction of becoming more *negotiated*, rather than simply being conferred by parental expectations and family traditions. We usually witness a transformation from the unquestioned, hierarchically organized relation- ships of preadolescence, so that years later, perhaps between the ages of seventeen and twenty-five, we find a greater approximation of equality, with a capacity for relatedness, between comfortably separate persons whose differing outlooks, ambitions, and interests present (potentially, at least) an opportunity for more interesting and mutually rewarding relationships.

The Evolving Contact Boundary

Gestalt theory is uniquely suited, for a number of reasons, to talk about the comprehensive nature of the changes observed during adolescent development. For one thing, Gestalt theory is essentially a *field model* of human experience and behavior. As such, it encourages us to address the pieces of the developmental puzzle as constituents of a larger, sense-making whole. All human psychological phenomena, according to Perls, Hefferline, and Goodman (1951), must be understood in terms of the dynamic interactions of the *organism*, or person, and his or her *environment*, by which is meant above all the social world: "There is no simple function of any animal that completes itself without objects and environment. . . . Let us remember that no matter how we theorize about impulses, drives, etc., it is always to such an interacting field that we are referring, and not to an isolated animal" (p. 228). The ways in which the organism or individual connects to and forms its relationships with the surrounding world is of central importance to Gestalt theory.

In Gestalt language, we speak of such relationship phenomena in terms of *contact* between the individual and the environment and between the individual self and other selves. Contact, to be precise, is the "functioning of the boundary of the organism and its environment" (Perls, Hefferline, and Goodman, 1951, p. 229). And *boundary*, in this context (although it is certainly a physical, spatial metaphor), refers to the *processes* of interconnectedness. These processes join the individual to his or her surroundings but simultaneously separate or "bound off" the self from others, "limiting, containing, and protecting" the self (Perls, Hefferline, and Goodman, p. 229) so as to ensure its organizational integrity and identity. In everyday language, my contact with you joins us as a "we" but also separates us as two I's. The organizational structure of our encounter makes up our contact boundary.

The Gestalt meaning of the term *boundary* is worth emphasizing because it will play a central role in what we will find to be true of adolescent development. In ordinary parlance, the term *boundary* is used to refer to the barriers that people erect to limit their involvement with others. The Gestalt notion of boundary—or, more precisely, *contact boundary*—is much richer and dynamic, for it is an expression of our essence as beings whose nature it is to interact with our surroundings: assimilating and incorporating, accommodating and adjusting.

Boundaries do separate, to be sure, but they are also the place of our meeting. Thus the term *boundary* expresses the fundamental dialectical structure of contact itself: it is a two-stroke process: one stroke is the capacity to join and merge, give out and take in, influence and be influenced; the other is the capacity to separate and bound, resist influence and maintain one's unique and essential characteristics.

These concepts, *contact* and *boundary*, are uniquely suited to the project of describing adolescent development, for this development is essentially an evolution and a reorganization of the child's modes of relating to (that is, *contacting*) its environment. In this connection, it is perplexing that Gestalt therapy has not produced a more substantial theory of human development. Gestalt therapy's primary emphasis has always been on adult functioning, and specifically on supports for and interferences with lively contact. But this very capacity for lively contact is, to state the obvious, a *developmental achievement*, and adolescence plays a major part in creating both abilities and limitations for making contact in adult life. We might say that developing the capacity for contact (that is, for establishing boundary conditions that support both joining and separating) is what adolescence is all about. We could even (if we wanted to take a teleological view of development) go so far as to say that the capacity for contact is the primary underlying organizational and motivational purpose of adolescent development.

This reorganization of relationships and evolution of *interpersonal* contact boundary processes is only part of the larger picture of adolescent development, as anyone who works closely with adolescents knows. Blos (1979) and other psychoanalytic writers have also emphasized the change and reorganization that goes on in the recesses of the adolescent's private experience. In other words, there is a revamping of the adolescent's relationship to self. Private experience becomes notably intensified and more complex, and much about it gathers up and absorbs the adolescent's attention. The body comes alive in exciting, confusing, sometimes frightening ways. Sexual arousal, acute body consciousness, concerns over physical strength and attractiveness, sudden storms of anger, strange sensations of heaviness and emptiness—all of these conspire to alter the internal landscape dramatically. Intense new experiences, some painful (loneliness, shame, poignant vulnerability and hurt) and some delicious (exhilarating freedom, intense excitement, seemingly unbounded power), arrive unsolicited. They are deranging and confusing, but they also render the adolescent's inner world alluring, even hypnotizing.

The effect of all this change is to disrupt and reorganize, chaotically at times, the adolescent's relationship to self. In fact, it is here in adolescence that we can really speak with phenomenological accuracy of the child's having such an internalized, reflexive relationship—an *experienced* relationship of self with self. That is, there is an opening up of new boundaries of contact, internal or *intrapsychic* boundaries, and these become the vehicle for what will eventually be differentiated adult experience and the depth, subtlety, and complexity of the adult personality. This expanding and sometimes exploding inner world of private experience is what adolescents are so often intent on keeping bounded off from adults. It is also what therapists (in one-to-one therapy, at least) work so hard to gain access to. It readily finds its way into fantasy and reverie, diaries and journals, sometimes into English papers and graffiti—but not often or easily enough into the conversations of psychotherapy.

The Gestalt Notion of Self

This private, inner world of experience has usually been designated by the formal term *self*, or *inner self*, in psychological theory. Conversely, self has been conceptualized as an internalized, encapsulated structure, something residing on the subject side of a dichotomized subject-world relationship. Adolescents certainly undergo a radical transformation in the experience of self, which opens inwardly to become more complex, more confusing, more ambivalent, and more deeply felt. Later in adolescence, this experience of self will become more stable and solid, more consistent over time, and more capable of providing the individual with autochthonous support and management. It would be acceptable to say, along with Erik Erikson, that healthy development involves the "successful alignment" of inner life with outer opportunities, an achievement that Erikson calls "ego synthesis" (Erikson, 1959). But this formulation is acceptable only if we set aside the limited psychodynamic notion of the ego as an intrapsychic structure and adopt a Gestalt formulation of the self and its development.

The Gestalt conception of self is spelled out in the work of Gordon Wheeler (1991, 1994). Assaying the contribution of Paul Goodman, the principal architect of Gestalt therapy's seminal work, Wheeler notes that *self* is located neither in the internal world of private experience nor in the outer world of interpersonal events but precisely in the "creative tension" between the two. To put this another way, the operation of the self lies in its organization of contact processes, "the more or less satisfying resolution of the 'external' world of resources, obstacles, perceived threats, and sought-after goals, with the 'internal' world of felt needs and known desires, memories, aims, past learning and future hopes" (Wheeler, 1994, p. 17).

When we understand the concept of *self* in this way—no longer as something purely internal to the organism or psyche but as the "system of contact functions" (Perls, Hefferline, and Goodman, 1951, p. 373) organizing the organism's relationship to its environment—we arrive at a somewhat different way of thinking about human and specifically adolescent development. Development, from a Gestalt perspective, involves both the reorganization of interpersonal relationships *and* the differentiating of internal experience. But in the Gestalt approach, no domain of change is prior to another; both of these are expressions of a more comprehensive reorganization of the *field*, an evolution of the contact functions and boundary processes that define the very meaning of *self*.

Intrapsychic and Interpersonal Contact Boundaries

If we agree to think of the self as the organ and process of integrating the inner and outer worlds of experience—or, again, as the structure of the field that allows us even to make this distinction—and if we think of human development as the evolution of this self over time, then adolescence emerges as a singularly interesting and important phase. Adolescence is the period when most individuals begin to segregate the inner (or intrapsychic) and outer (or interpersonal) worlds precisely as phenomenologically distinguishable domains of personal experience.

For many adolescents, this distinction becomes a salient phenomenological reality. They lose the fluid, preadolescent sense of belonging to the world, of fitting in with their families and playmates, and begin to experience themselves as standing out from or apart from the world and having an inside that does not always match up with what is expected or required on the outside. Many teenagers can describe this differentiation of intrapsychic and interpersonal experience quite vividly and, in fact, they may experience the self quite differently when it is for themselves and when it is for others.

Adopting the language of Gestalt therapy, we might say that in adolescence there is a sorting out of the *intrapsychic* contact boundaries from the *interpersonal* contact boundaries and, in this sorting, a working out of their relationship. This is really nothing more than another way of saying that the underlying and unifying theme of adolescent development is the maturation of contact functions and boundary process.

If we read the literature on adolescent psychotherapy published over the last thirty years, it is perplexing not to find more emphasis on the interrelatedness of the intrapsychic and the interpersonal. Typically, clinicians writing on the subject have emphasized one domain or the other. Therapists in the psychoanalytic tradition generally look at developmental struggles as fundamentally intrapsychic, and only secondarily as interpersonal. Therapists in the family therapy tradition, on the other hand, emphasize the interpersonal processes that contextualize the individual adolescent's intrapsychic process, typically giving little if any attention to the internal experience of the adolescent.

Consider the following clinical vignette. A fifteen-year-old girl has become very difficult for her parents to manage. She is openly defiant of their rules and authority, challenges them at every turn, and comes and goes as she pleases. She makes it no secret that she has become sexually active. She makes herself as attractive as possible and intensely invests herself in heterosexual relationships, much to her parents' consternation. Perhaps she is openly flirtatious, even promiscuous. Perhaps she leaves home and shares an apartment with an older boy or young man. Does this scenario express intrapsychic conflict projected onto the family field? Or does it express a breakdown in family field functioning, which inhibits the incorporation of internal superego structure?

Similar vignettes are offered in the clinical literature by both John Meeks (1971) and Charles Fishman (1988), who can be regarded as master therapists in the psychoanalytic and family therapy traditions, respectively. Meeks describes the inpatient treatment of Pattie, a fifteen-year-old whose rebellious acting out and sexual promiscuity pushed her parents to seek psychiatric hospitalization for her (his description is paraphrased here). On the ward, her behavior and dress were outrageously seductive and provocative, stirring up her peers and generating much concern among the hospital staff. She was being seen in "emergency" individual therapy sessions on a daily basis. In one of these sessions, Pattie leaned over her therapist's desk and provocatively asked, "Do you see anything wrong with these clothes?" The therapist paused and then replied, "I think you feel terrible about yourself." Pattie stormed from the session in a rage. Within several days, however, her behavior became more controlled, and she remarked to a ward nurse that the therapist "was pretty sharp." As her therapy proceeded, it developed that Pattie's extravagant delinquency was "simultaneously an effort to disclaim and escape a rigid superego, and an unconsciously calculated effort to force others to control her behavior" (p. 27). This became clear to her therapist and, presumably, to Pattie also. This is a wonderful example of a conceptual approach that emphasizes underlying intrapsychic conflict, and its emergence into the adolescent's awareness, as the essence of therapeutic intervention.

In contrast to psychoanalytic approaches, family therapists as a rule stress the family field processes that underlie adolescent behavioral patterns. Fishman (1988) tells the story of Maria, an extraordinarily beautiful fifteen-year-old who left home after a major fight with her parents and went to live with her eighteen-year-old boyfriend. She had been living with him for about a month when family therapy began. Maria agreed to attend the sessions but refused to move back home.

Fishman's therapeutic focus was on the marital and decision-making dynamics of Maria's parents. In the first therapy session, he discovered that the parents were inveterate avoiders of conflict. They vacillated between presenting themselves as powerless and making authoritarian pronouncements. They failed to communicate with each other, and each invariably undermined the other's attempts to negotiate with Maria. As a team, as an externalized superego structure, they were thoroughly ineffective. It is interesting and noteworthy that Fishman was not particularly interested in Maria's possible or potential conflicts about her own behavior. Instead, he directed his attention to the broader family field and asked Maria's parents about their fears for her. Maria's father confided his fantasy that her behavior, left unchecked, might evolve into prostitution. What is also noteworthy is that in this therapy the theme of sexual excess or exploitation—the fear that Maria might become a prostitute—surfaced in the *parent's* fantasy rather than in the child's and, by contrast with what happened in the case described by Meeks, was understood as an organizing theme of *interpersonal* rather than intrapsychic boundaries. Maria's behavior was contained, and she moved back home, only after her parents managed to organize themselves as an effective and realistic superego structure within the family field.

The polarity dynamics in these two cases—the tension between impulse indulgence and realistic impulse containment—are essentially the same. In Meeks's psychoanalytic approach, the focus is on the emergence of this polarity in Pattie's intrapsychic field, at the boundary of her relationship with herself. In Fishman's family therapy approach, the same essential polarity emerges in the broader field of family experience and interpersonal relatedness. This is not a matter of discovering which conceptualization is correct; both, as far as they go, are accurate descriptions of the phenomena.

To draw a distant but useful analogy, in physics in the early 1900s the question arose of whether light is a particle or a wave, because it was found to behave sometimes like a particle and sometimes like a wave. The answer provided by quantum mechanics seemed paradoxical: light is *both* a wave and a particle, although the definition of each seems to exclude the other; its properties at any given moment depend on the instrumentality of the observation. The same can be said of many adolescent psychological structures. The conflict that an adolescent experiences between impulse and superego, between the wish to act out sexually and the capacity to contain and limit that impulse, *is both an intrapsychic and an interpersonal field process.* But at any given point in adolescent development, or in any given adolescent, the conflict may seem primarily interpersonal or primarily intrapsychic. And so it is with the relationship between the psychoanalytic and the family therapy approaches to the adolescent struggle: one approach discovers the struggle as a wave, the other as a particle.

One important advantage of a Gestalt developmental approach

is precisely that these alternatives are not alternatives at all. As Wheeler points out (1991, p. 153), psychological field theory allows us to use a single set of concepts to integrate phenomena related to different "levels of system," that is, occurring at intrapsychic as well as interpersonal boundaries. Wheeler writes that "what we are claiming for the Gestalt model . . . is the ability to move between and among different systemic *levels*—intrapsychic, interpersonal, whole-system—in the same language, and to do this whether the initial presentation, the presenting client, is an individual, a couple, or a group. [If we conceive of the] presenting . . . symptoms as a set of contact *strategies*, as well as contact and awareness problems, in a structured ground . . . , the presenting dynamic meaning of figure can be considered in various grounds (individual, family, and so forth)." Another way of saying this is to say that the intrapsychic and the interpersonal, as expressions of an overarching field, stand in a *figure–ground relationship* to each other. Whichever boundary grabs our attention, whether it has to do with what goes on in the adolescent's family or what goes on (so to speak) in the adolescent's head, the other boundary always functions as the implicitly organizing context, or ground. What the adolescent experiences in the deepest and most private recesses of his or her private fantasy life is organized, in some essential fashion, by the interpersonal workings of the family milieu. And, conversely, what is transacted between the adolescent and significant others (parents, siblings, peers) in his or her world is organized by the shifting and evolving forces of intrapsychic life. This view of "mutual causality" is an essential requirement for an adequate theory of adolescence, precisely because the adolescent self, reflecting the developmental reworking of its relationship to the family, as well as its internal relation to itself, is *unavoidably ambiguous* as an intrapsychic and interpersonal field process.

In many actual clinical situations, the organizing themes of experience emerge in a flickering fashion, alternating between intrapsychic and interpersonal boundary manifestations. At one point, the adolescent may struggle with herself; at another, she may polarize and struggle with the adults in her life. Like the fluctuating organization of reversible perceptual figures, one boundary becomes *figural* as the other recedes to ground. In the longitudinal developmental process, we find a gradual shift occurring as family field articulations become less the rule, and intrapsychic articulations become more common.

It is a pleasure to find younger adolescents who are capable of exploring their experience along intrapsychic boundaries, reflecting on their beliefs or putting their feelings into words, but this is certainly not the norm. And it is distressing to find an older adolescent, a seventeen- or eighteen-year-old, who is incapable of configuring his struggles as belonging to the self and who instead continues to struggle with his parents or with other adults. As a general developmental rule, conflicts that were fought with one's parents yesterday are fought with oneself today. And, as we will see in later chapters, this development amounts to the adolescent's taking ownership of the functions of the self.

In well-functioning adult personalities, we look for the capacity to move fluidly between the figural experience of self and the figural experience of the other. The capacity for each kind of experience supports and reinforces the healthy functioning of the other kind. To make contact with oneself, one's innermost nature, requires the supportive and mediating context of relatedness to other people. Wheeler makes this point dramatically, stating that "it is through *being treated as a self*, which is to say as a being with a valid internal experience, . . . that we learn to regard ourselves . . . with a firm sense of this reality" (1994, p. 7). And, again conversely, it is by virtue of one's attunement to and comfort with this inner domain of experience that one is able to move outward and engage others in a lively and life-affirming way.

The mature interrelatedness of the intrapsychic and the interpersonal is not something to be taken for granted, however. On the contrary, the emergence and differentiation of these boundaries within the larger field is a matter of developmental *achievement*. There are adults in whom one boundary or the other is decidedly underdeveloped—individuals with little awareness of their affective life, and individuals with barely developed interpersonal sensitivity. One way of defining both maturation and health, each of which is earmarked by the achievement of the capacity for lively contact, is to do so in terms of differentiation and fluid intercourse between the intrapsychic and the interpersonal. Well-functioning adults seem able to move between the inner world of private experience and the outer world of transactions with others, and to do so in a way that heightens their sense of being whole and integrated. Dysfunctional adults are characterized precisely by their inability to do this.

Adolescents who are struggling with maturational issues display many of the same characteristics of disturbed adults, becoming stuck in the figure–ground organization of their experience around one boundary or the other. Some adolescents, typically those who present symptomatic acting-out behavior, rigidly limit their awareness to interpersonal boundaries. These clients focus their awareness "out there," on the problems and frustrations that occur in their relationships with other people—their parents, their peers, their teachers, and so on. Intrapsychic process remains very much a ground phenomenon for these youths, silently but powerfully shaping the figural awarenesses that emerge at the interpersonal boundaries. Getting these adolescents to shift their focus, to forgo blaming and projection in favor of reflection on themselves and their feelings, is extremely challenging, as any clinician knows.

Other adolescent patients develop exquisitely heightened sensitivity to their internal experience, readily forming figures related to their feelings, fears, and urges, but have great difficulty forming clear figural perceptions at the interpersonal boundaries with their peers, their parents, or their family system. With these individuals, the figure–ground relationship of intrapsychic and interpersonal is reversed, with the interpersonal (usually family) phenomena invisibly contextualizing their heightened, figural, internal awareness. It is not uncommon, for example, for adolescents who present acute psychosomatic problems to have little or no figural awareness of the painful family processes that their figural symptoms express.

In one case, experience truncates toward the interpersonal boundary; in the other, it truncates toward the intrapsychic boundary. With adolescents in both situations, the fulfillment of development, or therapy, must involve a filling out of the experiential field, so that awareness can flow from the interpersonal to the intrapsychic and back again. It is in adolescence that the intrapsychic and the interpersonal begin to differentiate themselves clearly in experience, and that their integration becomes organized as a more or less stable ground structure of experience. But this does not happen all at once, nor does it happen smoothly in many instances. Even in relatively untroubled adolescents we commonly find extremes of contextualization. Inner life may fall slavishly under the dominion of pressures and expectations coming from others, or interpretations of external reality may be radically appropriated by intrapsychic needs. The same

extremes in adulthood might signify significant psychopathology. In
adolescence, they represent interesting and important convolutions
in the developmental journey.

CHAPTER TWO

The Child Self and the Family

The adolescent, we might say, struggles to escape from childhood. And in order to do so, he must find a way to renegotiate his relationship with his family. But why is this so? What is it about human growth and development, in our culture and at this time, that makes this differentiation necessary? The answer to this question lies, I think, in the nature of childhood experience itself.

In this chapter, we will explore the meaning of childhood experience and family belonging, specifically from the vantage point of adolescent development. Insofar as the adolescent is developmentally compelled to separate from childhood and family, we will explore in some depth the nature of this *ground of inclusion*, and how this ground gives birth to the phenomena of adolescent development.

The Family as a Field

At least since the advent of psychotherapy, the study of child development has paid attention to the contextual influences that shape the psychological experience of the child. Initial emphasis on the infant–mother relationship has been broadened to include the wider context of the family as the relevant milieu of the developing child (Ackerman, 1958). The family constitutes a matrix, or field, for the emergent experiential and behavioral makeup of its members, particularly its children. Whatever the specific phenomena may be that we choose to isolate and attend to—behavior patterns, cognitive phenomena, intrapsychic dynamics, or personality traits—these phenomena are shaped within the broader field of family culture.

In the language of Gestalt therapy, the behavior and emergent personality of the child stand against the family field as a figure stands against its background. Background—or *ground*, as the Gestaltists called it—has been shown since the earliest Gestalt perceptual research to exert a contextualizing, organizing effect on our *figures* of perception (what we are attending to and aware of at the moment), influencing even such fundamental properties as the size, shape, and color of an object (Koffka, 1935). In similar fashion, the figural properties of the child—behavior patterns, emotions, cognitive style, and so on—are powerfully organized by the contextualizing ground of the family's process.

Field Forces and the Family Milieu

Probably the earliest broadly subscribed expression of this insight is to be found in Freud's theory of the Oedipal conflict. Although Freud's interest was clearly in assaying the depths of the individual psyche, he did so against the backdrop of the child's evolving experience within the family field. Before he formulated his intrapsychic theory of psychosexual development, Freud was intensely interested in the interpersonal dynamics of the family field—initially, in the possible incest of his patients by family members and, later, in the child's presumed incestuous desires toward the parent of the opposite sex (desires that Freud postulated in order to explain the very intensity of the family bonds and the power of the family context to organize the psyche of the child).

It is worth noting that the breakthrough of Freud's Oedipal theory followed the trauma of his own father's death (a disruption of Freud's family field), as he sought to understand the swell of emotional distress that resulted (Jones, 1961, pp. 206–207). In other words, the *figure* of Freud's theorizing activity took place against the contextualizing *ground* of his own deep rootedness in a family system.

Although Freud's theory conceptualizes the child's psyche as an isolated system, his formulation of the Oedipal theory—that the child becomes desirous of the opposite-sex parent and must then work through issues of competitiveness, anxiety, and eventually identification with the same-sex parent—preserves, at least implicitly, the insight that the child's psyche is configured within the context of ongoing family relationships.

The field forces identified by Freud are essentially instinctual in nature. And while this insight represented a significant contribution

in its day, theorists since Freud have gone beyond his narrow conceptualization. Initially, therapists and researchers focused on two-person
systems (such as mother and child) as the field from which individual
psychological process, particularly pathological process, emerges. As
the field of family therapy evolved, three-person and whole-family
fields became increasingly understood and charted. We will look at
each of these levels of context in turn, ultimately with an eye to
understanding their relevance to adolescent development.

The Contribution of Family Therapy Theory

The field of family therapy theory has exposed and catalogued a
broad range of the contextualizing forces indigenous to family fields.
Among the many variables that have been identified and studied are
system homeostasis (Jackson, 1957), marital dynamics (Lidz, 1957),
the rigidity and flexibility of family roles (Wynne, Rycoff, Day, and
Hirsch, 1958), the level of the parents' emotional maturity (Bowen,
1978), patterns of communication (Bateson, Jackson, Haley, and
Weakland, 1956), the interpersonal and subsystem boundaries
(Minuchin, 1974), and the family's systemic life cycle (Erikson, cited
in Haley, 1973).

The family field is not a homogeneous, unitary system but a col-
lection of overlapping interpersonal fields. A child engages one way
with a favorite sibling, differently with each parent individually, and
differently again with the entire family gathered together. (In Gestalt
language, we might say that the self actualizes or comes into being
differently under different contact conditions.) Generally speaking,
the interpersonal field is reconfigured as more family members are
involved. In other words, two-person or dyadic fields are *absorbed*, or
reintegrated, into three-person or triadic fields, which in turn are
taken up and reconfigured by the larger family field.

For example, a seven-year-old sits comfortably in the kitchen,
talking casually with her mother, amusing herself as she draws in a
coloring book. She and her mother are enjoying the ease and openness of their field together. But then her twelve-year-old brother enters the room to ask his mother for some help on a school project.
The seven-year-old's mood suddenly changes. She becomes whiny
and demanding, insisting that her mother look at the picture she is
coloring. Her relationship to her mother and, correspondingly, her

experience of self change as the interpersonal field shifts from two to
three persons. The mother–daughter field is reconfigured as it is integrated into the more comprehensive three-person system. The
daughter may now find herself competing for her mother's attention,
and the mother herself may subtly reorganize aspects of her own functioning as the field changes. For instance, she may shift from being a
calm, nurturing presence when alone with her daughter to becoming
a more animated, verbal, cognitively active presence once her older
child enters the scene, and each member of the family may experience this shift differently.

The specific field organization can vary from situation to situation, or from family to family. In some cases, the dyad is reorganized
as it is absorbed into a larger field. Many parents report pleasant relationships with their children individually, which erupt into conflicts when the entire family gathers together. In other instances, the
dyad rigidly retains its character, organizing the larger field around it.
For example, the same twelve-year-old boy may be emotionally close
to his mother and serve as her confidant and supporter within the
family. When his father comes home, this dyadic field may remain
intact but go underground, so to speak, and become an important
organizing influence in the interaction between mother and father,
amounting to what family therapists have called a *covert alliance*.

In assessing the contextualizing forces of a family field, it is useful
to think in terms of an ever more complex *gestalt*, or meaningful
whole, whose parts are taken up into more comprehensive configurations, contributing to the qualities of the whole but also being
changed by its contextualizing forces. The simplest units are the dyadic fields of the individual child with each parent and with each
sibling separately. These fields are contextualized by triadic fields,
whole-family fields, and, finally, by societal and cultural fields.

What is important here is to appreciate that the self of the child
is configured in various and simultaneous interpersonal contexts.
Very early on, the child self becomes multifaceted, complex, and
even contradictory, according to the field forces of the various relational contexts in which the child learns to be in the world.

Dyadic Fields.   Both in the psychoanalytic tradition and in family
therapy, the clinical relevance of dyadic fields has been emphasized
through scrutiny of the mother–infant relationship. The work of

Harry Stack Sullivan is probably the best example of this endeavor in the psychoanalytic tradition. Working with young schizophrenics in the 1920s and 1930s, Sullivan gave pioneering attention to the dyadic milieu and to relationship dynamics in the understanding and treatment of "mental disorders." He introduced the notion of the field to psychiatry and showed how traditionally conceived intrapsychic processes are always a function of interpersonal context. For example, Freud's "erogenous zones," presumably the foci of biological instinctual development, became for Sullivan "zones of interaction," and personality itself became "the relatively enduring pattern of recurrent interpersonal situations which characterize a human life" (Sullivan, 1953, p. 111). It is not surprising, since it reflects the biases embedded in the cultural field of Sullivan's era, to find in Sullivan a tremendous emphasis on the infant–mother relationship as the context in which the child's emergent "self system" is configured. In fact, it was one of Sullivan's students, Frieda Fromm-Reichman, who first proffered the term *schizophrenogenic mother* in elaborating the Sullivanian view that serious individual psychological disturbance is a function of a highly disturbed interpersonal field (Fromm-Reichman, 1948).

This attention to the pathogenic potential of the mother–infant dyad also characterizes the early work of several important family therapy theorists. Murray Bowen (1978), in his early research at the National Institute of Mental Health, described the relationship dynamics of mother–child dyads that contributed to the emergence of learned helplessness in schizophrenic offspring. Bowen postulated that the mothers of his subjects managed their own deeply internalized sense of inadequacy and insufficiency by adopting a polarized posture of overadequate caretaking toward their children. The children complemented this posture by taking on their mothers' projected inadequacy and helplessness, eventually acting it out in the form of psychological symptoms. In Bowen's formulation, what had been a feeling for the mother became a reality for the child. Today, as we learn more about the biochemistry of schizophrenia, we are inclined to see some of this earlier work as "blaming the victim"—or, at any rate, one of the related family victims—of this terrible disorder. At the same time, these perspectives on the importance of the dyadic system have shed a very useful light on the whole question of the child self's development in the family.

Triadic Fields.   Triadic fields have been the focus of a great deal of
interest in family therapy, especially in the work of Minuchin (1974),
who has pointed out that symptomatic children often become caught
up in their parents' relationship issues. This development occurs in
several typical ways. In *triangulation*, the child becomes paralyzed between two warring parents, each of whom demands the child's loyalty. Divorced or divorcing families are especially vulnerable to this
configuration. In *detouring* configurations, spouses deal with relationship stresses by maintaining a focus on a "problem child," implicitly
reinforcing the deviant behavior because it enables them to avoid
dealing with their own differences. For example, a mother may battle
openly with her child because of the child's failure to complete
household chores, and she may solicit her husband's disciplinary
support while avoiding the issue of his own lack of helpfulness in
household matters. In a third pattern described by Minuchin, the
cross-generational alliance, one parent covertly allies with the child
against the other parent, drawing solace from the child's support
rather than dealing directly with marital problems.

Whole-Family Fields.   The family as a whole can be conceived as
a milieu within which two- and three-person relationship fields are
organized. Numerous family therapy researchers and theorists have
identified the dimensions that describe whole-family fields. An early
example of this approach is the work of Jackson (1968). Observing
that as identified schizophrenic patients got better, other family
members often developed difficulties, Jackson was among the first to
conceive of the family as a system. He used the biological notion of
system homeostasis to conceptualize this feature of families, whereby
changes in one member's behavior trigger reorganization of the family field.
     The example par excellence of whole-family field theorizing as
applied to adolescent developmental issues is found in the work of
Stierlin (1981), who studied the psychological and behavioral dynamics of adolescent runaways. Stierlin identified "centripetal" and
"centrifugal" field forces as the "covert organizing transactional background" for adolescent-parent relationships. Centripetal family fields
have a variety of ways of binding their offspring, holding children
within a gravitational field charged by the emotional and personality
needs of parents. A failing marriage or a depressed parent may serve

as a powerful magnet, holding a sensitive eighteen-year-old close to the family and perhaps undermining her or his attempts to leave home for college. Centrifugal family fields are characterized by an "expelling mode." In these families, the parents' own developmental crises cause them to become preoccupied with personal issues—marital strain, occupational changes, new relationships, and so on. Teenagers may come to be viewed as hindrances, and a family climate with insufficient "gravitational pull" may release them prematurely to fend for themselves in the world.

Cultural Fields.   The very meaning of being a self differs from one cultural context to another, and the uniquely Western tradition of psychotherapy has been slow to incorporate this fact at the practical level (McGoldrick, Pearce, and Giordano, 1982). Presented with an unfamiliar cultural or subcultural context, the therapist would be wise to ask, "What sort of children is this family's culture designed to produce?" In cultural traditions emphasizing viable extended-family networks—for example, in rural agrarian societies—the closeness of family members and the individual's sense of being part of a larger whole have always been crucial to the community's survival. In contemporary affluent American society, individualism, achievement, and mobility are generally regarded as the hallmarks of effectively reared offspring.

The Contribution of Gestalt Therapy Theory

Gestalt therapy's genius has been twofold: the illumination of *contact process* as it unfolds for a client in the present moment; and the understanding of all the ways in which full and immediate contact, with parts of oneself or with others, can be interrupted, or resisted. Nevertheless, Gestalt therapists—with a few exceptions (Kaplan and Kaplan, 1978; Kempler, 1974; Papernow, 1993; Wheeler, 1994)—have not attended to the unique workings of the family field or to the role played by family process in shaping the self of the child.

From a Gestalt standpoint, the family may be thought of as a *contact milieu,* a context in which children learn a basic repertoire of contact skills and a style of contact process. Zinker and Nevis (1981) have articulated such a view, essentially proposing a phenomenology of the family field, a look at how the family organizes and manages

the experience and contact process of its members. To chart and describe a family's characteristic style of organizing and regulating contact episodes among family members, Zinker and Nevis introduce the
idea of an "interactive cycle of experience." Families, they point out,
develop signature patterns for organizing awareness, negotiating individual wants and interests, and generating conjoint projects and
involvements. In other words, each family develops its own contact
style, and this style organizes the ways in which individual experience and intrapsychic process get transacted within the family field.
This style determines whether private experience is expressed or
withheld, whether or not there is mutual give-and-take, and whether
or not the family as a whole is able to move through contact episodes
in a manner that supports the integrity and satisfaction of its constituent selves.

A given family's contact style may emphasize any of the so-called
Gestalt resistances, which are themselves various ways of favoring or
avoiding particular *kinds* of contact (see Wheeler, 1991). A family
may be highly *confluent*, emphasizing areas of likeness and sharing, or
it may be highly *differentiating*, emphasizing individual difference and
the uniqueness of each family member. As a contact milieu, the family field may support introjection, whereby family truth is handed
down by parents and swallowed whole by children, or it may support
active discussion and dialogue, whereby thinking for oneself is encouraged. Family members may be highly expressive and therefore
easy to read, or they may be generally reserved, which will necessitate
projective interpretations and mind reading. Individuals may readily
enact their impulses toward contact, or they may be inclined to hold
back and retroflect these impulses back onto the self. Individuals
may, as a family, be very straightforward and clear about their deeper
concerns, or they may be highly deflective, tending to dilute contact
with humor and casual chatter. In short, a family's contact style can
be described and characterized in many ways. My intention here is
simply to point out that the family field is the training ground for
children's learning how to organize their private experience and
manage it in their interactions with others.

In the language of contact boundaries, we can say that the interpersonal contact style of family interaction, introduced primarily by
parents, becomes the template by which individual children learn to
organize the private worlds of their intrapsychic experience. In other

words, the contact style of the family field *is* the "unconscious mind" of the child, if that term has any meaning at all.

Embedded Experience

Another way of putting it is to say that the child, as a being who is coming into the world and whose self is beginning to take on some identifiable shape of its own, is embedded within the family field. Since embeddedness and the process of disembedding are essential dimensions of adolescent development, we will spend some time with these terms here.

Differentiation and Embeddedness

Human psychological development is a process of ever-increasing differentiation. This elementary but powerful notion has been articulated by developmental theorists from virtually every theoretical perspective, from psychoanalysis (Mahler, 1963) to phenomenology (Schachtel, 1959) to family theory (Bowen, 1978). Differentiation implies at least two things: that internal or intrapsychic experience becomes more complex and articulated, and that interpersonal experience progressively takes on more of a quality of boundedness or contactfulness (in other words, that there is more and more differentiation between persons as separate and—by virtue of their separateness—related selves in the interpersonal field).

The complement of this principle is that each phase of development expresses a degree of embeddedness that is relative to what follows it. For example, infancy is more embedded than toddlerhood, and toddlerhood is an expression of greater embeddedness than is found in the early-childhood phenomena that emerge later on. Embeddedness and disembedding, in other words, are continual processes throughout childhood and beyond, and they take on new meaning and urgency in adolescence.

Introjection

Compared to the experiences of adolescence, childhood experience within the family is characterized by relative embeddedness. This means that the otherness of the family—and, correlatively, the distinguishing uniqueness of the self—are relatively deemphasized, perhaps even hidden to the child. Differences, where they necessarily exist, are largely embedded in the ground of experience. The boundary of the child self and the family field is highly permeable, and so the child's experience (perception, motivation, cognition, and emotion) is significantly shaped by the field forces of the family environment. Parental views and prejudices are typically absorbed by the child not as views per se but as *what is.*

For example, many of us grew up as believers in the one true religion, myself included. I can remember feeling genuine compassion as a child for others who were not so blessed (of course, I was completely unaware of the condescension hidden in my compassion). Only when I was well into adolescence did I discover that this belief reflected a point of view rather than an objective reality. Most prejudices are transmitted in this fashion, by way of the permeable membrane between the child's experience and the surrounding family milieu.

In the tradition of Gestalt therapy, this relationship between child self and family field has been called one of *introjection.* In his early writing, Perls (1969), citing a "structural similarity of the phases of our food consumption with our mental absorption of the world," described introjection as a sort of "swallowing whole" of environmental input (p. 128). For example, a parent may order a child to respect her elders, and the child may accept this maxim uncritically and incorporate it, unchewed and undigested as a directive for her behavior and as implying a definition of her place in the world.

In more strictly phenomenological terms, we might say that the organization of the child's experience, her framing of reality, is imposed by the environment. The term *introjection* refers to the process by which meaning is *organized for* the child more than actively *constructed by* her. But, as a normative phenomenon, meanings are largely inaugurated and confirmed by the child's interpersonal, family, and cultural milieu. Thus the child does not "make up her mind" in certain matters (for example, the assessment of her own essential value) as much as she "receives" her mind from the contextualizing family field. Introjection, in other words, has essentially to do with authorship, initiative, and agency in the business of making meaning and organizing reality. This is an important ground condition, as we shall see later on, for adolescent development, where the appropriation of the meaning-making function becomes an essential theme of growth.

Introjection as Figure and Ground. A useful distinction can be made between introjection as figural and ground phenomenon. The example of respecting one's elders, like most parental teaching, illustrates *figural* introjection, since these meanings are offered in an explicit and thematic way. But the most powerful organization of the child's experience is mediated by introjection of the *ground* of experience. Ground is implicit, inhabited more than known. We are accustomed to thinking of the broader cultural milieu in terms of ground. For example, linguistic anthropologists have shown that the self-evident givens of reason, perception, and, indeed, reality are organized for us by the language that we speak, and that they differ significantly from one cultural milieu to another. The ground of family meaning is absorbed the same way a culture or a language is absorbed, shaping experience by implicitly defining the nature of what is, without itself becoming a figural theme of experience.

The Necessity of Introjection. To understand this critical process of introjection fully, it is necessary for us to recognize its undeniable necessity and utility in organizing the child's reality. In the psychoanalytic tradition, in Freud, and certainly also in the Gestalt therapy of Perls, introjection has been presented in a decidedly pejorative fashion (although Freud, at least, was certainly of two minds at various times about whether the superego, a mental structure he regarded as wholly introjected in this sense, was ultimately a good or a bad thing). Children, we have been told, would grow up less inhibited and more in tune with the needs of the organismic self were it not for introjection. But this is simply not true. Introjection, for all its obvious involvement in adult neurosis, still reflects the environment's supportive response to the young child's need for structure—ready-made structure, to be sure, but essential structure nevertheless, which assists the child in the overwhelming task of organizing experience and making meaning in the early years of life.

For example, consider young males who grow up in environments without older male role models. In my view, role modeling is related to the broader, more comprehensive process that has been labeled *introjection*, which in this sense would include identification as a special case or type of introjective process. The role model constitutes a ready-made configuring of diverse shards of traditional male experience—having a penis, managing anger and violence, competing in the world of commerce in order to provide for others, and so on. The role model says, in effect, "Here's how these things go together." The male child may imitate the model, or he may differentiate himself from it, but in some fashion he uses the model, the whole introjected configuration of maleness, to support the task of figuring out how these things might go together in his own life. Male youth who grow up without role models exhibit curious and predictable phenomena. On their own, they attempt to figure out how to use their penises, what to do with their capacity for anger and violence, and how to manage in an economic world. Without models—that is, without adequate introjects—adolescent males sometimes organize the "stuff" of their maleness in odd permutations. It is not at all uncommon to find a fifteen-year-old boy whose best effort at organizing his gender role includes blustery sexual conquest, a reputation for being savage in fist fights, and a well-honed knack for stealing and fencing car radios. It is well known that delinquent boys, as a group, very often come from homes from which the father is absent. It is perhaps not so obvious that their delinquency often represents their authentic efforts to figure out what it means to be a male (or to be independent, or competent) in the absence of introjected structure.

Intrapsychic and Interpersonal Field Process in Childhood Experience

The boundary between the child self and the family milieu is permeable. In childhood, the intrapersonal and the interpersonal are not yet clearly differentiated, so that there is not always a clearly developed boundary between the two.

It is easiest to illustrate the embeddedness of childhood experience through instances of pathology, particularly when this embeddedness has been carried forward as an adult psychological disorder. The early research linking family process and severe individual psychopathology is rich with descriptive examples of embeddedness. For example, Bateson began work in 1953 on a project that would lead to his famous double-bind hypothesis of schizophrenia (Bateson, Jackson, Haley, and Weakland, 1956). Bateson noticed that schizophrenics often exhibit confusion about levels of communication. In any communication process, Bateson pointed out, there is not only a denotative message but also a metacommunicated iden-

tification of the context, or "mode," of the message. Nonschizo-
phrenics metacommunicate that what they are saying is playful, or
metaphorical, or friendly, or to be taken seriously, and so on; that is,
they communicate the message's mode, as well as the message itself.
Schizophrenics often fail to do this, typically confusing modes or failing to identify them at all. Metaphorical thinking may be offered as
literally true, as when one of Bleuler's patients, expressing his personal love of freedom, claimed to *be* the country of Switzerland (cited
in Arieti, 1974).

Bateson's research indicates that this intrapsychic confusion in
the thinking of the individual schizophrenic is matched at the level
of interpersonal communication in the family system by a general
incongruence between messages and contextual qualifiers. Human
beings, Bateson and his colleagues wrote, use the interpersonal context to guide them in discerning modes of communication, and the
mental habits of the individual are internalized versions of the interpersonal process of the family field (p. 253). Again, our view of
the causes of schizophrenia itself has evolved considerably since
Bateson's work, but his and his team's insights into the structure and
process of communication, and its impact on the developing child,
are of enduring value.

An eighteen-year-old patient of mine displayed this confusion.
Her parents, when they were angry with her, would play jokes on her.
For example, they would reprogram her car radio so that all the
buttons tuned in to the same station. My patient, understandably
annoyed, complained about this, and her parents pointedly criticized
her for having no sense of humor and taking their "jokes" too seriously. Not surprisingly, in her individual therapy sessions she showed
confusion about the difference between humor and hostility. She
made jokes that seemed oddly hostile to me, or she became confused
by remarks that I had intended as friendly and humorous.

A similar point is made somewhat differently in a fascinating series
of articles by Wynne and Singer (1963) and Singer and Wynne (1965).
The authors asked entire families with schizophrenic or nonschizo-
phrenic offspring to reach consensus on the meanings of Rorschach ink-
blots, and they found a relative isomorphism between individual-level
thought disorder and family-level communication process. For example, patients with "amorphous type" thought disorders typically came
from families "in which undifferentiated, often symbiotic relationships

[had] been formed" and "amorphous forms of handling attention and communication [were] shared." Elsewhere, Wynne formulated his view as follows: "The fragmentation of experience, the identity diffusion, the disturbed modes of perception and communication, and certain other characteristics of the acute reactive schizophrenic's personality structure are to a significant extent derived, by processes of internalization, from characteristics of the family's social organization" (Wynne, Rycoff, Day, and Hirsch, 1958, p. 215).

In the work of both teams we can see that embeddedness includes some degree of one-to-one, or isomorphic, introjection of the family's process into the child's organization of experience. The same correspondence is found in nonpathological functioning. A friend of mine, describing how her thoughts and ideas slide and flow into one another in classic right-brain fashion, calls her cognitive process "kaleidoscopic." Her ability to metaphorize one idea in terms of another is striking. Sometimes, however, she is frustrated at not being able to draw boundaries between topical areas in her thinking; and, indeed, this boundary confusion is sometimes apparent in her day-to-day behavior, as when her conversation rambles on without focus, or when she finds herself talking to relative strangers about very personal issues. Recently, we were talking together about family patterns, and she began to describe how her family of origin was organized, and how changeable and fluid the family's style of operating was. From one night to the next, she said, she didn't know which bedroom she would be assigned to. What struck me immediately was that her description matched, in the words and images she used, her description of her intrapsychic cognitive process. In other words, she thinks in the same way her family behaved. Most of the rest of us, if we stopped to think about it, could come up with our own parallels of this kind, out of our own experience of our families and ourselves.

The Child Self

To describe the child self as embedded is to say that its relationship to its milieu is an essential part of its very nature. The child self is precisely a self in the family field. This field structure of the child self accounts for the fact that, in adult depth psychotherapy, where the child-self core of personality is brought to awareness, the recollecting and reworking of family field relationships is virtually always a central part of the work. To say that the child self is embedded is essentially to say that our earliest experiences of self are configured according to the relational field of childhood. As adolescence gets under way, the experience of self includes more and more separateness, ownership, and organizational integrity. The self becomes more of a gestalt—a segregated, coherently organized whole. In earlier childhood, however, the organizational integrity of the self is still the organizational integrity of the family field from which the child self emerges.

By comparison with what occurs in adolescence, the child self is also unreflective. This means that the child self is essentially part of the ground of the experiential field. It is *lived* rather than *known*, not yet standing in a reflective relationship of ownership to itself. The preadolescent child is generally not given to the spontaneous experiences of self-consciousness that occur so readily in adolescence. For the child, experiences of self—self-image, self-concept, and so on—remain an implicit aspect of the ground. If a child is the family favorite, he probably will not organize this as an explicit figural theme of reflective experience. Instead, this self-concept will reveal itself implicitly in the way he organizes figural perceptions within the family environment. He may perceive his parents as warm and approving, his siblings as unnecessarily troublesome and argumentative. Figures of experience during childhood are focused largely *away from* the self; those that do pertain to the self tend to be fragmentary and primitive ("I'm bad," "I'm helpful," and so on). This is why, in therapy, preadolescent children do not talk about themselves, and why child therapists utilize methods (play therapy, guided fantasy, drawing) that allow access to the ground of the child's experience.

But, whatever the nature of this self in the family field, it serves as the backdrop for what is to follow: the differentiating from the family that defines adolescence. The specific form that differentiation takes in any individual case—congenial confluence, angry rebellion, spirited contact, intense ambivalence—is determined to a considerable extent by the developmental work of childhood. For example, the extent to which individual differences have been recognized and supported within the family will influence the identity-creating process of adolescence. Some children arrive at adolescence with a sense of themselves (although a presynthesized one) as valuable, interesting, potent, and capable, with an intuitive grasp of the boundaries that define their psychological space within the family field. Other children arrive at adolescence with an abiding sense of their own insufficiency and a pervasive confusion about what is included in and what is excluded from the boundary of the emergent adolescent self.

Whether or not a particular child can develop, in adolescence, a sharp figural sense of self will depend on the ground of the child-self experiences that have accrued over the years. When the ground of the child self is confused or amorphous, the adolescent may be compelled to import a figural identity from his peer environment (complete with costume, ideals, philosophy, musical tastes, attitudes toward authority, and so on).

Embeddedness and differentiation are meaningful only in relation to each other. The figural process of adolescence stands against the ground of childhood experience, ultimately seeking to alter it by drawing it up into a new, more comprehensive configuration. And the work of adolescent development is always, especially in the beginning (ages twelve to fourteen), a matter of reacting to, attempting to compensate for, the sense of oneself as a child, which organizes the ground of experience. For some teenagers, this child self is readily integrated into a new, more comprehensive, more reality-oriented configuration. For others, particularly those for whom the ground experience of the child self has included feelings of being inadequate, unlovable, or loathsome, the business of adolescent self-configuring takes on a largely self-protective quality. These teenagers often organize their newly claimed selves in a manner designed primarily to compensate for or correct their underlying ground of child-self experience. Thus we often find adolescents who desperately organize their experience of self around rigid figures like the self as invulnerable or the self as completely independent or the self as not caring about the parents' divorce or the self as unconcerned about schoolwork. These adolescents are certainly the most challenging for the psychotherapist. Still other adolescents approach the work of development as a polarity struggle, an experience of being pulled between two alternative organizations of self, one that expresses the impulse to pull out of the family milieu and become one's own person, and one that retains the lingering organization of the self as embedded in the family milieu. We will return to this important developmental tension, this tug-of-war between competing organizational paradigms, in Chapter Six. For the time being, it is sufficient to keep in mind the importance of the child self as the ground from and against which the adolescent struggles to emerge and establish a figural integrity.

Case Example

Dan, a seventeen-year-old high school junior, was referred to me by his parents and came to therapy willingly. His family had just returned to our city from a four-year stay overseas, the result of a business assignment for Dan's father. Dan was not in any particular difficulty, according to his mother, but needed someone to help him with the adjustment process as he reacquainted himself with his former school and classmates. He had seen a therapist for several months before leaving his temporary home overseas and had found the experience helpful.

Dan's mother took pains to assure me in our initial phone contact that Dan had no real problems and just needed someone to talk to. When pressed a little, however, she conceded that Dan was "very sensitive and emotionally immature" as well as "exceptionally bright." She theorized that his emotional development had not kept pace with his "prodigious" intellectual development.

When I saw them together for an initial office visit, an interesting picture emerged. Figural in their thinking were a host of problems that they both saw as attendant to Dan's superior intelligence: other students found him odd and intimidating; teachers often felt threatened by his challenges in class; Dan had trouble finding anyone who could relate to him "on his level."

Dan's descriptions of himself, which emerged in subsequent sessions without his mother, were somewhat more evenhanded and less self-aggrandizing. He said that he felt anxious around his peers. He oscillated between being quiet and restrained and being verbose and intellectually assertive. His experience of self in social situations seemed to be organized around his use of words. Words, he felt, were real and substantial and could be used to define his personal boundaries and regulate the distance between himself and others. He dreaded the rare situation in which someone used a word he did not understand; he felt this as a minor humiliation, at least. He himself, however, often and quite intentionally, used strings of words that left others in the dark. Indeed, Dan's conversational vocabulary was the most extensive I had ever encountered. I did not hesitate to ask him (as I sometimes needed to do) to use another word or explain what he meant in simpler terms. His command of language, although clearly used in the service of his need for emotional security, was still extraordinary.

Dan often felt his psychological integrity threatened and his self-esteem under attack in social situations. He described interchanges with his teacher in English class (a class for gifted students), where he would argue with passionate certainty for a point of view that differed from the teacher's. In my office, he would reflect with curiosity on the intensity of his feelings during these "discussions," observing that he engaged in them almost as matters of life or death. The same sort of passion had brought him some trouble at his former school too, where his constant challenges came to be viewed as serious disruptions. He ended up in the principal's office at one point, and he in turn escalated the issue to one of "intellectual freedom versus censorship," mounting a one-man crusade against the school's attempts to "squash" him and prevent him from speaking his mind. This was an important theme of Dan's experience in his public life as a student: he often felt that classmates and teachers were out to control him, and he had instinctively mobilized his personality and intellectual resources to prevent this from happening. As a result, he had gained a reputation, to quote Dan, for being "contrary, obstreperous, and pugnacious." He was a sort of verbal warrior, making his lonely, heroic way in an unsympathetic Orwellian world.

Our first four sessions together were fairly straightforward. I attempted to learn about Dan's experience, and he checked me out. We seemed to be a good fit, and he was beginning to relax while in the office.

Our fifth session began with an unexpected moment of discovery. I opened the waiting-room door to find Dan sitting quietly, holding in his lap a canned soft drink and a bag of pretzels. As he entered my office, I observed casually, as a conversational aside, "Ah, you've brought a snack." Dan sat down and looked at his two hands, one holding the can, the other holding the pretzels, as if they were foreign objects or belonged to someone else. He stared at them for a full minute, and then he looked up at me.

"My mother gave me this snack as I left the house," he said slowly. "She said 'Take this, you're going to be hungry.' I hadn't really realized it until you just mentioned it. She just gave it to me like I was a little kid, and I just took it without thinking. I never even noticed it, really. I don't even like pretzels."

What followed was one of those wonderful dawnings of awareness that adolescent clients share all too infrequently with adults. Dan sat courageously with his new experience. "I can't believe it!" he exclaimed, smiling sheepishly. "I feel like such a little kid."

He began to describe other ways in which his mother treated him like a kid. He talked about her "controlling every aspect" of the family's home life, and about how much his father's "weakness" bothered him. His description of his parents was an angry, demeaning caricature (and perhaps considerably one-sided, if we take adult reality as the measure of truth). But it was a first attempt, on Dan's part, at an objective, disembedded assessment of the family field—a field that until now he had simply inhabited as the ground of his awareness.

Before this session ended, Dan turned his focus on himself. He described his constant, underlying sense of himself as a young child: powerless, without boundaries and definition of his own. His mode of organizing his awareness at home was thoroughly introjective; the meanings that defined his experience of self were meanings pressed upon him by the family field. And the boundary of self that defined his place in the family was confluent and permeable—a boundary conferred by the ground, rather than asserted as a figure.

Dan's ability and willingness to reflect on and verbalize his experience were somewhat exceptional for an adolescent client, but the organizational dynamics of his experience were not. We have seen that the main task of adolescence is, in a sense, to reorganize experience. This means coming to terms with the given organization, the child self, and reworking the self's paradigm. It is not at all unusual for adolescent experience to be reorganized as a sort of polarity correction of the child self's experience, and such polarity dynamics were clearly a powerful force in reorganizing Dan's experience. In his life outside the family—that is, in the regions of his experience where he had assumed responsibility and authorship—he was acutely sensitive to loss of boundary. He was uncomfortable agreeing with anyone. He was an expert at taking the contrary position, and he had developed the verbal skills to stake out his autonomous point of view in almost any situation. He simply loved the experience of being the only person in the room who knew the meaning of a particular word. When he felt threatened by his peers—specifically, when he felt their power to *define* him, to confer meaning upon him ("Dan, you're such a dweeb!")—he would let loose with a string of esoteric epithets, creating an impermeable boundary. He confided, later in therapy, with a smile, "Sometimes *I* don't even know what I'm saying!"

The developmental work of adolescence stands always against the ground of a prior organization, a way of experiencing the family and the self. It is a ground that never leaves us, even when the work of adolescence is done; mature, well-adjusted adults in their thirties or forties still find the experiential paradigm of the child self evoked in certain situations (for example, in an argument with a spouse, or during a visit to parents at Thanksgiving). The field of experience is flexible; otherwise, we would never change. It is also indelibly furrowed. And this elasticity, this capacity to stretch the self into new shapes while retaining the dynamic forces of the self's given organization, is nowhere more evident than in adolescence.

CHAPTER THREE

Reorganizing
the Interpersonal World

In adolescence, as we have seen, the organization of experience changes. The child begins a process of disembedding from the familiar world of childhood and family experience and sets a course of progressive delineation and ownership of the self. The fulfillment of adolescent development will be marked by a heightened sense of integrity and an increased capacity for self-support. On the way, the figural experience of self will be intensified, becoming more salient and centered, as contact boundaries are renegotiated.

Disembedding the Self

As this developmental process unfolds, the embedded self in the family field of childhood gradually gives way to the more differentiated patterns of adolescent experience. The emergent adolescent self establishes itself as a charged pole within the field, pulling itself out and attempting to stand apart from the milieu of parents and family. This development is analogous to the physical reorganization that occurs in weakly polarized magnetic fields when an electric current is passed through. The electric current causes opposing poles to define themselves, creating a pattern of forces, or a force field, which rearranges the material within the field. Likewise in adolescence, the current of temporal passage, of time passing, of growing up, polarizes the experiential field, setting up psychological "flux lines" that reshape the contact field of self and others. In other words, the development of the adolescent self is essentially synonymous with its disembedding from the field of childhood experience and its progressive reorganization of this field.

In early adolescence, the embedded self of childhood takes its first tentative steps toward existential selfhood. The adolescent begins to develop awareness of having a place in the world, of being a *phenomenologically* separate and potentially free-standing human being. Whereas the childhood self is a sort of franchise to the adult selves in its environment, the adolescent self is more of an entrepreneurial operation. The newly organized self of adolescence, in standing over and apart from the parent milieu, begins to exist in the etymological sense *(ex-istere)* of standing out, standing more as itself and under its own authorship, having a life for which it is individually responsible.

From this developmental moment on, the adolescent's world, beliefs, parents, and morality all seem less absolute, less the way things have to be. He begins to hold these realities out at arm's length so as to see them more clearly and more objectively. In other words, he begins to differentiate himself from the familiar world of parents and childhood assumptions and to inherit the responsibility for defining his own place and direction in life.

As the adolescent self disembeds from the family field of the child self, the contact boundary of self and others (particularly of self and parents) becomes engorged, as it were, and this situation gives rise to new sensitivities and awareness. Interactions that for years have been familiar, even routine, now become awkward and problematic. As the adolescent self emerges, it no longer unquestioningly accepts the contours and boundaries conferred on it by its milieu. The adolescent begins to take over these self-defining functions, and this process, at least in most families, does not happen without a certain degree of chafing and grinding. Accordingly, the contact boundary of adolescent self and parents, the place where the relational field must be renegotiated, becomes as sensitized as a swollen membrane, as responsive as newly grafted skin to vibrations within the family field, and we see the heightened reactivity and moodiness that characterize so much of adolescent behavior.

Contact Boundaries

In the language of phenomenological field theory, adolescent experience is marked by a new sense of *boundary*, a heightened differentiation of "me" from "them," of inner from outer, and a markedly different investment in the processes that organize contact between self and others. To say that the adolescent develops a heightened sense of self is tantamount to saying that the experiential field becomes organized more vividly around contact boundaries. In Gestalt therapy theory, as we begin to see in Chapter One, the notion of the *contact boundary* is used to capture the interactive essence of human experience. Polster and Polster (1973, p. 102) write that "the contact boundary is the point at which one experiences the 'me' in relation to that which is 'not me,' and through this contact, both are more clearly experienced." In other words, self and nonself can be identified only through processes at the contact boundary. Gestalt therapists refer to these processes as *contact functions*. These functions, which regulate the way in which an individual takes in and acts on the environment, also serve to shape and identify the experience of self.

The notion of the contact boundary derives from the experiential data of *difference* and *relatedness*. In any one contact, there are two complementary moments of experience: a sense of difference or separateness, of being differentiated from something else, and a sense of connection or involvement, of being engaged with something else. Adolescence is about these complementary phenomena: differentiating or becoming separate from, and negotiating the terms of involvement. With different individuals, or at different contact boundaries for a given adolescent, we may find one or the other of these complementary dimensions being emphasized. A teenager, diligently separating from the influence of his family and creating clearer boundaries, may at the very same time be struggling to rework the terms of involvement with the same people. But, whatever we witness at the contact boundary of the adolescent and his environment, we are witnessing the developmental work of recreating, organizing, and identifying the self.

The transformation of adolescence is essentially a transformation of the child's experience of relatedness in various fields. At some developmental moments, the heightening of differences is paramount; at others, the negotiation or renegotiation of involvement is figural. In the service of clarity, let us examine these complementary moments of the contact process separately. We will see how the adolescent cultivates both the experience of differentness and the business of reshaping involvements in the interpersonal world.

Boundaries as Separation

We are concerned here with interrelated but distinct fields of adolescent experience. We will consider, in turn, the adolescent's experience of family and parents, his relationship to the wider adult world, and his involvement in the world of peers.

Differentiating from Family and Parents. A great deal of so-called typical adolescent behavior is designed to generate an experience of boundary, or separation, between teenagers and adults. This is behavior that polarizes, sometimes through conflict, sometimes comfortably, the worlds of adult and adolescent experience. In most families, it is not difficult to find examples of behavior that functions precisely to make this difference palpable.

The act of pulling away from the family is transformed from a murky psychological impulse into a substantial, concrete reality through behavior that is almost ritualistic. Meals become an issue: a son wants to spend less time at the table, or sometimes he wants to eat with his friends instead of with the family. A daughter resists going to church, complains about dinners with her grandparents, or asks to be released from the obligation of attending family functions. In public, a son avoids physical proximity with his parents, actively disassociating himself from the family group. At the theater, he sits in a separate row. At a football game, he goes searching for his friends. At the mall, he walks fifteen paces behind his mother. In all these events, and in the minor struggles that accompany them, the pulling away of the adolescent becomes a reality of the relationship.

One client of mine, a fifteen-year-old boy named Robert, described how powerfully this experience can take hold at the visceral level. Robert and his mother had lived together as a two-person family since his birth and had enjoyed a mutually rich and stimulating relationship over the years. Robert described to me how in recent months he had begun to feel engulfed by waves of revulsion when he was with his mother. Like her, he was exceptionally bright and verbal. They had often spent time, after school and in the evenings, discussing politics and the arts. As long as they could remember, each had found in the other a resonance of unusual degree. Recently, however, Robert had begun to find these conversations unfulfilling, then boring, and finally downright irritating. He felt it, he said, right in the pit of his stomach, and it flooded up through his chest in a rising wave of nausea.

A psychoanalytically oriented therapist might interpret Robert's revulsion as his reaction to a heightening of sexual feelings in the context of his enduring attachment to his mother. But such an interpretation arbitrarily truncates the richness and ambiguity of the situation, reducing to libido a pervasive change in the entire field of Robert's experience—a field that does incorporate his emergent sexuality, to be sure, but only as a minor subtext of the evolving contact process. Robert was nauseated more by his tendency to swallow his mother's penetrating ideas—that is, by his introjecting of her views and his deference to her wish to shape his thinking—than by any impulse to attach or act out sexually.

In many households, the sharing and withholding of information is another important focus of separation rituals. Many adolescents become secretive, no longer wanting to share the stories of daily life with their parents. Instead, and with an intensity quite different from that of the childhood years, they turn to friends for sharing and support. They talk with friends about their parents, a simple but significant challenging of one of childhood's implicit taboos. And, interestingly, parents begin to do the same thing. They seek out adult peers who have children of similar ages and commiserate with them about the tribulations of raising teenagers. This mutual turning away represents a developmentally significant and essentially healthy metamorphosis of the parent–child field.

At times, the adolescent conspicuously keeps his parents in the dark about what he is doing. His reports of an afternoon's activity become increasingly vague, less descriptive of concrete events: "We were over at Rick's, just hanging around." And he may or may not have been over at Rick's. He may have been at the mall, or driving around, or at his girlfriend's. He becomes visibly annoyed when pressed for more detail, taking the questions as invasions of a new and private space. This ritual of not letting his parents know exactly what he is doing is not simply a matter of covering up forbidden activity (although that, too, becomes part of the picture, in many cases). Its meaning is more essential. It creates a buffer zone of parental unawareness, a sort of moat behind which the configuring of a heightened experience of self can proceed. The non- and misinforming that adolescents do serves essentially to diffuse and lessen the field forces of the parent–child relationship. Forbidden activity sometimes serves as an anchor or rationale for creating this buffer. And even adolescents who are not, objectively speaking, engaging in forbidden activity—those who keep themselves out of trouble, and whose parents are flexible and accepting—will sometimes manufacture the belief that they are doing forbidden things. "My parents would kill me if they knew" is frequently a mistaken but developmentally useful myth for the separating adolescent.

Forbidden activity is a ritual of separation familiar to those therapists who work with adolescents clinically. Our clients ignore, stretch, bend, and break rules. They defy authority and get themselves involved in behavior that no responsible adult would condone. The self-destructive potential of such behavior is painfully clear to the clinician, but the successful passage through adolescence is usually characterized by the separation ritual of forbidden activity. In other words, forbidden activity is part of the subcultural identity of adolescents in our society.

Drinking and drug use are examples par excellence of forbidden activity that serves to heighten the adolescent's experience of boundary between self and the family or childhood milieu. Approximately 80 percent of adolescents will experiment with alcohol by the age of eighteen. And for some of them, alcohol consumption will become dangerously woven into the personal tapestry of coping methods. Approximately 15 to 20 percent will develop patterns of consumption serious enough to disrupt their eventual adjustment to adult life, warranting diagnoses of chemical abuse or dependency. For the remaining 60 to 65 percent, alcohol experimentation and use serves the ritual function of forbidden activity, its meaning and attraction provided in part by the fact that it takes one unmistakably beyond the limits of adult (specifically parental) acceptance. It takes them beyond the boundary of the "known map," into the uncharted realm where adult cognizance and purview disappears and the disengagement of the self from parents evolves from wish into fact.

The discernible shift in the adolescent's own phenomenology is that the family now becomes experienced at times as a constraint—something apart from the self that gets in the way. The family's role as a support and necessary framework for living, while by no means at an end, may be relegated to the *ground* of experience, where it can be conveniently ignored. Most teenagers, even (or perhaps especially) those rebelling against parental influence, react strongly when family support is somehow disrupted. Divorce, a parent's loss of a job, or the remarriage of a single parent are common examples. But this support function of the family is frequently denied or devalued, especially among boys, while the polar image of the family as constraint is heightened, sometimes to an absurd degree. This is particularly noteworthy among younger adolescents, who are often more invested in bounding themselves off from the family of childhood than in accurately assessing reality. It is not uncommon for thirteen- and fourteen-year-olds to claim, without the slightest sense of hyperbole, that they could live entirely on their own, without any support from their parents, if only given the chance.

The developmental point of all this distancing is that it serves the essential and important task of creating an experience of boundary between the adolescent and his parents. The gravitational pull of the parental orbit is not ultimately made up of all these particulars (the meals together, the sharing of information, the enforcement of rules and limits). The "stuff" of interpersonal field forces is much more subtle and at the same time much more powerful: the adolescent *cares* what his parents think of him. He cares too much to be capable of becoming a free-standing agent in the world at large. The task of learning to depend on his own agency, of empowering his own capacity to approve and disapprove of things (including his own behavior), can be accomplished only if the power, real and imagined, of his parents is diminished.

Another important expression of boundary creation is the experience that many adolescents have of the gulf between the generations. This gulf is most painfully salient when the adolescent is in crisis or in need of support—for example, when he or she becomes the victim of abuse at the hands of peers. It is not uncommon to find youths who are literally frightened for their lives because some predatory bully has marked them as targets, but who feel so disengaged from the adult world that seeking out adult intervention is not even seen as an option. It is difficult for adults to grasp the intensity of this experience. I have had patients who were willing to consider suicide before they would consider reporting their situation to adults.

This experience of the gulf, and the acute emotions that so often accompany it, reflect an underlying existential and developmental reality of adolescence. Adolescents often feel isolated and lonely, not

because they are neurotic, and not necessarily because support is unavailable to them, but because their separateness has become a fact
of life, an organizing principle of the experiential field. It becomes a
given and an imperative. It is liberating, and it is terrifying. Emergent
boundaries identify an emergent self. Psychological segregation from
the family field opens up an interiority that is delicious and fascinating and at the same time insulating and engulfing. With the creation
and heightening of boundaries, the belongingness of childhood—the
sense of being a part of something larger than oneself—is counter-
posed with an equal and opposite truth. The adolescent is on his own.

Separating from the Wider Adult World.   Beyond the immedi-
ate family field, adolescents also engage in the less focally defined
task of differentiating themselves from the world of adults in general.
Typically, this arena is not nearly so charged as the family field, but
it is still extremely important for trying out and testing new boundaries in the experience of self.

   Dress and appearance are probably the most obvious expressions
of this enterprise. Fifteen-year-old Kerry was a case in point. She
dressed primarily in black, and her lipstick was either black or shock-
ingly red. She shaved one side of her head and wore her hair, streaked
with white, down over her face much of the time. Unlike many of her
punk friends, Kerry was an excellent student who clearly valued and
enjoyed schoolwork and learning. Nevertheless, she loved to complain about adults who could not "accept" her, citing as examples
people in stores who turned to look at her, shaking their heads. Indeed, at school her teachers almost always tended to dismiss or avoid
interacting with her at first, until they discovered her sharp and facile
mind. Kerry's was a large extended family, and although she had enjoyed it as a younger child, she now found her family too close for
comfort. Her appearance functioned like a fence and put her in control of the gate. Her dress, insofar as it provoked a predictably distancing judgment from adults, supported a critical, rejecting (bounding)
counterresponse from her.

   A good part of the outward trappings of adolescence—those expressions and affinities that leave adults, as if by design, scratching
their heads and wondering aloud—serves this important function of
generating an experience of difference, or boundary. They define and
identify a transitional culture, a way of organizing behavior and ap-

propriating reality. Examples are everywhere: on the covers of record albums, in graffiti on school walls, in preferred literature, in music, in language, and so on. Consider the use of sexually explicit and scato-logical language. Anyone who has had the experience of sitting near a group of teenagers in a movie theater or at a high school football game knows exactly what I mean. Language that the adult generation considers vulgar, or at least inappropriate in mixed company, is com-monplace in these situations, and this has been true forever. I recall howling with laughter when my dear old grandmother wished my brother and his new bride, who were married in the early 1970s, a "long and wonderful intercourse." She would have been mortified at our ready sexual interpretation of such a remark in mixed company. But most of my own generation would never dream of sprinkling our mixed-company conversation with "Fuck you" and "Blow me," al-though I recently trailed behind a group of wholesome-looking teen-agers at a shopping mall who included these expletives liberally in their banter. My experience at that moment was a sharp one, an ex-perience of the differences between our generations. And this is pre-cisely the purpose of that sort of behavior. Again, the function is unmistakable: to separate a transitional culture from both childhood and adulthood, allowing it to serve as a nourishing milieu for the disembedding and reorganization of the individual self.

Teenagers sometimes generate boundary experiences in ways that adults find hostile or offensive. Years ago, I worked at the outpa-tient mental health clinic of a Catholic hospital. The reception desk was managed by a sweet, elderly nun who always dressed in the tra-ditional all-white habit of her order. One patient, a boy of about sev-enteen, would regularly engage the sister in unwelcome debate about the dehumanizing effects of uniforms. Several times he left her in wordless tears after his stop at the reception desk. His own uniform was a T-shirt, which he wore religiously on his appointment days. It said in bold letters: "Harley's the Best. Fuck the Rest." When I asked him what effect he supposed his shirt might have on adults in general, and on elderly nuns in particular, he replied simply, "That's their problem."

Adolescent bounding behavior is not limited to these sorts of high-profile enactments. It runs through the broad range of experi-ence and behavior and can be as experientially subtle as it is behav-iorally bold. One such expression of bounding is found in the adolescent love of the absurd. Let me illustrate with a story of my own children. Some years ago, I was sitting with my son, then fourteen, and my daughter, then twelve, watching David Letterman's television show. At one point, Letterman came onto the set wearing a suit covered with Velcro hooks. Opposite him was a wall, ten or twelve feet high, covered with Velcro loops. With full ceremonial drumroll, he jumped onto a small trampoline and catapulted high onto the wall, where he stuck, suspended by the Velcro. My son, who had been sitting on a small stool, fell onto the floor in a fit of convulsive laughter. My daughter, decidedly preadolescent, looked at the screen for a moment and then turned to me. "That's dumb," she said.

Of course, there are cognitive differences between twelve- and fourteen-year-olds that help explain why adolescents grasp the higher-order, abstract illogic of absurdity, whereas concrete-operational twelve-year-olds tend to see absurdity more two-dimensionally, as silliness. But the difference between the adolescent's and the preadolescent's contrasting responses to absurd humor goes beyond cognitive development considered in isolation. The difference has to do with a larger, more comprehensive shift, an existential transformation, which underlies the strictly cognitive, affective, and interpersonal changes. The adolescent's appreciation of the absurd signifies that he has discovered the very borders of common sense, that is, the common cognitive currency of adult-world thinking and reality construction.

In adolescence, more than in any other developmental phase, the individual is exhorted by the culture at large to organize meaning a certain way: to use good judgment, to be practical and realistic, to subordinate private reality to the demands of the "real world," to begin planning for responsible adulthood, and so on. This is a constant and intensely figural message for adolescents in our culture today, and while they are busy absorbing it, they delight in discovering its perimeter. In the same way that adolescents are beginning to relativize their experience of the family, disembedding from that field and seeing it in a wider context, discovering family reality precisely as a frame (albeit a compelling one), they are also discovering common sense as a frame of mind. And so, just as the adolescent is beginning to organize a self that transcends the family field, he also delights in organizing cognitive experiences that transcend the borders of common sense. Once again, the experience of boundary is what holds the allure.

Some wonderful examples of the adolescent romance with humor and absurdity are provided by Richard Hawley, who writes, "Because school is so serious, humor is salvation: not polite humor, not the clichéd posturings derived from television programs and other commercial culture—but the instinctive, spontaneous, sometimes anarchic impulse to deny the seriousness of everything, to set up an alternative system in which the preposterous reigns" (1993, pp. 56–57). Hawley, who has spent a lifetime educating adolescent boys, is a remarkably astute anthropologist of adolescent culture. His observations of youth behavior are penetrating and instructive. He offers the following example, from his personal experience as a teacher, of the boundary-making function of adolescent absurdity. Four boys in the school where Hawley was teaching, each of them a bit odd in his own way, collaborated on publishing an unofficial school newspaper. They called it *The Voice of Cheese*. At irregular intervals, the paper would be "published," which meant that a single copy would be tacked neatly onto a prominent bulletin board. Hawley says, "For some reason, everybody in the school, including faculty, seemed to read it. The wonder of it was that the surreal drift of the articles made no outward sense whatsoever, except perhaps to members of the [group] whose in-jokes and private irreverences were no doubt encoded in the text" (pp. 58–59). What followed was predictable. The faculty as a group became vaguely convinced that the boys were up to something, precisely because it made no sense. And the less sense it made, the funnier the students found it. Eventually, one faculty member recognized some reference to himself in the pages of *Cheese*. The reference, according to Hawley, was completely oblique and nonsensical but nevertheless prompted the faculty member to make a dramatic show of tearing the paper from the bulletin board, in front of its assembled readership, and righteously ripping it to shreds. Again predictably, this response from an official adult triggered even more straight-faced lampooning from the student body. The editors, feigning bewilderment and incredulity, launched an extensive inquiry into the reasons for the faculty member's odd, aggressive behavior, wrote serious letters to the school newspaper, and so on, all of this activity masking a private undercurrent of subdued hilarity at the absurdity of the whole thing. The beauty of Hawley's story is that it accentuates the developmental and psychological context of the adolescent affinity for the absurd—namely, the bounding of the adolescent culture from adult culture, and the diffuse but foundational enterprise of challenging and creating meaning.

Boundaries Within Peer Culture.   Simultaneous with the disembedding and bounding that begin to develop between adolescents and adults, there emerge differentiating boundaries among adolescents themselves. In early adolescence, fissures in adolescent culture develop along the same lines that separate youths from their parents and teachers. Seventh graders, for example, typically differentiate themselves according to those who are still adult-world embedded and those who have become invested in pulling away from adult influence. Perhaps the clearest example is related to the development of heterosexual interest in early adolescence. Girls who may have been popular and socially successful in sixth grade often lose status if they fall behind their peers in terms of developing interest in boys. They may be seen as too childlike by their peers. A teacher of seventh-grade girls has told me that on their annual overnight field trip, the girls roughly segregate into those who have brought some sort of stuffed animal and those who have brought *Seventeen* magazine.

It is usually around the age of thirteen that teenagers begin to identify themselves with particular groups or crowds, rather than with specific individual friends. The fast kids, the brainy kids, the nerds begin to emerge as discrete segments of peer society. By the middle phase of adolescence, the social topography of peer culture becomes richly differentiated. There are jocks, metalheads, geeks, stoners, brains, punks, losers, hoods, and so on. Interestingly, individual adolescents often identify themselves across multiple groupings, using the variegated social topography to concoct a personal recipe of identifications. A typical statement from a fifteen-year-old boy asked to locate his position in the social landscape would be: "I get along with the jocks and the metalheads, and a couple of my friends are brains, but I'm not completely in any one of those groups." The point is not so much that individuals segregate themselves into one group or another but rather that the adolescent's perception of the peer field undergoes a rich diversification, testifying to the reorganization of adolescent experience.

Boundaries as Connection

The adolescent's work of bounding from the adult world, creating a phenomenological sense of separateness and autonomy, is in the service of connecting to that world in a fuller, more lively, more powerful way. Contact, as I have pointed out, is a two-stroke process, a mode of relationship that establishes separation and connection at the same time. The separation boundary of adolescence, in other words, serves ultimately to support the young adult's engagement of the adult world as an empowered participant, a relative equal.

There are gender differences in how adolescents integrate the work of separating and the work of connecting. I can recall vividly the transformations of my own children and their friends as they covered this ground. When their friends arrived to visit, they would pass through our kitchen on the way to more private corners of the house, often encountering my wife and me. At the ages of twelve and thirteen, my son's friends would pass through oozing smiles and deference, stopping and politely answering any questions or remarks we might have for them. At fourteen, this picture changed dramatically. They passed through with heads hung and eyes averted, mumbling if directly addressed but doing their best to escape the kitchen as quickly as possible. By the age of seventeen, a new posture had emerged. Heads were held up, faces broadcast a tentative (and somewhat self-conscious) confidence, hands were sometimes thrust out in greeting, and occasionally a sort of "old boy" greeting was proffered: "Hi, Mr. McConville. How's your golf game?"

With my daughter and her friends, the kitchen procession evolved quite differently. There was no period of averted glances and awkward slinking escapes, just friendly conversation that became more engaging and horizontal as time went on. By the time they were seventeen, it seemed as if our daughter's friends had become *our* friends, too, and my daughter would sometimes have to extricate them from the kitchen conversations that so easily developed.

The investment that adolescent girls have in maintaining and developing their connections has been beautifully described by Carol Gilligan and her colleagues (Gilligan, 1982; Gilligan, Lyons, and Hanmer, 1990). Much more than adolescent boys, and especially with their mothers, girls struggle to preserve their sense of relatedness even while they expand their experience of self beyond the restrictive boundaries of childhood traditions. Boys are often content to experiment with change and keep their experimentations to themselves where their parents are concerned. Girls are more likely to disclose their experimentations and their evolving experiences of self, and to push for acceptance of these changes within the framework of existing relationships (Rich, 1990).

I am reminded here of Leslie, a sixteen-year-old who asked her parents to take her to a therapist. When I met with her alone, she announced her intention of using my services to get her parents to accept some changes that she was in the process of making. Leslie had recently attended a sleepover where she and her friends had been "busted" for alcohol consumption. As it turned out, Leslie was not particularly interested in drinking, but she felt it essential that her parents accept "in principle" that she was now at an age where drinking was going to be part of her life. She and her mother had debated endlessly about this before she came to see me, and neither one had budged an inch. Our work together, which included a series of five sessions with Leslie and her parents, resolved the issue quite satisfactorily—not because anyone on either side changed position but because both sides learned and came to accept that there were now issues on which there would simply not be a meeting of the minds (as distinct from what had been the case during Leslie's childhood), and that this was now an acceptable term of their evolving relationship. By my scorekeeping, their *debate* ended in a draw and transformed itself, in form and spirit, into a thoughtful *discussion*. Leslie was delighted with the result.

Adolescent girls may maintain connection with their parents more obviously than their male counterparts do, particularly in the fighting and sharing that they do, but the ultimate objective of adolescent males and females is the same—namely, to rework the contact boundary, and with it the emerging sense of self. To emphasize this point, the emergence of uniquely adolescent selfhood is tantamount to the reworking of important relationships. In some respects, this reworking emphasizes the separation-differentiation dimension of the contact process; in other respects, it emphasizes (as in Leslie's case) the cultivation of new terms of involvement. There are gender differences, to be sure; but, for both sexes, both dimensions of contact are undergoing change.

Traditional psychoanalytic developmental theory has emphasized the separation process as the essential theme of adolescence. And if one works primarily with adolescent boys in therapy, this may indeed seem to be the case. I have often seen adolescent boys who disengaged emphatically from their mothers, sometimes (in divorced families) refusing to see them for prolonged periods. But the developmental point of these separations is not simply to get away, to "escape from an overwhelming regressive pull to infantile dependencies" (Blos, 1979, p. 147). It is also to make a different sort of connecting possible, a new mode of contact that creates changes on both the adolescent's and the parent's side of the relationship. For Robert, the sixteen-year-old who described his visceral revulsion to his mother's presence, these feelings diminished, along with the urgent need to escape, once his mother joined him in the work of reorganizing their field. She did this by adjusting her behavior and her expectations, and by mourning the loss of her own childrearing self. And Robert, once he had learned how to withdraw from his mother, once this had become a confirmed part of his contact repertoire, relaxed and resumed their relationship, although on a somewhat different footing.

Another boy, fifteen-year-old Terry, remained entrenched for almost three years in his refusal to interact with his mother, but his entrenchment reflected the fact that he was doing all the work himself. At the age of fourteen, Terry had literally bolted from his mother and gone to live with his father. He avoided his mother in every possible way because he could not figure out how to be with her without feeling like a child. When I invited her to several sessions, he lost his ability to speak his mind and hold his ground, reverting inevitably to his childhood configuration of guilt and passivity. Only much later, and then only once he had a steady and serious girlfriend, did he permit himself any contact with his mother. His mother had stubbornly refused to acknowledge that Terry's discomfort with some of her behavior (her cooing voice, her insistence on touching him) had any legitimacy whatsoever. Terry's distancing from his mother was best interpreted as an effort not to exit the relationship but to change it, to make new forms of contact possible, to create a more differentiated connection with her that might endure the vicissitudes of development.

A psychoanalytic understanding of these developments would rest primarily on a construction of Terry's awakening libido and his fears of regressive dependency. But such an explanation would account for only a limited part of the developing field. Terry's mother was at least as much altered by the addition of the girlfriend as Terry was. In the process of heightening boundaries, both the adolescent and the parents are changed. It is the *field* that must come to terms with its "regressive tendencies," not the adolescent alone.

CHAPTER FOUR

Taking Ownership of the Self

At the most concrete level, the adolescent self coalesces as the child begins to appropriate sensory experience in a new way. He begins to take ownership of his experience—that is, to appropriate vision, hearing, smell, and touch more precisely as his own.

Every family, intentionally or not, teaches its children a certain view of reality. Some of this is obvious as parents pass on their biases, prejudices, and values concerning the world at large. But, more subtly, parents also pass on a way of organizing and defining both intra- and extrafamilial reality. How they see the child, whether their view is communicated explicitly or not, shapes the way the child sees himself. Furthermore, how parents see themselves will largely determine how the child perceives them. But as the experiential field of the adolescent begins to differentiate, these habitual and unquestioned perceptions begin to lose their aspect of objective reality. As the adolescent himself begins to synthesize a point of view of his own, he discovers that much of what he formerly took for granted had actually issued from someone else's point of view, and he becomes pointedly aware that his own perceptions do not always coincide with the family's reality.

Appropriating Sensory Experience

In a very real sense, the adolescent begins to experience ownership of his sensory experience. He begins to see things with his own eyes. He begins to notice things that have been there all along but that he has not synthesized as perceptual figures or formulated as observations or opinions. What is perhaps most obvious, the adolescent begins to see his parents in ways he did not before. I have often listened to twelve- and thirteen-year-olds in therapy as they "discovered" that

51

a parent is alcoholic, untrustworthy, or insincere. The adolescent shifts from accepting reality as proffered by the adult world and begins to notice the obvious. And if he has noticed the obvious all along, he brings it more clearly into focus and holds it there, making it available for reflection and conversation. He sees, for example, that adults are sometimes quite arbitrary. He may well have known and felt this before, but now he begins to see it as a substantial perceptual reality.

I remember James, a compulsive, tightly controlled boy of fourteen whose various rituals had the unmistakable quality of passive-aggressive behavior, which was directed primarily at his mother and his sister. James was charm-school polite. He had no conscious awareness of his anger or of the meaning of the many operations he undertook to keep it in check: the stiff, straight-backed posture; the habit of folding his hands tightly in his lap; the various minor rituals that kept potential assertiveness under wraps. What James was aware of, or at least what he could formulate, was that his family was "fine" and that there was something vaguely but pervasively "wrong" with him. This view was essentially the one his parents had conveyed when they first consulted me, and although they had never put it quite so bluntly to him, their view had shaped his own. Over a series of sessions, months into therapy, James's ability to *see* his family gradually emerged. He began by noticing the various ways in which his older sister manipulated him (or "controlled" him, as he said). Soon thereafter, he began to see how her behavior was partly a reply to their mother's insistence on controlling all of them. This picture of the family, its members and its dynamics, was revealed to him like a landscape through a morning fog—in vague, suggestive outlines at first, and then with progressive clarity and detail as time went on.

Younger children experience their parents' characterological traits more kinesthetically than cognitively. They *feel* the effects of one parent's rigidity, or of another parent's need to be needed. Phenomenologically, the parental character is a *milieu* for the psyche of the child, an environment that shapes the child's experience all the more powerfully because of its invisibility. The adolescent, however, by virtue of beginning to differentiate an *authentic* (that is, an *authored*) self out of the family milieu, steps back, as it were, and begins to see. He quite literally begins to use his eyes and ears in ways that have been implicitly discouraged, perhaps even prohibited, and his perceptions are all the more authentic for that. This emergence of perspective, which reveals the surrounding world in greater detail and truth, sets the stage for the heightened awareness of inner life that will develop as adolescence progresses. At this point, the emerging adolescent self announces itself as a point of view, a psychological space from which the world is seen.

Parents often feel this change in their relationship with their child. They can sometimes even sense the moment when the child accumulates enough psychic ballast to become a center of experience (at least in this relationship) in his or her own right. That moment signals a change in the relational field whereby the child is able to sit back and look at his parents, and formulate observations and opinions that deviate from the adults' definitions of reality. One thirteen-year-old boy told me how he suddenly realized one evening at a restaurant that his father's treatment of the waitress was a self-serving exercise in power: "He was just showing off. He wanted everybody to know he was in charge." Such moments mark a significant shift in the distribution of psychological power in the parent-child relationship.

As any junior high school or high school teacher can testify, this is the age when kids begin to mimic and caricature adults, copying their gestures and their familiar verbalizations and vocal mannerisms, and acting them out for each other as a way of solidifying and substantiating these new perceptions. Teachers of children in this age group see how scrutinizing their students have become. A friend of mine who teaches history to ninth-grade girls noticed one day that his students seemed particularly distracted and skittish. As the day progressed, he observed the same behavior in each successive class. Finally, at the end of the day, he asked one of the girls about it, and she confided the horrible truth: a white thread, awkwardly trailing out of his back pocket, had held the fascination of the entire class for most of the day. This "flaw," and the students' ability to identify it and hold it perceptually, had dominated the field of their collective experience for much of an entire day.

Of course, adolescents also begin to see themselves and each other with the same sort of zoom-lens clarity, and they often convey how transparent to others they feel. They notice skin tone, facial hair, the shapes of people's heads, the length of legs, the swelling of nipples, the color of clothing. They notice odors, voice pitch, eye movement, the suppleness or rigidity of body posture, and so on. They are attendant to a broadly new and articulated domain of perceptual reality, and this development reflects both a blossoming of sensory experience and an appropriation of sensory experience as an instrument of the self.

The phenomenon of taking possession emerges across the spectrum of the senses. Adolescents appropriate their hearing in part by their intensified interest in music, which typically redefines or refines their earlier, preadolescent preferences. Fairly specific musical tastes often develop, which are more self-consciously identified with. While they may not be unique from an adult perspective, they are experienced as such by the adolescent, for they are chosen, not introjected, and this is the important point.

In general, the adolescent identifies with his tastes in a way that younger children do not. Tastes become a way of knowing the self. Long before the crystallization of a preliminary adult-world identity, as described by Erikson (1959), the rudiments of this eventual gestalt emerge in the form of a preliminary constellation of sensory identifications. Cigarette brand, footwear, clothing label, and favorite fast food are all chosen. This one "rules" while that one "sucks," all in the service of delineating and defining the new adolescent sense of self. For the most part, it is not the content of these choices that ultimately matters, because they may change overnight. The process of choosing is what heightens and makes real the adolescent's ownership of sensory experience.

The Synthesizing Function of the Self

If adolescence is a period of taking possession of the self, then its most concrete expression is the adolescent's beginning to organize contact with the world in new and more personal ways. *Taking possession of the self* means to appropriate that function whereby we, as human beings, make meaning of our experience.

Crocker (1988) has pointed out that this process occurs not only at the level of specific sensory awarenesses, in "discernible moments" of experience, but also at the more holistic level of organizing a personal history and a world view. Among the most important essential abilities of the self is its *synthesizing function*, that capacity whereby we appropriate the larger contexts of our experience into relatively organized wholes. Crocker writes, "This spontaneous and ineluctable activity of organizing one's experience into a temporal whole, of having access to that complex whole of past experiences through memory, and of being able to anticipate the future imaginatively on the basis of past experience, is the work of [the self's] synthesizing function. The sense of personal identity is one important result of the self's referring all of its experiences to itself" (p. 106). She goes on to point out that the synthesizing function of the self is what makes possible the sense that each of us has of owning our experience, the "indisputable sense that these are MY experiences, that this is MY life" (p. 107). The appropriation of this capacity, this synthesizing function of the self, is one of the defining characteristics of adolescent development. Its emergence signals the beginnings of the shift away from introjection as the essential mode of creating and organizing meaning in the world.

Adolescents reveal this shift in countless ways. Most begin to organize a perception of their families as something apart from themselves. They remain tied in many ways to the family context, of course, but they also begin to see that context, to hold it perceptually at arm's length and identify its figural properties. They no longer simply *inhabit* the family milieu. When asked in therapy to tell about their families, most adolescents can do so, however halting or self-serving their characterizations may be. When an adolescent responds to this request with a shrug or an uncomprehending look, as preadolescent children often do, that is always a significant indicator of immature differentiation.

Sometimes the adolescent's reorganization of family experience is striking and reflects a dramatic, self-authored reinterpretation of family reality. One fourteen-year-old girl, Tammy, had undergone what her parents called a "personality change" over the course of about a year. The outward picture told a familiar story of adolescent metamorphosis. Tammy had lost interest in school and changed her appearance from "preppy" to "tough." She wore black jeans and a leather jacket, spurned makeup, and wore her hair straight and unadorned, pulled back behind her ears. Her parents described corresponding behavioral changes at home. She had become angry and argumentative, referring to the family as "a bunch of assholes" and adamantly refusing to take part in family functions. She even refused to allow her laundry to be mixed with that of other family members,

and she became enraged whenever she felt that her parents had in-
vaded her boundaries, even in the most innocuous fashion.

Tammy's parents had been married for sixteen years. Her mother
had been married once before and divorced before Tammy's birth.
From her previous marriage she had a daughter, now nineteen, who
lived with the family. Tammy's father, a sensitive and gentle man, had
maintained an active caretaking relationship with his own parents,
who were getting on in years and were in failing health. The precise
historic dynamics of this marriage and this family were somewhat
hard to determine, but several things were clear. Her father's attachment and attention to his own parents left his wife feeling set aside,
and she had compensated by maintaining a special bond with her
daughter from the first marriage. In effect, beneath the surface of an
adequately functioning and unremarkable family life (there were no
significant problems during Tammy's childhood years), there existed
two families grafted together as one.

Tammy's mother seemed depressed to me in her rounded shoulders, stooped posture, and low energy level, although she denied that
she ever felt "any more depressed than anyone else." Tammy's adaptation as a child to her family field was to be as pleasant as she could
be. She had been a "sweet kid," by her parents' description, someone
who "sort of pulled us together and never made any trouble." Sensing
her own parents' primary emotional preoccupation with other things,
Tammy satisfied her own need for a special attachment and sense of
importance by becoming her grandfather's "little girl." And, in this
family of covert emotional loyalties, her grandfather had let Tammy
know that she was his favorite.

Then, when Tammy was twelve, her grandfather died. Her grandmother became depressed, and, as in a chain reaction, so did her father and her mother, although no one became depressed enough to
acknowledge it or seek treatment. In effect, Tammy was abandoned
in a family of sad, preoccupied people. For several years, she continued in her childhood role of all-purpose daughter, trying as best she
could to make people happy by being the best that she could be.

As Tammy turned fourteen, near the anniversary of her grandfather's death, she began to look at her life through new eyes. She began, literally, to synthesize her experience differently, and what
emerged for her was a whole new crystallization of the family's history
and reality. The underlying patterns of attachment and loyalty now

emerged as *figural* in Tammy's experience. As this occurred, her hitherto *ground* sense of not belonging, of not having a place in this family, became acute. She began to see her mother as rejecting and as
favoring her older sister. Her father now emerged in her perception
as "wimpy," unable to establish himself as a force within his own family. She saw him as a grown-up "mama's boy" and hated him for it.
She didn't belong in this family, she said, and concluded that no one
had a right to tell her what to do. She recalled numerous incidents
from childhood when she had wanted and needed her parents' attention and support, and (sidestepping the fact that she had often suppressed her needs in order not to make trouble) she now became
furious at her parents' unavailability.

Tammy's new synthesis of her world was extreme, but certainly
not uncommon. With many, perhaps most, adolescents in clinical
treatment we find similar if usually less dramatic reinterpretations of
the larger picture—of their parents, the family, their place in the
world. What Tammy's story also illustrates, something not the least
bit uncommon among adolescents, is the painful and disruptive outcome of this emergent capacity to see the world and parents more
accurately. The idealization of parents, which in childhood supported
the sense of security and order, now begins to crumble before the
adolescent's eyes. And, as in Tammy's case, these revelations are
often accompanied by a sense of disappointment and betrayal, and by
emotional reactions of sadness, grief, and rage.

Synthesizing the Self

In the same way that the adolescent begins to organize meaning in her
perception of her parents and family history and in her assessment of
both peers and adults, she also begins to synthesize an experience of
an identifiable, personal self. This development is a process that starts
with the heightened identification and ownership of fragments, or
moments, of experience and it grows uncertainly and ungracefully
over a period of years. From the burgeoning field of experience (the
vast array of feelings, motives, wishes, goals, ideals, and perceptions
that constitute the adolescent's experience of self), and from the burgeoning complex of emergent partial self-gestalts and of polarities that
begin to organize these constituents, she begins to make figural what
she identifies as belonging to the self. That is, she begins a delicate

process of organizing this field into figure-ground structures, perhaps weakly or loosely constituted at first. These structures bring to the foreground of awareness what is claimed as the self's own, and relegate to the periphery what is not. As part of this process, the adolescent will most likely disassociate herself from and polarize with certain portions of the field, disclaiming or renouncing ownership of whatever seems too childlike, too adult, too unfamiliar, too unflattering, too other—in short, of whatever is experienced as "not me."[1]

This aspect of the self's process, whereby it accepts things into or deletes things from the field of its own experience (including some portions while excluding others, configuring self and bounding from nonself, owning and disowning), is a special, reflexive expression of the self's synthesizing function. It is another expression of the self's growing capacity for organizing its experience by taking over tasks formerly carried out by the environment. This transition from *environment-synthesized* (introjected) to *self-synthesized* process is by no means an all-or-nothing proposition, and it is certainly not an all-at-once occurrence.

Adolescence is a time, as we know, that is notorious for conformity. On the surface, it may seem gratuitous to speak of the adolescent's growing capacity for self-definition. Conforming to peers, however, is distinctly different from childhood-era family embeddedness, especially when some degree of choice is exercised with respect to peer relationships. It is certain that adolescents experience a degree of agency and choice in peer-group identifications that is not experienced in family identifications. Even youths who to adult observers

---

[1]In Gestalt therapy theory, *self* is identified as "the system of contacts" of the organism and its environment (Perls, Hefferline, and Goodman, 1951). Accordingly, Gestalt theorists have emphasized, in sharp contradistinction to psychoanalytic writers, that self is defined *by* the *process* of contact rather than *as* a hypothetical *structure* existing within the organism (McLeod, 1993; Yontef, 1993). But Gestalt theory has tended to neglect the fact that one derivitave of the organism-environment contact process is a *reflexive experience of self*, that is, of a structure (or gestalt) that emerges in experience and that I identify intuitively as "myself." (This sense of self is more intrinsically given in experience than is the "verbal replica" of the self that Perls, Hefferline, and Goodman identify as "personality" [1951, p. 382]). The self, in other words, is *both synthesizer and synthesized* within the field of experience. Certain phenomenological writers, especially Straus (1963) and Merleau-Ponty (1963), have captured and emphasized this *irreducible ambiguity* in the meaning of the term *self*, as that which organizes contact, and that which is organized by the process of contact.

seem slavishly conforming and peer-group dependent tend to experience themselves as having made choices in these matters, and they may become quite defensive if it is suggested that they have succumbed to peer pressure.

Phenomenologically, the emergent synthesizing function may manifest itself in the adolescent's growing awareness as a "true self," which he or she sharply distinguishes from identifications of self originating in the expectations and attributions of others. About parents or other familiar adults, the adolescent may say, "They think they know me, but they don't." The very *right* to define themselves becomes an issue with many teenagers, and many will pointedly object when someone else attempts to define their inner reality for them. If a parent says, "You seem awfully angry today," the adolescent may become furious that the parent has the gall to tell him what he is feeling. If a parent observes, "You have seemed depressed lately," the adolescent may deny this attribution on principle and confide to friends, "I hate it when they try to tell me what I'm feeling or thinking." This right to self-definition is appropriated by the adolescent in the emergence and development of the self's synthesizing function, and he or she may become acutely sensitive to interactions where this right is not respected and confirmed.

The emergence of this capacity and disposition to identify the self sharply augments the adolescent's sense of boundary between self and other. And while this is essentially a process of growth, it has painful side effects. The dark side of this budding self-definition, and of the heightened sense of ownership that comes with it, is occasionally a sense of isolation and aloneness, which is likely to surpass anything that the individual has experienced in childhood. In other words, the adolescent's sharpened and intensified sense of who he is gives rise, paradoxically, to an intensified sense of being unknown by others. Thus we have the virtually universal adolescent complaint of not being understood by parents and teachers, which arises especially when the individual's experience of self is discrepant with feedback received from the environment.

Owning and Disowning

In synthesizing its own identifications, the adolescent self creates the internal boundaries of conscious and unconscious, of ego-syntonic and ego-dystonic, of awareness, potential awareness, and unawareness. In external perception, it organizes acuities, blind spots, and projections. In essence, the self synthesizes for the adolescent the experience of "me" and "not me." Zinker (1977), describing the intrapsychic experience of self, writes, "One's inner reality consists of those polarities and characteristics which are ego-syntonic, or acceptable to one's conscious self, and those which are ego-alien, or unacceptable to the self. Often, the self excludes painful awarenesses of the polar forces inside of us. I would rather think of myself as bright than dull, as graceful than clumsy, as soft . . . than hard, as kind . . . than cruel" (p. 97). One task of the synthesizing function, in other words, is owning and disowning aspects of the self. Like any other organizational process, owning and disowning create dynamic tensions throughout the field being organized. Energy is required for segregating one aspect of experience as "me" and maintaining a boundary, a differentiation, from the larger field of potential experience of self.

In Gestalt language, the process of taking ownership of the self is essentially a matter of organizing the field of potential experience of the self in figure-ground terms. The young adolescent, for example, may identify with her interpersonal skills, making figural her experience of self as social, friendly, or popular. She may own her interest in making connections and enjoy thinking of herself as a "people person." She may candidly talk about the importance of being popular among her peers. Her sociability thus becomes part of the way she identifies herself, part of how she comes to know who she is, and one of the ways she differentiates herself from others. At the same time, her interest in schoolwork and her desire to maintain the approval of her teachers may recede to the ground of her experience, becoming a recessive, subordinate aspect of her newly configured system of contacts. If her parents are not particularly enthusiastic about her emergent identity, and if they complain that she is socializing at the expense of her schoolwork, she may feel a painful separateness from them. She may say that they don't understand her, or that they are trying to make her into someone she is not. She may then begin to understand her sociability as something that differentiates her from her parents, something that contributes to her emergent sense of boundary with them. As she begins to integrate her newly valued sociability and the contact skills that it comprises, it will attain a figural clarity (and soon a relative stability) in the emergent gestalt of her experience of self. And as her experience of self is reorganized in this way, it will come in time to be taken for granted. What was initially a tentative, energetically held *figure* of experience gradually becomes part of the *ground*, where it will help to frame and contextualize new figures in the experience of self as they emerge.

The other side of this process is the disclaiming and relegating to ground of what is identified as alien to the self. In fact, to adults who work clinically with adolescents, it is disowning that often seems the more salient phenomenon. Younger teenagers in particular have a remarkable capacity for projecting unwanted aspects of themselves, often seeing themselves as victims and making others responsible for the outcomes of their own behavior. Youths whose anger is explosive typically resist seeing themselves as having a temper; it is easier on self-esteem to see others as hostile or provocative. Suppose that the same adolescent girl has missed an after-school appointment with a tutor and spent the time talking with a good friend. She explains to her irate mother that her friend had been rebuffed by another friend. But her mother "just doesn't understand." Instead, she lectures about commitments and responsibility. ("You agreed to the tutoring, and we scheduled it for Tuesday because this was convenient for you. It's your responsibility to get to your appointment.") Her daughter argues, "She needed me, and my friends are more important than some lady I don't even care about." The daughter's moment of forgetting her appointment, irksome though it is from a practical standpoint, is still important for its function of fixing in her experience a fledgling autonomous ability to structure her own identity. She disowns her forgetfulness and her failure to honor a commitment, but she heightens her figural sense of herself as a loyal and supportive friend. This self-identification becomes real in the moment when she takes her stand and engages her mother in argument, in the concrete business of renegotiating their relationship. She is saying to her mother, "I am who *I* take *myself* to be," and she is asking to be recognized and accepted on this basis.

Owning and Identity

The self's emergent capacity to own and disown is related to but not identical with Erikson's notion of "ego identity." For Erikson, ego identity represents "a gradual integration of all identifications," characterized experientially by "the accrued confidence that one's ability to maintain inner sameness and continuity . . . is matched by the sameness and continuity of one's meaning for others" (1959, pp. 89, 90). It is the integration, or configuring, of the individual's history of identifications into a viable and relatively stable structure of experience. Erikson borrows from Gestalt perceptual theory in formulating the concept of identity, pointing out that identity constitutes "a whole [that] has a different quality than the sum of its parts" (p. 90). Identity, as defined by Erikson, represents an achievement of adolescence, an organization of self that supports the individual's movement into early adulthood. Our emphasis here, however, will be more on the development of the underlying *process* than on the specific *contents* of the achieved identity.

The crystallization of a viable identity in later adolescence, or in early adulthood, is made possible by the emergence in early adolescence of the synthesizing function of the self. In some instances, early identifications of self may appear to be anything but useful preparation for eventual adult living. But they are unmistakably useful. When a thirteen-year-old boy begins to think of himself as a computer wizard able to impress his friends and attract the attention of his teachers, he is not just laying a groundwork of pride in intellectual ability that will support academic accomplishment and possible career opportunities. He is also, at the level of psychological process, cultivating the nascent capacity to define himself, to make figural certain aspects of self while differentiating and disassociating from others.

A less comfortable example is furnished by an adolescent boy I saw in therapy. This boy developed an uncanny ability to entertain his classmates without quite getting himself into trouble. He would ask apparently serious questions in class, which contained skillfully embedded in-jokes. His classmates would chortle while the teacher became confused. My patient would artfully appear to share the teacher's confusion, occasionally evincing mild annoyance with his classmates. In private, his peers referred to him as The Razor, and he himself took pride in his underground reputation as a master prankster. This hardly seems the stuff of viable identity formation; and, at the level of content, we might suppose that it was not. But at the process level, what was blossoming was the capacity to define the self, to appropriate cognitive and interpersonal skills in a manner that felt to him uniquely his own, and that defined a contact boundary with peers and with the adult world. Even in youngsters whose behavior is blatantly self-destructive—for example, adolescents who identify themselves as gang members, or "druggies," or as stridently anti-authoritarian—we must concede that the underlying *process* expresses an essential developmental impulse: namely, the impulse to take ownership of the self and define its boundaries of contact with the interpersonal world.

The difficulty that befalls many struggling adolescents is that well-meaning adults, out of genuine concern for them, disconfirm the *process* of self-definition because they become blinded by the *content* of the choices being made. A fourteen-year-old client of mine, a boy with a history of academic failure and indifference to anything that looked like work, developed an intense interest in computers. As he began to develop some competence, he announced his immediate plans to become a computer consultant and advertise in the local newspaper. His well-intentioned father stepped in and advised him against this idea, suggesting instead that he apply himself more diligently in school and think about some long-range career goals. That was a shame, because this was the boy's first attempt even to think of himself as capable enough to do something useful in the world. This fragile seedling of a knowledgeable self deserved more careful watering than it received, and my client soon returned to adventure games as his primary computer preoccupation. This outcome illustrates why, in working therapeutically with younger adolescents, it is so critically important to take them seriously, out of respect for the sometimes delicate processes that underlie their outward behavior.

The Self as New Gestalt: The Problem of Figural Integrity

The synthesizing function, as described here, is the newly claimed capacity to organize personal experience into meaningful patterns and wholes that have at least some authentic ties with the adolescent's organismic functioning. A sense of internal coherence, cohesiveness, and figural integrity is established, and the adolescent's sense of self becomes a newly synthesized gestalt. Gurwitsch (1964, p. 115) defines *gestalt* as "a unitary whole of varying degrees of richness of detail, which, by virtue of its intrinsic articulation and structure, possesses coherence and consolidation and, thus, detaches itself as an organized and closed unit from the surrounding field." The transformation of adolescent experience is more than the addition of new components (sexual feelings, intellectual skills, social anxiety); it is a global reconfiguring of mental life, a new integration of emotional patterns, motivational vectors, specific feelings and impulses, memories, personal history, experienced time, cognitive capacities, and skills. It is a reorganizing of habits and learning style, of tastes, preferences, and interests, of values and beliefs, of social roles and identifications. These multiple parts are subtended by a more comprehensive development: the newly configured whole to which they belong, according to a specific gestalt coherence. This new configuration, with its initially tentative internal coherence, is what sets the adolescent apart from his familiar world of childhood experience.

The reorganization of the adolescent's interpersonal fields, and the emergence of personally valued contact skills and styles, have as a by-product a newly heightened sense of self. When we speak of the adolescent's new sense of self, we are talking about his sense of his own psychic organization, his own configuration. The adolescent recognizes many parts of the self that are familiar from childhood, and these provide his sense of continuity. He knows that he is the same person who was once six years old. But he also experiences himself as different. He feels a discontinuity in his history, and while he is able to recollect his childhood, he is also curiously able to disassociate himself from parts or even all of it. That was then and this is now, he tells himself. This change amounts to a paradigm shift, and as Kuhn (1970) points out with respect to scientific paradigm shifts, any new paradigm emerges tentatively at first, as much from faith as from evidence; the new paradigm breaks new ground, and if it is shown to be wrong, the price is humiliation and loss of face.

For the adolescent self to establish its viability—that is, its capacity to hold a place and function effectively in the world at large—it must first establish its *figural integrity* as an organized portion of the experiential field. In other words, its first challenge is to resist the forces that would lead to its destructuring, to the loss of its tentative gestalt coherence and to its regression to an earlier organizational state. And, as a new gestalt, the figural integrity of the adolescent self is *necessarily* problematic. Its viability, in the eyes of the adult world and of the adolescent himself, is open to question. It will take time and experience before this new self becomes a stable structure, before its boundaries, its contact style, and its internal cohesiveness can be taken for granted.

The development of stable gestalts of the self can be illustrated by an examination of simpler perceptual gestalts. Figure 4.1 is an example of an embedded perceptual figure. At point A, a rabbit is concealed, its contours absorbed by the surrounding weeds and brush. At point C, however, its boundaries have been accentuated, and it clearly emerges as the figure against the background of the brush and weeds. This figure illustrates the progression from weak to strong gestalt. Initially, the figure of the rabbit is tentative and readily destructured, but as its boundaries are accentuated and defined, the image gains configurational integrity. At point C, the rabbit is simply there, and it is virtually impossible to destructure the rabbit and return it to its original tentative organization.

Figure 4.1. Embedded Perceptual Figure

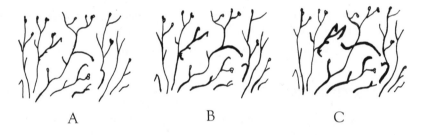

A   B   C

In everyday life, the organized patterns that emerge are more complex and multidimensional. For example, consider the perception of an individual's social identity. Over a number of years, I watched an associate of mine transform herself professionally and personally. She began as a kindergarten teacher and eventually was promoted to head of the primary school where she taught. Later she earned a doctorate, which qualified her as a learning specialist. She resigned as head of the primary school and became an expert consultant. In time, she published a book on children's brain development and learning styles, and this book was received very well. It was interesting to observe the changes in her image (that is, her identity in the eyes of her colleagues and herself) and her ways of making contact with others in various situations throughout this transformation. The gestalt of "expert," like the rabbit in the bushes, emerged tentatively at first, as her colleagues maintained their former ways of thinking about her. Not surprisingly, she did, too, and occasionally she told me that she thought she had no special knowledge to offer, a feeling that came through in the sometimes tentative nature of her consultations. Over time, and through the accumulation of concrete experiences in which she enacted her expertise and made it palpable, the gestalt of "expert" eventually established its configurational integrity. There emerged from her a quiet, implicit confidence, which drew people to seek her counsel. It is now difficult to see her in any other way. Her special expertise is now something "everybody knows," something comfortably taken for granted by others and by herself.

The developmental situation for the adolescent is similar, but with one very significant difference: the stakes are higher. They are higher because they are both developmental and existential. They include not only the content of a new self gestalt but also the very process of authoring a self and the determination of whether this authorship is viable. Once we recognize the vulnerability of the new self-organization, certain familiar and problematic phenomena of adolescent experience and behavior can be understood from the standpoint of their purely developmental function.

The Subjectification of Experience

I have already described the adolescent's newly intensified capacity for objective observation and interpretation of the people and events around him. At the same time, perhaps paradoxically, there is a marked tendency to subjectify experience. The adolescent's interpretations of reality become noticeably (and literally) self-serving. Generally, the adolescent is likely to skew his interpretations of reality so as to support and enhance the integration and strength of the newly configured self. And, because of the self's tentative integration, the degree of distortion, even with "normal, healthy" teens, may be considerable. The same youngster who is so uncomfortably vulnerable to other points of view will block out alternative perspectives and construe events in a remarkably narrow-minded fashion. The usual trigger for the tendency to subjectify experience is some threat to the experienced wholeness and adequacy of the self. As the self matures, the adolescent will accommodate conflict and allow for more honest self-examination and self-critique. But before the self has established its basic solidity over time, self-examination and self-critique are powerful destructuring forces that can be devastating for the individual, tantamount to a disintegration of the newly synthesized self.

This trait of subjectifying experience sometimes makes even normal teenagers resemble adult character-disordered patients. As Millon (1981) notes, adult character disorders represent constrictions in the individual's capacity to relate to reality. They are systematic distortions that serve to control anxiety and maintain a minimum level of self-esteem. These distortions serve essentially the same functions in adolescence. The difference is that in adolescence there is a legitimate developmental need. Once this need is met and the self has established a preliminary viability, the degree and intensity of reality distortion diminish considerably.

Anger and Projection

Adolescents are often more angry than they seem to have any right to be. Interactions between teenagers and their parents—in the consulting room, in public places, at family gatherings—regularly reveal the angry "overreactions" of adolescents to parental behavior that seems innocuous to an outsider. Parents bring their children to therapy and describe them as "moody" and "touchy," relating incidents of not quite comprehensible anger. A thirteen-year-old recently stormed out of my office when her father asked her to clarify something she had just said—a request that sounded to me both respectful and reasonable. Assessed in light of the adolescent self's developmental process, however, such anger loses its aura of mystery.

An individual who is angry is generally more clearly and firmly bounded than when she is not. When I am angry, I experience and convey to others a sense of solidity in my position. I and others know where I stand. The stability I achieve may approach rigidity. "It's no use talking to him when he's angry," someone close to me might say. For an adolescent, anger is a temporary and extremely effective antidote to the experience of losing center and risking disintegration. The conditions of permeable boundaries and tentative gestalt coherence, so readily triggered in interactions with certain adults, are immediately reversed in the state of anger. That is why so many adolescents bait adults into conflict precisely when they are being confronted about issues or behavior where their own ground is shaky. Anger is often adopted as an antidote to the guilt and shame that might otherwise emerge at these moments (and which often does emerge later, in private, after the anger has spent itself), threatening the self's precarious sense of integrity.

Therapists who work with adolescents also know that projection is a contact style that seems indigenous to this age group. This, too, is not accidental. Projection is particularly suited to the developmental needs of the emergent adolescent self, since it focuses tension and conflict away from the phenomenological "inner" self, relegating the tension and conflict to the contact boundary between the self and the surrounding environment. While the self is still tentative, internal tension poses a particular threat to its integration and cohesion.

Guilt is a particularly virulent destructuring experience for adolescents. The mature experience of guilt involves internal differentiation, a polarization of self with self. When I am guilty, I am down on myself, I take myself to task over some aspect of my being and behavior. A certain internal relationship is implied, a configuration of parts that creates tension inside the field of my experience of self. For this to be a useful experience, there has to be sufficient tensile strength in the self's gestalt coherence. The self must be able to absorb its own internal confrontation, and it must be able to respond to this confrontation without feeling crushed. Useful guilt usually involves some variation of an internal dialogue which, like any other healthy dialogue, moves toward resolution and closure. Older adolescents become capable of this sort of internally differentiated experience. Generally speaking, younger adolescents, or adolescents who are struggling with issues of self-definition and coherence, are not. Thus the child who is tending toward guilt and self-reproach because of some recent behavior (say, some excessive drinking, or sexual acting out) may provoke a parental scolding as the internal conflict begins to materialize. Once the scolding begins, the child turns his attention to the parent, becoming defensive and angry. The elements of conflict remain the same in terms of its content: one side urges greater impulse control, and the other wants greater impulse indulgence. But the struggle is shifted *away* from the interior of the self, to the *boundary* of self and environment. What would otherwise have been a conflict *inside* the boundary, a struggle of the adolescent with himself, becomes a conflict *at* the boundary. This happens because the internal struggle would pose a threat to the integration of the emergent self. The battle with parents, however, reinforces (temporarily at least) the adolescent's sense of internal coherence and consolidation.

The same sort of dynamic makes both anger and projection effective antidotes for shame, another virulent toxin for the emergent adolescent self. Self, for adolescents, is often organized as "face" held out to the social world. As face, the self requires that others implicitly confirm the individual's posture toward the world. Adolescents are forever holding themselves out in tentative and experimental ways (one could almost say *performing* themselves) and so are constantly in danger of disconfirmation (losing face). The moment of losing face, of being involuntarily reorganized—as a child, as incompetent, as uncool, as wrong, as at fault—is the moment of shame. Anger and projection forestall this possibility by polarizing the interaction, deflecting the spotlight and turning it to someone else, reasserting, perhaps desperately, the adolescent's own organization of the field.

Adolescent Narcissism

The self in adolescence, in spite of its intensely interpersonal nature and highly sensitized contact boundary—or perhaps because of it—is transiently but markedly narcissistic. Its narcissism is generated by developmental necessity rather than characterological pathology. Parents of teenagers, even high-functioning, nonsymptomatic teenagers, are sometimes greatly alarmed by their shocking capacity for inconsideration and selfishness. A fifteen-year-old boy comes into the kitchen with several friends, and within minutes they have eaten an entire rack of cupcakes intended for a younger sibling's birthday party. "Didn't you stop to think, even for a minute?" shrieks his mother. "You *knew* it was your sister's birthday! You *knew* she was having her party this afternoon!" "I forgot," the boy answers, and later his friends comfort him for having to put up with a mother who is such a bitch. From a commonsense perspective, such self-absorption seems incredible. But the adolescent is operating not so much according to commonsense as to developmental necessity. To become a self, the individual must become interested and invested in himself.

This means—literally, in a psychological sense—withdrawing energy and interest from the surrounding world and investing it narcissistically: becoming self-absorbed. As the adolescent is busy losing interest in his family, segregating himself from the family milieu, he is heightening his experience of self as figure and relegating family concerns to ground. Perceptual theory teaches us that what is figural commands and absorbs our attention, whereas ground is comparatively dull and lifeless, possessing little contour or definition of its own. When our fifteen-year-old cupcake pillager says, "I forgot," he is telling the truth, unbelievable as it seems. His remarkable loss of interest in the "obvious" ("The candles and party hats were *right next to* the cupcakes! How could you *not* have known they were for your sister's party?") is matched by an equally remarkable (and temporarily necessary) interest in himself.

A corollary phenomenon is the peculiarly uneven empathy that adolescent children have toward the interpersonal environment. Particularly in the family, empathy may dry up temporarily in a formerly caring youngster. Indeed, in one of those strange convolutions of human development, the capacity for familial empathy poses a temporary danger to adolescent self-development. In clinical consultation, it is very often the more empathic youngsters (invariably described by their parents as "sensitive") who get tangled up in family business. The teenagers who are unable to limit their empathic responses are the ones who become dysfunctionally preoccupied with their parents' emotional pain in a difficult marriage or in a divorce. The symptomatic behavior (failing grades, chemical abuse, argumentativeness, night terrors) may seem anything but empathic, but the catalyst for the symptoms is the child's undampened empathy for the parents.

Acting Out

Acting out of one sort or another is a feature in well over half the cases of adolescent children referred to mental health professionals. Much of this acting out is clinically significant, since it places the individual at risk or impinges on the rights of others. What is it about the nature of adolescent development that makes acting out so common in this age group? After all, even adolescents who are not referred for psychotherapy still display a relatively high level of acting out, even if theirs is more benign.

The function of acting out in adolescence is the *enactment* of the self. The adolescent's sense of self is not yet so strong that words and thoughts—symbolic representations—are enough to anchor its reality in the world. The adolescent self is a tentative reality, not yet proved. In many instances, the answer to "What is he trying to prove?" is simple. He is trying to prove that he *is* who he takes himself to be. Acting out, in other words, is an important mode of *contact* during adolescence; a means of integrating, establishing, and defining the organism's relationship to its environment. It is a mode of contacting the environment that makes the self real and actual, giving it substance and ballast.

When my friend the learning specialist first completed her doctorate, she had difficulty taking her role as an expert seriously. But as she embarked on a course of *action*, giving consultations, presenting lectures, and finally writing a book, this new gestalt of self became a more solid and public reality, something that organized both her own and others' experience. She did possess this gestalt, however tentatively, when she completed her graduate work, but not until she *acted it out* could she reshape her contact style in the world. So it is with adolescence, but at a more bedrock level of the self's reality. By acting out, the adolescent begins to make the self real and substantial. Until he does so, his experience of self remains ephemeral, even phony. Certain accomplishments of adolescent development—the challenge to parental dominion, the capacity to make choices of one's own, sexual maturation—must be acted out in order to become real. This is why adolescents, as a group, are so remarkably strong-willed about learning from their own experience, a cause of endless frustration to adults: "I'm just trying to help you avoid some of the same mistakes *I* made." Against all reason, when the youth insists on acting against parental advice, he repeats the same mistakes. "I told you so," intones the exasperated adult.

This scenario is not just an example of the adolescent's poor judgment and false bravado. He has come to the point in life when introjected information no longer suffices to organize experience. "I've got to learn for myself," he says, and the painful truth is that he is right, in a very basic developmental sense. The action he takes produces *some* result that is *real* and substantial in the public world; it is seen and recognized by others. It may be an act of defiance or an incursion into some forbidden domain of adult life. It may be some laudable accomplishment. In either case, it is public and undeniable, and the weight of the result is absorbed back into the self, giving it substance and ballast of its own.

Organizational Needs and Tasks

The emergent self of adolescence is both a structure of experience and an integrator of experience, both something organized and something that organizes. It is a new paradigm for experience, different from the earlier paradigm of childhood and family. Its most salient phenomenological aspect is its heightened identification of and with itself, enabled by the appropriation of sensory experience and self functions that make *ownership* a central theme of adolescent development.

As an organized entity of perception, the self obeys many of the same organizational properties that psychologists have identified for perceptual configurations in general, particularly configurations that are synthesized over time. Thus the developmental needs and tasks of adolescence are largely *organizational*, serving a new integration of mental life, personal identity, and interpersonal relatedness—a new gestalt, called the *adolescent self*.

Like any other configured whole, whether physical, perceptual, social, or political, the adolescent self, once it has emerged from the field of embedded experience, is inclined toward its own preservation and integrity. Much of the character and quality of adolescent behavior is simply dictated by the developmental needs of the new gestalt's process as it attempts to establish its own viability. In this sense, adolescent narcissism and adolescent projection are no more mysterious than the distributive properties of a soap bubble, or the flux lines of an electromagnetic field. They are expressions of the underlying process of configuring a viable whole.

CHAPTER FIVE

The Polarities of Adolescence and Development

For the early adolescent, time is visceral. This quality of time may announce itself in a twelve-year-old boy's odd discomfort when his mother hugs him, or in the flush of a young girl's cheeks as she finds herself fixed in the gaze of an older boy. In the academic literature, much is made of the physiological changes at puberty, but the psychological impact of the changing body is also important. It is primarily through the changing body that time becomes real, that it takes on flesh, so to speak, and that the child feels caught up in its current. Time and change are no longer external or impersonal realities to the developing fourteen-year-old; they are immediate and palpable. The experience, however dim or penumbral, is of growing up, moving out of one era and into another. It is the experience of passage.

Time and the Polarization of Experience

This experience of time passing runs through the intrapsychic field like an electric current, polarizing it and arraying its components around an axis of old and new, childlike and becoming adult. The field of experience of self becomes stretched between past and future, between the archaic self of childhood, with its legacy of introjects and childhood affects, and the emergent self of adolescence, with its nascent self-conscious sense of ownership and autonomy. This polarization of the intrapsychic field is directly reflected in the adolescent's organization of and response to the environment. In the sixth or seventh grade, peers are frequently dichotomized into those who still try to please adults and those who self-consciously attempt to diminish adult influence. Adults tend to be similarly dichotomized into those who treat adolescents like children and those who treat adolescents as more grown-up. The most concrete and elemental expression of this reorganizing is the emergence of *polar tensions* in experience. Rudimentary polarities, snatches of ambivalence, present themselves in isolated moments.

Consider the following scenario. Several of a boy's associates tell him they are going to cut study hall and go down to the lunchroom before their scheduled lunch period.

"All the good-looking girls are down there now," they argue, "and besides, no one checks attendance. Come on."

The boy freezes momentarily, dimly aware of the tightness in his chest as he considers their offer.

It would be neat, he says to himself; but he also feels the need to do what he is supposed to do. He finds himself strangely pulled between two possibilities, one familiar and one unfamiliar.

What may evolve into a conscious ambivalence or well-defined polarities in the older adolescent will emerge as polar tension in the younger adolescent. These may appear as a momentary experience of divergent possibilities, as in the preceding example, as a dim awareness of differences between self and other, or as vague rumblings of conflict within the self. With the emergence of polar tensions, the adolescent begins to experience divergent possibilities in the experience of self. The actual (or at least the familiar) and the possible begin to stretch the field of potential experience of self. He may be intimidated, but he fantasizes himself as fearless. She may smile sweetly, but she feels the push to speak her mind assertively. He feels himself pulled between being polite and brash, compliant and impulsive, inhibited and adventuresome, bad and good, and so on. Typical adolescent polarities include the following:

scared	fearless
little	big
dependent, needy	independent, self-sufficient
sweet, childlike	sexy, sensual
other-pleasing	selfish, self-absorbed
family-loyal	peer-loyal
good	bad
obedient	rebellious, willful
lazy	industrious
disciplined	impulsive

controlled	angry
passive	active
masculine	feminine
obligated	carefree
caring	uncaring

The proliferation of polar tensions is both terrible and wonderful for the adolescent. On the one hand, it signals a literal disintegration of the familiar as the comfortable, organized meanings of childhood give way to alternative possibilities. On the other hand, it signals a new experience of freedom for the self, an opportunity to trace out new boundaries of the self's identity. And this happens at the most mundane and concrete moments—for example, in the decision about whether to greet or ignore a former teacher, whether to be friendly to a socially isolated peer or poke fun at him, whether to masturbate or not, whether to sit in the back or the front of the classroom, whether to come to the dinner table when called or linger awhile in one's room, whether to wear one's jacket collar up or down, whether to button the top button of a blouse or not. These are moments of experiential and behavioral self-definition in miniature, all organized by emergent polar tensions.

The polar tensions of the younger, less reflective adolescent may develop into the conscious ambivalence of the older, more mature adolescent, in whom we recognize the healthy self-exploration that leads to inner richness and diversity. The earlier adolescent has more a sense of opposites than a clear awareness of alternatives. From this sense of difference, this sense of divergent possibilities, *awareness* itself begins to expand in adolescence. Indeed, awareness is cultivated in experiences of difference.

This is a principle of development long recognized by perceptual and cognitive psychology. Koffka (1935) shows that the perceptual awareness of *any* object is organized by its boundary, by the portion of the field that marks the *difference* between figure and ground. Cognitive development is likewise mediated by the grasp of difference, as when a small child first notices that some "doggies" are different from others and warrant other names—horsies, cows, kitties. As an individual progresses from early to middle and finally to late adolescence, his or her capacity for awareness—of the surrounding environment and other people, of experience of self, of feelings and urges and motives—will deepen and expand.

As polar tensions emerge in experience, there develops a sense of *choosing the self*, becoming responsible for its contours and its configuration. One thirteen-year-old boy from a devoutly religious family and a small religious school gave me a detailed chronicle of learning to swear. He recalled his sense of shock at having heard his older brother swear during a sandlot football game. At that time, my client was about ten years old. He clearly experienced the difference between himself and his older brother, but it was a difference at the boundary of the *family*, not at the boundary of the *self*. His brother had stepped outside the family's value boundary and joined the world of swearers, and my client wondered more what his parents would think than what he himself thought. A year or two later, several of his boyhood friends began to spice their casual language with intentionally shocking expletives. My client, who by then had begun the transition to adolescence, was still not a swearer himself, but the difference between himself and his associates felt more personal than the difference between himself and his older brother had. His friends had decided that swearing was all right. He had not, and this difference defined a boundary between them. Swearing versus not swearing defined a polar tendency that organized the interpersonal boundary of *self* and *other*. Shortly before I met him, my client had begun to experiment with language and to swear sometimes. He waffled on whether to swear in particular situations, and he fluctuated between phases of swearing and not swearing. The *polar tendency* was evolving now into a *true polarity*, an organizing theme of his own intrapsychic field, a boundary between newly differentiated parts of the self, one part representing the investments of his child self, and the other interested in experimenting beyond the boundary of family values.

Thus polarities are organizers of experience. They emerge in concrete situations from a ground of embedded experience, and they contribute developmentally to the adolescent's emergent sense of self. In the preceding example, there is a migration of awareness from the family boundary to the interpersonal boundary and, finally, to the intrapsychic boundary. This transition is marked by a growing sense of personal relevance, an explosion of awareness, and an increasing capacity for choice and responsibility in the question of who the self is becoming.

Differentiation of Self Gestalts

If we look for a moment beyond adolescence, to the field of adult experience of self, we get an idea of the highly differentiated functioning toward which adolescence points. Even in adult experience, what we mean by the term *self* is actually a complex and changeable series of partial organizations. The self is in fact a confederation of profiles, of self gestalts, that are unified as a whole but are never given all at once in experience. Each self gestalt represents a particular organization of contact functions, and each is accompanied by a particular configuration of intrapsychic experience. I organize myself one way when I am with my patients, another way when I am with my friends, and yet another way when I am with my children. I may be more open and receptive in one situation, more active and direct in another. A given constituent of my personality—say, my selfishness—may occupy a particular place in my overall comportment when a particular interpersonal field and its corresponding self gestalt are called forth.

The adolescent likewise begins to make much sharper distinctions than he did in childhood. Probably the clearest example is the line drawn between peers and adults. Teenagers are much more conscious of this boundary than younger children are, and they often treat the boundary as unbreachable. Thus, as we have already seen, a teenager in grave trouble with peers may never seriously consider going to adults for support or intervention. A similar divergence is found in the field of experience of self. Many teenagers develop one organization of self for adults and another for peers. The difference is not always extreme, but it can be. A boy may be serious, respectful of authority, task-oriented, and prudent in school or at home with his parents, but he is a relatively impulsive and devil-may-care person with his friends. Contact styles may also be quite different in the two situations. He may be confluent and retroflective with adults but forthright, assertive, and ready to argue with his peers. He may feel like two different people, and may appear that way to those who observe him in these two contexts. This is part of what often gets called "moodiness" in adolescents. In reality, however, it is a shifting of much more than mood. These divergences are not just superficial role adaptations. They represent different self gestalts, differing organizations of the experience of self, and so they give rise to a growing subjective sense of inner diversity and complexity.

The adolescent's sense and organization of self are truly interpersonal and field-dependent. It is difficult for many adolescents to hold an intrapsychic state that is unsupported by the immediate interpersonal field. As the adolescent moves from one interpersonal field to another—say, from an after-school meeting with a teacher to a ride home with peers—he or she may undergo a relatively comprehensive and almost instantaneous reorganization of the intrapsychic field, involving dramatic shifts in self-esteem, mood, contact style, and priorities. If we as adults find this fluctuation hard to comprehend, we might do well to tickle our own awareness. What adult has not had the experience of visiting the home of his or her own parents and feeling the still powerful interpersonal field forces of that environment? One friend of mine confided that it takes only minutes in his parents' home for him to begin to feel like a twelve-year-old again. His mother gestures wordlessly at the floormat, reminding him to wipe his feet, and in that instant the gestalt structures of his intrapsychic field begin to reorganize themselves. For the adolescent, who has so little accumulated intrapsychic ballast, the shaping forces of any given interpersonal context are powerful indeed. (This simple fact explains why certain adolescents can find traditional individual psychotherapy so overwhelming.)

Further examples of different self gestalts are easy to find. The same youth who cannot remember his commitment to empty the dishwasher after dinner is described as committed and reliable by the supervisor at his after-school job. This youth will tell us that he literally feels himself at different ages in the two environments. He may attribute this difference to the different treatment he receives from his boss and his parents, but it is unmistakable that he "does his self" differently at work and at home. At home, he may be thin-skinned and overreactive to feedback. At work, he may accept criticism as a necessary aspect of the employer-employee relationship. Interpersonal boundaries that are permeable and tenuous in one field are resilient and flexible in another.

The self gestalt that is organized in adolescent romantic relationships is also different from other organizations of self. Adolescents characteristically allow dependency, attachment, longing, and vulnerability to reemerge in these relationships. The same boy who tells his parents that he needs nothing from them, who puts his burgeoning self-sufficiency at center stage in that relationship, may organize romantic experience of self around his needs to be touched and admired, telling his girlfriend that he can't live without her. Again, contact styles evolve that are specific to particular self gestalts. The boy who is direct and open with his girlfriend, sharing his most intimate hopes and fears, may develop a highly deflective contact style with same-sex peers, diverting serious conversation with wit and repartee.

This differentiation of self gestalts in adolescence is important for development because it allows different aspects of the experience of self to develop more fully. There is, we might say, a degree of dissociation in service of the self. One consequence of this dissociation is an asynchronous quality of self-development. The same girl who seems worldly and confident in one situation may become strikingly unsure of herself in another. For example, one client of mine, a class officer in her school, was required to organize a complicated fundraising project for a class trip but was afraid to call her dentist to reschedule an appointment, fearing that he might yell at her.

Adolescence as Paradigm Shift

In a general sense, the field of experience of self for the adolescent comes under the sway of competing paradigms, one organized more by the introjected structures of childhood and the other having more to do with the new experiences of adolescence. Underlying specific instances of ambivalence is a more comprehensive polarization between old, family-embedded configurations and new, self-synthesized configurations of experience. Thus, as similar and related experiences tend to coalesce into a configuration, a sense of the self as adolescent emerges as an alternative to the more familiar organization of the self as child.

With the figural emergence of this new adolescent self-configuration, it is as if the basic psychological "cellular mass" tears itself apart, destructuring the field of self experience and giving rise to a more confusing but also more richly differentiated range of possibilities. In many instances, it is as if the adolescent has two separate selves, two nearly discrete self paradigms, each with its own configurational organization of internal and external experience. The teenager feels the inertial pull of personal history. The earlier, established gestalt of the child self does not simply disappear as the individual begins to disembed. This self gestalt remains embedded in the world of internalized adult proscriptions, and its organizational paradigm is largely a legacy of childhood introjection. This self colors its perceptions to conform with a given reality, clinging to family standards and definitions of value and achievement, and monitoring and configuring the feelings and urges that emerge. This old self of childhood, still alive and well, continues to derive self-esteem from adult approval. It accepts the adult world more or less at face value and, without a great deal of conflict, adopts an existential posture of dependency. This paradigm typically includes introjected notions of what it means to grow up. Adolescents under the sway of the child-self paradigm do not necessarily remain childlike in appearance. On the contrary, sometimes these adolescents seem very much (even too much) adult in their demeanor. But this seemingly grown-up behavior is organized by introjects rather than authentically crafted and synthesized by the individual self.

Thus, the child self persists as a powerful paradigm for experience, but there also emerges a new, tentatively configured, adolescent self gestalt, one that is tied more directly to the individual developmental project of appropriating sensory experience and self functions. As adolescence gets under way, the individual begins to feel the differentiating internal tension, not just of fragmentary polarities, but also of significantly different paradigms for organizing the entire field of self experience. Another way of describing this state of affairs is to say that the intrapsychic life of the adolescent comes under the organizational sway of an *overarching developmental polarity* made up of opposing paradigms for knowing the self and the surrounding world.

Perhaps the best descriptive model for this phenomenon of competing paradigms is found in Gestalt perceptual psychology's study of ambiguous figures. In one well known drawing (see Figure 5.1), the figure of an old woman alternates with that of a younger woman; as one figure emerges, the other recedes and becomes background. The old woman, becoming the younger woman, does not cease to exist but is relegated to ground as a potential organization. When the viewer least expects it, she reasserts herself and dissolves the younger woman to ground.

The psychological development of adolescence is likewise characterized by competing gestalt organizations, which typically emerge

Figure 5.1. Young Woman or Old?

as opposites, or alternatives, in experience. The desire to attach and depend, which is comfortably integrated in the gestalt of the child self, may be rigidly controlled or denied in the organization of the adolescent self, but it remains in the ground of experience as a potential organizing desire, a recessive organization of the field. Considerable tension and anxiety may be generated as the individual hovers in the gray area between these two articulations of the self.

In the simplest and most straightforward case, development proceeds as a sort of dialogue between these alternative possibilities. For most teenagers, there is an evolving interplay between the introjected organization of childhood and family and the budding, authentic, experimental self of adolescence. Each pole of this emergent duality informs and tempers the other, and their interplay is readily apparent. The individual is able to identify with, own, and feel responsible for the contact style, affective tones, and cognitive states that belong to each pole. Each serves to limit and challenge the other, which promotes contact between the two and, ultimately, their growth and mutual accommodation. The experimenting adolescent self challenges the constricted, archaic morality of the introjected child self. Old rules, uncritically obeyed in the past, are measured against the evidence of current experience. The adolescent observes that adults do not always know what they are talking about, and that some do not deserve respect. Or he asks questions of himself:

"What's really wrong with swearing, drinking, sex, fighting, thinking, challenging?"

The recently emerged self of adolescence actively brackets certain affects that belong to childhood—feelings of attachment and dependency, of fearfulness and self-doubt. The new self may make itself purposefully oblivious to these feelings and, by doing so, often creates opportunities to master developmental challenges. A fourteen-year-old boy wants to try out for a sports team but is intimidated by his lack of athletic experience and fear of humiliation. His friends chide him for being a wimp, and so he tells them, and then himself, that he is not afraid. With this new (if tentative) face, he shows up for tryouts with only his own resolve for support, having denied the childlike feelings that would have held him back. In this way, the newly formed gestalt of the adolescent self serves to challenge and restructure the fixed gestalts of childhood.

It is not uncommon to find adolescents who have organized themselves in counterpoint to some painful vulnerability of childhood. One client of mine, a remarkably sensitive and thoughtful boy, who hid under an armor of leather, studs, and hobnail boots, developed a trademark paranoia and cynicism about adults in general. He sometimes railed against the scams that advertisers and store owners perpetrated against teenagers, and he prided himself on his ability to spot this sort of adult-world treachery. He reported once having gone to a hair salon and inquired about having his hair dyed shocking red. When he became indecisive, the woman at the salon suggested that he have it done first with a soluble dye; that way, she said, he could wash it out if he didn't like it, or he could come back and have the permanent dye applied if he did like it. "She must have thought I was stupid," my client told me. "She was just scamming to get me to pay twice."

What my client did not like to talk about was his unquestioning childhood faith in his father, and his devastated sense of betrayal when his father abruptly left his mother and the family for a woman who had been a close family friend. He had learned, in other words, that faith in adults was dangerous. Now, as an adolescent, he cultivated a cynicism that protected him from further hurt.

In this way, the adolescent instinctively seeks to remedy the inequities of childhood. And if the child self is transformed by its contact with the new gestalt structures of adolescence, it returns the favor by containing and pruning the impetuous inclinations of the burgeoning adolescent self. It provides a necessary structure for impulse expression, acting as a sort of braking system when experimentation ventures too far from the familiar. It dampens down narcissism, providing measures of guilt and self-reproach when the adolescent becomes self-absorbed to the point of hurting others.

By the latter part of the teen years, this ambivalence bears fruit. The adolescent's independence and worldliness become grounded in a realistic sense of limits, tradition, and responsibility. His feelings of attachment, obligation, and moral constraint become exposed to the light of empirical reexamination. And while the polarity of old childhood experience versus current experience will continue throughout life, the framework of a self that can accommodate both will be established, with any luck, by the end of adolescence, approximately between the seventeenth and the twenty-second year.

For some youths, the interplay of old and new is subtle and private. For others, it is stormy and theatrical. For most, it proceeds inexorably toward a more balanced and integrated mix, a workable blend of the sedimented wisdom of family teachings and the emergent authenticity and discovery of adolescent experimentation.

For the majority of teenagers who find their way to a therapist's office, however, the developmental projects of disembedding and self-definition have somehow become problematic. The polarity dynamics of child self and adolescent self lead neither to a heightening and broadening of contact between parts of the self nor to a richer contact boundary between self and others. For many teenagers referred for mental health services, the back-and-forth interplay of old and new has been interrupted, or perhaps it was never allowed to begin.

In the following paragraphs, I will trace out three examples of the polarity dynamics that underlie common presenting clinical profiles for the therapist who works with adolescent patients. The first is the relatively normal and healthy phenomenon that I have already identified as *ambivalence*. In the second dynamic, the polarizing process has become rigidly and protectively *frozen*. This pattern is characteristic of many of the more clinically and behaviorally dysfunctional adolescents referred for treatment. In the third dynamic, the developmental polarity process seems *interrupted*, or truncated. Half of the developmental polarity emerges fully in awareness, but the other is disowned and undeveloped. This pattern characterizes many of the conflicted or "neurotic" youths who enter therapy.

Ambivalent Polarity Dynamics

Dana, who had recently turned fifteen, asked her parents to arrange for her to see a therapist. Both of her parents had been in therapy in the past, and so the family culture supported this idea. Dana was a bright, pretty girl, somewhat unconventional in her dress, who engaged with me readily and used her time well in my office. She was seen for only three visits, by which time she had gained enough support and insight to proceed quite competently on her own.

Dana was not representative of the kind of adolescent who usually finds his or her way to a therapist's office. In fact, she was most representative of those who do not. At some point and in some fashion, most healthy adolescents turn to adults outside the family for those critical bits of support that are not possible with their own parents. They turn to coaches, English teachers, youth ministers, and the parents of friends. In sometimes barely visible ways, they draw sustenance from these real-world adults. They feel accepted, have their perceptions and insights confirmed, get taken seriously, and so on. Dana used her "therapy" with me in approximately this manner. Her story nicely illustrates the normal and healthy interplay of the child-self and adolescent-self polarities, and her ability and willingness to verbalize her experience will help us see these developmental dynamics with clarity.

Dana's initial focus was her father, whom she complained about. Her reason for asking to see me, she said, was to figure out how to handle him. He had changed, she said, about the time when she was ten or eleven. Before that, she said, her father had been warm and involved; their relationship was good. But then he had changed careers, from social work to sales, and his new job involved traveling, which took him away from the family on a regular basis. Dana recalled this change with sadness. Asked how it had affected her personally, she answered that he had stopped coming to her ice-skating performances. Ice skating had been a big part of her childhood (in fact, it was an important organizing force for the entire family field), but she had recently, and with considerable conflict, decided to end her training.

After his career change, Dana said, her father had become more distant and strict, playing out the traditional role of the father who, after being away, comes home to restore order and enforce discipline. In Dana's eyes, he became more stern and authoritarian, and they grew apart.

"It's like you had two different dads," I suggested, to which she enthusiastically agreed. "And you," I asked, "how did you change?"

Dana shifted the focus onto herself with little difficulty and began to describe how she had begun to "grow up" around the age of eleven, and how she had become less interested in and dependent on her parents' attention.

Eventually I said, "It's like there were two different yous, too." Dana responded with the slow, head-nodding, unfocused stare of someone reorganizing her thinking about herself. She was able to articulate in vivid terms what I have called the child-self gestalt and the adolescent-self gestalt. For example, she described how her social behavior had changed.

"Before," she said, "I was a leader but also a sort of conformist. The teachers loved me, and I was real popular with everybody. But I also remember that I was real careful about things, like how I dressed and who I liked."

At fifteen, Dana was experimenting with her social behavior and role in a fairly ordinary way, and to adult observers she would have appeared to be simply a normal adolescent growing up. But to Dana herself, these experiments were important and transformative. She described a day in ninth grade when she went to school in an old pair of jeans that she had decorated herself in ink, with elaborate designs. There was no fashion precedent for this style of dress in her school, and so it felt dangerously her own. "Most of my friends liked it," she reported with satisfaction.

Dana experimented in other ways with architecting her self and maintaining her nascent integrity against the force field of adult and parental expectations. She had been an excellent student all her life, but in the past year or so she had become less interested in her studies. With straightforward insight, she announced, "I used to get straight A's, and I still could if I wanted to. But it's almost like I purposely don't." She also confided a variety of forbidden behaviors, such as riding around with boys in cars after school—pretty benign stuff for a therapist whose usual clients are troubled adolescents, but significant experimentation for a young girl whose legacy has been compliance and obedience.

Dana then told me a little story, one that reflects the most ordinary sort of psychological process but is amazing for its uncluttered simplicity and clarity. It is almost a parable of adolescence. Dana had been grounded for a month on account of behavior that she could not even recall at the time of her telling me this story. She had been angry for a day or two, but then she softened. "I spent a lot of time with my family that month," she reported, "and I began to feel close to them again. I liked it, and I liked them, even my dad. But then, when I got off being grounded, I went right back to the way I was before, the way I am now. And I don't know why."

During that month, Dana had returned to her former self. She became once again the little girl who enjoyed her parents' company and cherished the sense of security and certainty that came with being part of a caring family. But then, given the opportunity, she resumed her adolescent journey away from childhood.

Dana and I talked about her "two sides," and about how each one felt important in different ways. She was clearly very able to feel and identify with both, much more than most adolescents are. What Dana took away from our conversations, which seemed to help her, was the reassurance that she was not "crazy" for having such different sides to her personality, as well as confirmation of her intuitive belief that each side was valuable in its own right. The business of reconciling the two sides, I speculated, might take some time, and by then the work of growing up, or at least the work of being a teenager, would be almost done.

It is a healthy sign when adolescents demonstrate awareness and ownership of both their childlike and adult-tending aspects, but this does not rule out clinically significant developmental problems. Rachel, another fifteen-year-old, provides a good example. Like Dana, Rachel had a preadolescent history of being a "good girl," to quote her parents. Her relationships with adults had been affectionate and free of conflict. Through the previous school year, her academic performance had been above average. At the time of her referral to therapy by school officials, Rachel was on the verge of being asked to leave the private religious high school where she was a tenth grader.

A description of Rachel's behavior in the three months before her referral sounds almost like a caricature of adolescent acting out.

She had become argumentative with her parents, sometimes shrieking at the top of her lungs. She had begun getting drunk every other weekend or so, and she frequently drank alone, particularly when she was angry with her parents. Her grades had dropped precipitously. She had become bulimic, purging herself daily for about a month. She had sexual intercourse for the first time and, finally, together with her best friend, she had shoplifted over a thousand dollars' worth of merchandise. Rachel confided all these developments to her friends, several of whom, out of concern for her, reported her spree to a school counselor.

When I first met with Rachel alone, she could hardly unburden herself fast enough, spilling out all these offenses in detail. She seemed relieved to have adults involved in such a way as to bring her behavior under control.

Nevertheless, except for the fact that Rachel had actually done every one of these things and had put herself at considerable risk in the process, all of this seemed a bit contrived. Like an immigrant who dons the trappings of an adopted culture with excessive zeal, Rachel seemed to have launched herself into adolescence and gone overboard. Her behavior, as if it were a response to her parents' description of her, said "I'm not a little girl, and I'm certainly not *good!*"

Somewhat less available to Rachel's awareness was her still powerful child self, which at first emerged in our sessions as something on the periphery of her consciousness. "I'm going through a little kid phase," she said, telling me that she had asked friends for such Christmas presents as crayons and a jump rope. She saw this as playful but in no way tied to her real experience of self.

Rachel's child-likeness oozed out of her pores, however, and it was only a matter of time before it found its way figurally into the therapy hour. Rachel had the odd habit of wearing mittens to therapy. She would take off her coat but keep her mittens on the whole time she was in my office. She also confided that she wore them to bed at night. Asked about her mittens, Rachel shrugged. "I just like it," she said.[1] But later in the same session, sitting cross legged on the

---

[1] A psychoanalytic framework might find conflicts regarding masturbation in a child who wears mittens to bed at night. This is quite probably a valid interpretation, but its meaning is embedded in the more comprehensive gestalt of being a child. The hands of a child are snuggly and warm, not stimulating genital pleasure.

couch and staring absently at her mittens in her lap, Rachel said, "It feels like being little. It's warm and safe." This awareness supported our exploration of her childhood experience—how it persisted into the present, and how deeply ambivalent she felt about it. Sixth grade, she told me, had been an idyllic time in her life, a time when she got along with everybody and pleased everybody—parents, peers, teachers—without the slightest sense of conflict. With adolescence, of course, that had all changed.

Even though she was more clinically problematic than Dana, Rachel also exhibited an ambivalent organization of the developmental polarity of child self and adolescent self. With a little work, she was able to bring both into her awareness and accept ownership of each. She gave them different names: Rache, as she had been known to everyone in childhood, and Rachel, as she now preferred to be addressed. The capacity to access and own such divergent aspects of the self often makes the difference between a transient developmental turmoil and a more enduring developmental problem.

Frozen, Protective Polarity Dynamics

One expression of an adolescent's taking ownership of experience is, as we have seen, a growing capacity to see and understand his or her life. The family, adults, and the social world are all experienced as they actually are, more in terms of the subtle complexities of their own makeup. This trend is no less marked in the adolescent's evolving experience of self: his or her vision of life, understanding of present circumstances and relationships, and grasp of personal origins and life history. But this growing capacity for awareness has its price.

Meaning that was formerly embedded in the field of childhood experience—that is, meaning that was *lived* more than *known*—now achieves a certain figural salience. It stands out and reveals itself to the adolescent. And because this is *his* world speaking to him, it tells him who he is. His life history—his family, his past—becomes for the adolescent acutely personal. These things come as an inheritance, as it were, from childhood to the new self gestalt of the adolescent.

For many adolescents, this psychological development is not problematic. But for many others, the meanings discovered—the inheritances of life as a child in the family—will crystallize at the price of great narcissistic pain. A mother's drinking, a family's poverty, a father's Old World ways: all these things may suddenly become sources of great personal shame. As the adolescent begins to synthesize meaning about his personal history more authentically, there may emerge powerful realizations of how awful life has been, how abusive and unfair, how rejecting, how deceiving, how illusory, how hypocritical.

I recently sat with a thirteen-year-old boy after a birthday visit to his father's home in a neighboring state. Since his parents' divorce years before, he had held steadfastly to the hope and belief that his dad would do anything for him, something that his father had often said. His father had promised him "something special" for this birthday. But the birthday came and went, and the something special never materialized. Now my client sat with the awful realization that his father had forgotten his promise or, worse yet, was the *sort of person* who often made empty promises. The accrued disappointments of his childhood relationship with his father had been contained over the years by his insistent hope and optimism and reinforced by his father's cheery tones, his evident sincerity, and his enticing promises. For this boy, as for so many other adolescents in therapy, the price of growing up, of taking ownership of experience and self, meant dealing with a backlog of disappointment, sadness, and hurt.

For adolescents who can tolerate these emergent awarenesses, this stage is accompanied by difficult insights and painful retrospective realizations. Insight always involves a reorganization of the field, and these invariably (at least for a time) wound the self, diminish the individual's sense of worth and value, and raise the developmental dilemma of whether awareness is even bearable. Many adolescents are not willing to pay the price of growth and integration, most often because there is not enough environmental support. When the legacy of childhood experience with which the adolescent must come to terms has included intolerable psychological pain, the enlivened inner world of adolescence poses a distinct threat. The pain is simply intolerable, the diminishment of self-worth is too cataclysmic, and the shame of acknowledging rejection and insufficiency is too great.

For these individuals, the developmental polarity dynamics between the child self and adolescent self become rigidly locked, in a manner designed to shut down all possibility of any painful awareness. The adolescent becomes a sort of dedicated antichild. Rudy fit this description, for the most part. He was brought to me by his aunt and uncle, who had been his legal guardians for the previous two years. Rudy was pleasant enough, but increasingly his aunt and uncle were discovering his deceptive and delinquent behavior. He was stealing, cutting school, sneaking out at night, and, they suspected, using (and perhaps selling) drugs. All of this was especially troublesome to them because they had accepted custody of Rudy as a way of rescuing him from a disastrous home situation (a rescue Rudy had welcomed) and had treated him always with support, love, and respect, just as they treated their own two preteen children. They had done everything they could to give him a family.

Rudy's own family had essentially disintegrated. His mother committed suicide when he was eight years old, and his father's attempts to hold the family together had deteriorated under the weight of his own emotional collapse and alcohol abuse. Rudy had learned to survive by using his wits and developing street skills—fighting, stealing, smooth talk, and conning. He was a well-mannered kid who could wrap most adults around his finger, but he had long since learned that the only person he could truly rely on was himself. With peers, he enjoyed a reputation for bravado and fearlessness. He was cocksure, charismatic, and clever. Everyone respected him. He was vulnerable to no one.

Rudy was something of an enigma to the adults who knew him. He had not been deprived as a young child, and he seemed to have survived early childhood as a reasonably happy and well-adjusted boy. He was very bright and had been successful in school. Nothing in his earlier history suggested a sociopathic or delinquent orientation. And now, as a teenager, he had an environment rich in resources that would support his maturation into adulthood. His aunt and uncle truly loved him, and they had intuitive parenting skills which would support and confirm his coming into his own. There was really no need for his delinquent behavior; it only made his life more complicated and difficult. "Why, Rudy? Why?" was the question his aunt and uncle plaintively put to him.

I myself could hardly imagine what it would be like to be an eight-year-old and have my mother, with no forewarning that I could discern, take her own life, and then to watch my father slowly unravel before my eyes, transforming himself from a competent provider to a raving, unpredictable drunk who could not hold a job. I could only imagine the shock and grief, the overwhelming sense of anxiety and vulnerability, the deep sense of betrayal and abandonment. In the face of such experience, Rudy had done exactly what he needed to do to survive: he had *vowed* to be a child no longer and *never again* to find himself in a position of need or dependency. For Rudy, adolescence began at about the age of eleven, the age when he got his streetwise persona, or self gestalt, together, and rigidly fixed it as the organizing configuration of his experience of himself and his contact with the world. In keeping with his vows, his relationship with his new family became one of manipulation and control rather than support and trust.

The hallmark of the client caught in a frozen polarity is the rigid fixing of an adolescent-self gestalt that prevents the possibility of any contact, with self or with others, reminiscent of the painful legacies of childhood. For many such adolescents, this project is far less competently and more desperately executed than it was in Rudy's case. One common thread is the prevalence of behavior that interrupts sensory and affective contact, both intrapsychic and interpersonal, either by heightening stimulation to the point of distraction or blunting it to the point of anesthesia. Chemical use and abuse are often a cardinal feature, as are purposeful excesses of risk taking, danger, sexual stimulation, conflict, anger, crisis, and so on. One is unlikely to experience the emotional pain of loss, failure, or rejection during an afternoon of truancy, shoplifting, speeding down a country road, or jumping forty feet from a railroad trestle into an off-limits swimming hole.

It is also unlikely, as every therapist knows, that an adolescent caught in a frozen polarity would welcome the opportunity to spend time with an adult, with the intention of learning about himself. In fact, most such adolescents are simply not candidates for outpatient psychotherapy. Nevertheless, in restrictive inpatient settings where their acting out can be contained, many of them "dissolve" to their child-self gestalts and become much more available for the work of therapy.

Rudy was unusual in this regard. It was true that he had no interest in attending to his sadness, sense of smallness, fear, and need for competent support, but he did tentatively accept my offer to teach him how to manipulate the adult world more effectively.

"After all," I pointed out, "you have done a pretty lousy job of not getting caught."

Our relationship was odd, by conventional psychotherapeutic

standards. Rudy manipulated me to intercede on his behalf, to reduce his punishments and expand his privileges. I agreed to do this for him, but only after he listened to my critique of his manipulative methods and took a lesson on how better to read and manipulate me. I identified our relationship in just this way, assuring him that, in light of his history, it was both understandable and acceptable. "You've simply got to get better at it," I insisted, and I proceeded to teach him what I knew about the arts of predicting adult behavior and negotiating deals that would work to his advantage.

When Rudy failed to hold up his end of a bargain, I pointed out that he still had much to learn about surviving in the real world. My pledge was to teach him everything I knew about survival: no moralisms, no little-kid stuff, just effective self-interest. In the end—and I considered this to have been a thoroughly successful therapeutic relationship—Rudy conceded his inability to stay out of trouble (although he had improved), even with my help.

When his aunt and uncle reached the end of their considerable tolerance and offered him the choice of returning to his father's house or attending a wilderness therapeutic school, he honored me with his trust by coming to me for advice. I thought the school was an excellent opportunity for him, and I said so.

"But you can't con the wilderness," I pointed out. "You're going to have to learn new ways to get by out there."

He nodded. He had already figured that out. The last I heard, Rudy had adjusted well to his residential school—doing schoolwork, getting good grades, and staying out of trouble.

In terms of the polarity between child self and adolescent self, Rudy had organized his adolescent-self gestalt in protective counterpoint to the ground of his childhood experience. For adolescents like Rudy, the new self becomes so rigidly figural that it does not permit alternative figures to emerge. In Figure 5.1, if we were to accentuate the features of the old woman, the figure would cease to be reversible at all; its figure-ground possibilities would become more rigidly fixed. This is exactly what happens with these damaged adolescents as the specific figural qualities of the new adolescent persona are exaggerated and highlighted. Frequently, such youngsters adopt flagrant badges and symbols of their toughened, affect-denying, nonchild self—shocking, surreal colors, or no colors at all (black clothing), hardened shells of leather and studded metal, T-shirts screaming against childhood's innocence, fear, and vulnerability. A central part of their adolescent resolution is to deny and avoid palpable experience of dependency on adults. This is what makes psychotherapy so nearly impossible with these adolescents. As was ultimately the case with Rudy, what they need is something that addresses a *larger field* of their adjustment than individual psychotherapy does. They need a therapeutic environment, one that simultaneously challenges their desperate survival mode of contact and makes available the sort of safety and competence that have been missing in the past..

Interrupted Polarity Dynamics

The majority of youths who enter outpatient psychotherapy fall somewhere between healthy ambivalence and rigid, defensive polarization. Ambivalence, as I have already pointed out, is a sign of healthy struggle. It is characteristic of teenagers who have already established enough solidity and permanence of the self gestalt to tolerate their own internal diversity. For them, the divergence of the child and adolescent strands of experience emerges in the form of experienced polarities. There exists a relationship of *ownership*, however vague and undeveloped, and however tentative or conflicted, to the various aspects of the self. The rigidly polarized adolescent, by contrast, has frozen the figure-ground relationship of self experience in a fashion that precludes the aware experience of polarity and ambivalence.

For those adolescents in whom the intrapsychic organization of self experience falls between these two extremes, the capacity to tolerate ambivalence while staking out ownership of the self is also limited, but not so rigidly as to preclude flux and variation in the experience of self. The reality of being, ambiguously, both in and out of childhood is subordinated to the necessity of developing an integrated and coherent sense of self. Thus, for these clients, the emergent polarity of child self and adolescent self is interrupted in the interest of a more immediate structural integrity. The individual in this circumstance identifies with one end of the polarity while actively dissociating from and disowning the other. Here, the meaning and motive of the disidentification will not be the management of overwhelming psychic pain. Instead, there is a need to limit internal conflict, in the interest of establishing the self as an integrated

gestalt. This means that many adolescents will synthesize and identify with only one portion of the burgeoning field of experience. That
portion is organized as "me," while other, contrasting or contradictory portions are dissociated from the self, denied, and often projected onto the environment, rather than emerging in awareness as
ambivalence.

What happens to those aspects of self that are disavowed is of
great interest to the therapist, because it is precisely the *loss of contact*
with those aspects that interrupts movement toward wholeness and
maturity. Typically, the interrupted polarity is projected, buried, or
both. One such client, Emily, appeared at my office wearing a dress
and a bow in her hair. She had a constant smile on her face. She was
sixteen but reminded me more of an eight-year-old on her way to a
birthday party. She worked at being charming and nice, and she seemed
concerned initially only with pleasing me. She described her classmates as coarse and wild—"immature," in her words. She had had
several boyfriends, but these relationships ended quickly because she
found them "too aggressive." She boasted of an "adult-type friendship"
with her mother; to my way of thinking, however, the two of them
seemed quite enmeshed. She valued this closeness, and although she
and her parents saw this relationship as a sign of maturity, it seemed
transparently like the closeness of a dependent younger child with a
parent. Even as an adolescent, Emily was thoroughly identified with
her child-self gestalt, including its aspects of attachment and dependency. She felt insufficient to the challenges of growing up, taking on
the wider world, and having genuine power of her own.

The aspects of experience that emerge in most adolescents and
signify the beginnings of differentiation were conspicuously absent
from Emily's experience. She occasionally became angry, but her anger was devoid of any thrust toward authentic contact with her parents; it was more of a temper tantrum, and it was not taken seriously
by Emily or her parents. These episodes were quickly forgotten. Likewise, Emily did not seem sexually awakened. Her interest in boys was
romantic, in the desexualized manner of old novels in which relationships are highly idealized, almost in fairy-tale fashion. And, not
surprisingly, Emily was having difficulty finding Prince Charming.
Her cognitive individuation was also lagging. Most of Emily's views
on matters of the world echoed her parents' views. "We're committed
Democrats," she announced when I asked her to describe her family.

For child-self teenagers like Emily, who have not yet synthesized a genuinely adolescent self, the business of change and growing up poses unavoidable intrapsychic and interpersonal problems. The child self, in effect, is being asked to carry a weight that it is not strong or flexible enough to bear, and something must break down sooner or later (sometimes not until midlife, in what we call a *midlife crisis*). Emily, for example, developed an abundance of psychosomatic ills. She had periodic bouts with stomach distress, occasional headaches that kept her out of school, and a variety of other, not readily diagnosable ills. It was as if the slivers of emerging adolescent experience had no psychological place to be taken up and drawn together. As a result, they were leached through her physical organism, to be expressed as unwanted pain and discomfort.

A variation on this theme, with a somewhat different emphasis, would be the youth whose experience of self is organized largely around the rigid parameters of introjected standards and ideals. This is the student whom teachers describe as perfectionistic, as an extremely hard worker who will settle for nothing but the best. Such adolescents frequently seem very adultlike. They relate well to their teachers and generally are liked by them in return. They often hold positions of responsibility (editing the school newspaper, presiding over the student government, and so on). Marnie, a sixteen-year-old junior in high school, fit this profile perfectly. But while her teachers genuinely admired her, her classmates basically ignored her, and she felt distant from them. She saw their playful, goofing-off behavior as "immature" and said that she much preferred the company of the college-age students of her elder sister's generation. Like many adolescents whose experience of self is organized around uncompromising introjects, Marnie was vulnerable to unexplained depressions. Her own potential lightheartedness, her capacity to challenge the rules and rework her rigid introjects, had gone undeveloped. Instead, these shards of experience surfaced in her projections as she became increasingly alienated from and bitter toward certain "irresponsible" classmates. Their playfulness and propensity for challenging the rules sometimes exerted an almost hypnotic pull on her, a fascination that she cloaked in righteous disapproval.

Adolescents like Marnie are often difficult to interest in psychotherapy, since the idea of needing help often clashes with the distorted ideal of perfection. Marnie acknowledged that she was miserable, but she insisted, "I'm perfectly capable of working this out myself." Unfortunately (to my mind, at least), her parents agreed with her. They themselves seemed wounded by the prospect of having a "flawed" daughter. This was years ago, and when last I heard, Marnie had graduated from college and was making a success of herself—but at what price, I wonder. And, I can't help feeling, what a shame that she never learned how to be an adolescent.

The complement of an Emily or a Marnie is the rebellious adolescent who reverses this polarization, identifying intensely with the newfound adolescent experience and rejecting anything reminiscent of childhood history. The potential conflict between new impulses and old introjects is circumvented by the projection of childhood introjects onto the environment. These are the adolescents who, by acting out against the limits and guidelines of authority, loosen the bonds of their own constricted childhood selves. But, rather than own this conflict as intrapsychic, they become experts at luring and provoking the adults in their environment into dancing out the polarity conflict with them. Barry, a fourteen-year-old, had begun to experiment with alcohol. He and his friends, while drinking on summer evenings, had begun a pattern of minor vandalism. Barry had always been "a good kid," according to his parents, and of course he still carried within him the spirit of attachment and obedience that had earned him this attribution. But the intrapsychic conflict was more than his fledgling adolescent-self gestalt could tolerate, and so he skillfully provoked his parents into playing out his introjects. After a night out with his hell-raising buddies, he invariably did something to attract their attention: coming home late, leaving a stolen bicycle behind the garage, getting mouthy when asked about his activities, and so on. Like many acting-out adolescents who are essentially in conflict about their own behavior, he seemed to make an art of getting caught, so that the conflict could be worked interpersonally rather than intrapsychically.

Clients like Barry most often earn diagnoses of oppositional disorder and conduct disorder. Many of them oppose therapy strenuously, seeing it as an adult conspiracy to get the upper hand. Even so, however, many such youths can be engaged, provided that the therapist can avoid the lure of their polarity conflicts. The problem for most rebellious adolescents is that they do not know how to be in conflict with themselves—how to be ambivalent about stealing another boy's bike, how to gracefully regret an outburst of anger, how to look at both sides of an argument—without reverting to and feeling stuck in the child-self gestalt. Their vehicle for managing these possibilities of experience is the interpersonal field, and particularly their relationships with adults. Rebellious adolescents have a way of orchestrating the interpersonal environment so that others carry the intentions and speak the lines of the dissociated child-self fragments while the "I" sits comfortably, with at least temporary integrity, in the role of adolescent rebel.

One of the identifying flags of adolescents struggling with interrupted developmental polarities is the stereotyped nature of their relationships with adults. Adolescents like Emily and Marnie, whose identification is with the self-organization of childhood, generally have friendly and accepting relationships with adults. They like adults—in fact, they usually prefer them to their own agemates—and frequently ally with them. Adolescent-self identifiers like Barry typically polarize with adults. They may accept relationships into which the adult tacitly agrees to enter as a buddy, but their relationships with most adults tend to solicit the "judging parent."

Case Example

Ben, a seventeen-year-old referred for depression, was a friendly but socially awkward boy. He had a small coterie of congenial acquaintances but no relationships that he found especially satisfying. He desperately wanted to have a "best friend" and a girlfriend but had been unable to find either.

Ben was the eldest of five children in a warm and relatively close-knit Catholic family. His youngest sister, adopted at age three, was retarded. That his parents would voluntarily take a retarded child into their family was emblematic of their genuine kindness and their practical commitment to religious values. Both parents worked hard to send Ben and his brothers to the academically challenging Catholic boys' high school that they attended.

Ben was very open about his appreciation for his parents. Although his relationship with them in recent months had begun to exhibit some of the strain and conflict typical of adolescence, Ben stated that his mother was still probably his "best friend." Periods of relative neutrality in their relationship were punctuated with occasional moody explosions and occasional heart-to-heart talks. His relationship with his father, who was himself vulnerable to depression, was warm but more distant. Until the time Ben was referred to me for psychotherapy, he had always found that his parents provided enough support for any difficulties he experienced.

Ben had a long history of academic mediocrity, in spite of testing that suggested his ability to do much better. He was a willing and committed student but acknowledged that he often had great difficulty following through on his good intentions where schoolwork was concerned. This had become an intense source of frustration for Ben as his senior year in high school got under way and he began the process of thinking about the future and applying to colleges.

On a typical school day, Ben would arrive home after school determined to start working on his several hours of daily assigned homework. After half an hour or so, he would find himself becoming lethargic and unfocused. He would fritter away large chunks of time in anxious wrestling with himself. He might get up from his desk to go sharpen a pencil, absentmindedly pick up the sports section of the newspaper and begin reading articles of little interest, wander downstairs to the family room and stop for fifteen minutes of disengaged trance in front of the television, drift into the kitchen and open the refrigerator, and then anxiously "snap to" and march himself back up to his desk, only to find that he still needed to sharpen his pencil.

Over the course of eight months, Ben's therapy dealt with a host of important issues concerning his relationships with his parents, his fears about the future, his management of his interpersonal needs, and his feelings about himself. About six months into therapy, Ben was earning a D- in algebra. He needed the course to graduate but had fallen behind. In spite of exhortations from his parents, his teacher, his counselor, and himself, he could not get himself to do the nightly assignments or attend after-school review sessions given by the in-school tutorial service. Ben was at war with himself, and algebra had become the battlefield.

What seemed abundantly clear to me was that Ben hated algebra. His struggle had richly symbolic meaning, and it was rooted in issues of attachment, dependency, and "graduating" away from the family and going off on his own to college. But Ben still hated algebra with a passion, and he simply did not want to devote time and energy to something he detested so much. Obvious as this was to everyone else, however, it was not part of Ben's awareness.

"How do you feel about this class?" I would ask him.

"It doesn't matter how I feel," he would reply, following with a lament about how he owed it to himself and his parents, who were working so hard to send him to this school, to at least do the work and get a passing grade.

Ben would readily discuss his deeper motives for not doing the work, but he was unable to experience his own sensory and visceral avoidance with any sort of ownership and identification. He simply could not admit to himself that in spite of all his good intentions, his gratitude to his family, and his appreciation of his teachers, he self-ishly, impetuously, irresponsibly *did not want* to do the work. Ben was a classic "good kid." As such, he organized his awareness of himself in terms of what felt right, appropriate, grateful, and responsible. He abhorred those nuances of his own experience that felt selfish, indulgent, or irresponsible. He begged me to help him figure out how to follow through on his good intentions for "busting" the algebra problem.

I agreed to do so, but only on the condition that he first carry out an assignment of my design.

"Anything," he replied.

I instructed Ben to devote time during the upcoming week to decorating his various spiral notebooks with anti-algebra graffiti. He looked at me as if I were crazy and protested that this was not at all what he had in mind. I insisted, and although he ultimately diluted the experiment by writing only on the insides of his notebook covers, he did comply.

In our next session, I had Ben read the graffiti to me aloud, and together we played with intonation and emphasis. At the time, I think, this seemed to Ben an incidental experience, a bit of off-the-wall playfulness carried out in collaboration with a trusted (if not quite conventional) adult. But it was clear to me that Ben had to break through some invisible inner membrane in order to allow himself these playful moments of genuine and selfish self-expression.

Two weeks later, Ben entered our session with a big smile on his face and reported the following impromptu experiment. Several nights before, his parents had gone out for the evening. As they left, they had supportively encouraged him to "get to work" and complete his algebra assignment. He assured them that he was about to do just that.

As they drove down the driveway and Ben stood watching them from the kitchen window, the most incredible thought struck him. He "realized" that he did not have do his algebra if he did not want to. He could pop a tape into the VCR instead, put his feet up, and watch a movie. In fact, that is what he did. The interesting thing is that it was the sort of thing that Ben had been doing all semester, but never had he allowed it to become figural, nor had he experienced it as an intentional part of himself. As Ben told me this tale of wild self-indulgence, he rubbed his hands gleefully and laughed heartily at the silliness of it all.

"You're right," he conceded. "I *really* hate algebra."

Predictably, within several weeks, Ben magically "found" the motivation to push himself through the distasteful task of doing homework and attending after-school review sessions. He finished with a C in the course.

Ben's stuckness, his inability to complete his separation from his parents and begin feeling himself to be a citizen of the world beyond childhood and family, was an expression of the perseverance of his child-self paradigm for organizing the field of his experience. Algebra became one of several arenas for pulling apart this restrictive paradigm and allowing a more diversified configuration of self to emerge. Ben's learning, at least in this one small episode of therapy, was of the most ordinary variety. He was a good, sincere, grateful kid. He was also selfish and antagonistic and occasionally in conflict with what the adult world had designed for him. He was, as he himself put it, "just a regular teenager."

CHAPTER SIX

The Tasks of Adolescence

Traditionally, writers on adolescent development have subdivided adolescence into three phases: early adolescence (roughly twelve to fourteen years), middle adolescence (roughly fifteen to sixteen years), and late adolescence (roughly seventeen to twenty years). I am not interested in breaking adolescent development down into tightly delimited, discrete substages, especially not substages that are tied to specific ages. Particularly for practicing clinicians, such schemas are probably more misleading than valuable. But I do want to sketch out the process of transformation and growth that stretches between the embeddedness of childhood and the potentially differentiated contact of adulthood, and I want to trace that evolution at the boundary of self and environment.

Adolescence and Contact

If we are to understand adolescence, it is important to be able to describe how the meaning and function of the contact boundary and contact process change from the earlier to the later stages of the adolescent's developmental journey. Adolescent development aims at maturation of the capacity for differentiated contact. The whole point of adolescent development is to reorganize the field of experience so that a certain sort of relationship between self and environment becomes possible. Mature contact involves the dual qualities of interpenetrating and differentiating, of joining and separating. It implies that the individual is capable of maintaining boundaries but at the same time is capable of relaxing boundaries, so as to give out to and take in from the environment. This formulation is the Gestalt equivalent of Freud's famous statement that the fulfillment of human development is "to love and to work." For the Gestalt therapist, loving and working are potentiated and made satisfying by the maturing of this capacity for differentiated contact. Thus what matures over the course of adolescence is the *contact boundary*—the boundary that defines the self and at the same time organizes and regulates its intercourse with the environment. What emerges, then, is a delineation of self, a crystallization of a difference between self and nonself, and an organization of a certain relationship between the two.

As an evolving system, the organism-environment field is oriented toward this achievement of *"developmental pragnanz,"*[1] a state of dynamic organization that constitutes the "best" organization that the field is capable of attaining. The field where full and satisfying contact is possible is one in which a dynamic balance is achieved between the organism's organizational integrity and its capacity to interact with its environment. This maturation of the field is the goal of adolescent development, the dynamic equilibrium toward which adolescent development tends.

In the course of adolescent development, the contact boundary passes through three evolutionary phases, each characterized by a specific organizational achievement. The first is the stage of *disembedding*, when the work of differentiating from childhood and heightening generational boundaries is figural. The second is the stage of *interiority*, when the deepening of inner life, the experience of ownership, and the phenomenological heightening of a private self become figural to development. The third is the stage of *integration*, when the goal of the figural work is a stable organization of intrapsychic and interpersonal experience and the roughing out of a style of integrating the differentiating and merging dimensions of contact.

There is some correspondence between these stages and the traditional timetable of early, middle, and late adolescence. The stages proposed here are not conceived as age-bound time periods, however, but as an ordered description of developmental work to be done, in functional if not always in temporal sequence. I have found it convenient to separate these stages, or tasks, to clarify the underlying logos of the developmental process. In fact, however, these stages are certainly in process simultaneously, and we should expect a great deal

---

[1] The "Law of Pragnanz" was formulated by Wertheimer as the general principle of the organization of configured wholes, namely that gestalts tend toward that organization which is most elegant, balanced, stable, whole, and complete.

of variation in the ways that individual adolescents work at accomplishing or avoiding each of these tasks. In some cases the work does emerge in discrete, sequential stages, but in others there is a sense of the adolescent shuttling back and forth—working at generational boundaries, deepening inner life, achieving a balanced field of self and other, and then renewing energies for some earlier unfinished work. I have had some clients in whom no clear delineation of these stages was apparent, although they seem in retrospect to have done the developmental work described here.

As a broad generalization, I believe that the developmental emphasis of each of these three tasks shifts as the individual moves from early adolescence toward adulthood. The tasks emerge as organizing themes of each successive era of adolescence. It has been my experience, however, that there are some fairly clear gender differences in the way the developmental work gets done. Boys are much more likely to follow a clear, age-related sequence, doing the work of bounding and distancing from adults before doing the work of deepening interiority or the work of reengaging with the adults in their world. Girls are more likely to do the work simultaneously, or in smaller loops, bounding and reengaging recursively throughout their adolescent years. But these statements, too, are broad generalizations, and exceptions are common.

The support that our culture and our traditions lend to adolescent boys and girls also clearly differs along gender lines. It is not uncommon to find boys whose adolescent development seems dominated by the need to suppress child-self gestalt and separate from adults, and whose capacity for interiority has been neglected or arrested. Nor has it been uncommon (although this seems, thankfully, to be changing) to find adolescent girls whose experiential sense of boundary, identity, and autonomy has been tentative and undervalued. Keeping in mind, then, that developmental schemas are only crude maps to an enormously rich and nuanced terrain, let us turn to the pattern of adolescent development.

Disembedding

In the stage of disembedding, the essential tasks of development have to do with establishing a sense of boundary—a sense of being demarcated and defined, of being set off, identified with one's own experience, differentiated from the milieu (both intrapsychic and interpersonal) of recent childhood. Sometimes the most striking feature of early-adolescent children is their experience of discovering, as if it were a forbidden truth, that they have left childhood. The point of development at this stage is precisely the establishment of a boundary, a sense of difference, and the forging *in principle* of the capacity to maintain this difference and define the contours of this new experience of self.

Early adolescence simultaneously involves characteristic developments of the intrapsychic and interpersonal spheres of experience. Intrapsychically, there is an intensification of experience, which derives in part from the physiological and endocrinological changes of pubescence. Thus the twelve- to thirteen-year-old's inner world is permeated with heightened experiences of physical power, emotional reactivity, and sexual arousal, which both necessitate and make possible a heightened sense of boundary from the family and from the familiar patterns of childhood experience.

The first organizational task of adolescent development is to establish, in fact and in principle, ownership of self—a preliminary sense of authorship, identity, and boundedness. For some, this will be a loud and public undertaking; for others, it will be quiet and covert. For some, it will entail a dramatic reorganization of the family field; for others, it will simply amplify the contact boundaries and interpersonal patterns that already exist. This first task of adolescent development is not a reorganization of the self as a segregated gestalt but a reorganization of the *interpersonal field* as a place where experiments with heightened authorship can take place. The intrapsychic growth of adolescence, which involves the familiar themes of psychosexual maturation and identity formation, is predicated on this restructuring of the interpersonal field. We could almost say that the first task of adolescence is to set the stage for adolescence—that is, to alter interpersonal contact boundaries and processes, so that intrapsychic emergence and maturation become possible. Thus, long before the adolescent *feels* genuinely and consistently different on the inside, he or she may inaugurate sweeping changes on the outside. Makeup, new haircuts and clothing, new musical interests, territoriality about personal space—these outward signs may abruptly announce the transition from childhood to adolescence, long before the adolescent feels genuinely and consistently reorganized at the level of intrapsychic experience.

This interpersonal boundary becomes the focus of much early-adolescent experience. This is the boundary where awareness first develops and articulates a new sense of self-definition. Adolescents at this stage, for all the presumed intensity of their physical and affective experience, have not developed the language to describe their inner worlds. What develops sooner is a richly articulate capacity to describe experience at the boundary of self and environment. In therapy, these younger teenagers like to talk about everyone but themselves—their friends, their teachers, their parents, and so on. They often draw a blank when asked to focus their attention on intrapsychic contact boundaries.

If we recall for a moment that childhood experience is organized under a paradigm of introjection, we can shed some light on the possibilities for early adolescence. Kepner (1987), writing about the young child's adaptation to toxic introjection, notes that introjection breeds two complementary styles for coping: *underbounding* and *overbounding*. The underbounded child, Kepner writes, "give[s] up the self in the service of the other, burying his or her own needs deeply out of reach," whereas the overbounded child "compensate[s] by closing his or her boundaries to any contact that might be foreign or unassimilable" (pp. 174–175).

We find very similar options open to the early adolescent who organizes a developmental response to the generic introjection of childhood. He or she may underbound, remaining enmeshed in the field of childhood experience, or overbound by disengaging from this field. In nonclinical populations, we find many early adolescents who do a bit of both, remaining very much engaged with the adults in their environment in some situations while emphatically pulling away in others. In clinical populations, we more frequently see youngsters who approximate the underbounded or overbounded extremes. The underbounded adolescent is the one who remains attached and dependent, who is confluent with adult expectations, and whose budding capacity for differentiation feels alien and dangerous. The overbounded teenager is the one who disavows dependency needs and childhood history.

Of more interest here is the bounding that separates the early adolescent from his family and his past, and that occurs as a normal part of the developmental process. What is important to keep in mind is that the variations on this process, whether healthy or pathological, are very much a function of the introjecting context from which the child is emerging (or failing to emerge). The fact of whether a family has prepared its children for their eventual differentiation is usually first apparent at the time of early adolescence. The discussion that follows is focused largely on the self-formation of the individual child, but it is nevertheless important to remember that pathological interruptions and distortions of this process are virtually always reflections of family process.

Intrapsychic and Interpersonal Process

At this first level or stage of adolescence, the intrapsychic and interpersonal dimensions of experience are related in a manner very specific to the developmental-organizational task just outlined. The self at this point is still very much a self in the family system, so that intrapsychic processes are unavoidably externalized—mapped, as it were, across interpersonal contact boundaries. Another way to say this is to say that the mind, or psyche, of the first-stage adolescent is very much an *interpersonal field structure*. Conflicts that in the older adolescent take on the quality of the intrapsychic, the struggle of self with self, are for the younger adolescent conflicts with others. The early adolescent orchestrates and choreographs his world as a medieval playwright does, assigning newly differentiated traits, qualities, and components of experience to various characters on the stage. The social field of the thirteen-year-old is almost like the psyche turned inside out. Parents may carry the role of dependency longings and moral restraint. Friends may carry the role of sexual interest and narcissistic self-inflation. Enemies may carry the role of underdeveloped or dissociated parts of the self. In therapy, as the thirteen-year-old describes his overprotective mother, his most loyal friend, the cutest girl in his class, the boy at school that he can't stand, he is also telling us, in the best and most precise language he has available, about the emergent boundaries and dynamics of his intrapsychic process.

The Projective Framework of Experience

The interpersonal world of the early adolescent becomes an extension or projection, in a sense, of the broader field of experience of self. More precisely, the early adolescent's interpersonal field is shot through with forces, organizing vectors, and boundaries that emanate from the intrapsychic process of the emergent adolescent self. This is a virtual reversal of the field conditions of preadolescent experience, where the environment imposes its imprint on the malleable psyche of the child. In early adolescence, we see the opposite vector assert itself as the environment begins to be appropriated to the organizational and developmental needs of the emerging self.

Early adolescents are notorious for their "poor reality testing." It is not uncommon to find thirteen-year-olds who begin to see their parents as thoroughly hostile and provocative, and who have a relatively weak grasp of their own moodiness and antagonism. Their perceptions of their environment are heightened to the point of caricature, but their awareness of the needs and feelings that organize perception remains undeveloped. Another way of saying all this is that the younger adolescent tends to organize experience of the self and environment in what might be called a *projective framework*. In a projective framework, it is the other, the environment, that stands out as figural, and the self is organized more implicitly as the ground of experience. This organization protects or shields the tenuous adolescent self from awareness and contact that might prove too intense or too threatening to its precarious integration.

In Figure 6.1, the lines may not be well enough articulated to suggest the image of two faces. The lines suggest faces only in the vaguest way. For most viewers, it is much easier to maintain the field

Figure 6.1. A Vase or Two Faces.

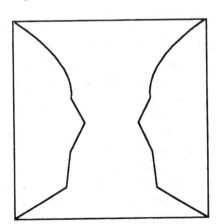

organization of a figural vase against a background; this is a more believable organization of the visual data. In the same way, a four-teen-year-old boy may find it difficult to maintain a figural percep-tion of himself as independent, no longer in need of adult support, especially in the face of so much obvious data to the contrary. It is much easier for him to maintain this organization of self-perception *implicitly*, as part of the ground, by organizing his parents figurally as impediments to his independence.

In therapy, it is much easier (and safer, from their point of view) to get younger, less mature adolescents to talk about the people in their world—their friends, their enemies, their parents and teach-ers—than it is to get them to speak reflectively about themselves. The developmental value, often lost to adults, of the disembedding adolescent's projective framework is that it regulates the contact process, allowing the adolescent's sense of self to solidify while mini-mizing the dangers of raw exposure and destructuring. For the adoles-cent, to enter into an honest and straightforward discussion about how she struggles to become more independent is far more risky than to discuss how her parents stifle her independence. Both statements frame the same existential-developmental issue, but the second way of organizing it leaves the self's tenuous integrity less at risk.

The capacity to define and maintain a boundary of the self in the interpersonal world, successfully established, makes possible the more differentiated and interactive contact of later adolescence. Be-fore this boundary becomes a mature organ of contact, it serves the preparatory function of establishing authorship and integrity of the self. As this task is accomplished, broader aspects of the experience of self that feel incongruent can be conveniently located "over there," outside the fledgling *I* boundary, projected onto others, where they can be used as a sort of whetstone for defining and sharpening the contours of the emerging self. The girl who is first learning what it means to have a woman's body and be sexual may locate her child-hood inclination to be a "good girl" in her parents and may use these projections to help her define, in counterpoint, what she is experi-encing Thus she may complain bitterly if her mother questions her choice of bathing suit, or if her father prohibits her from dating a boy several years older. At the same time, however, she uses her parents (and quite possibly exaggerates their position) to heighten and iden-tify her ownership of her attractiveness and sexuality.

In early adolescence, the scope and depth of awareness about the intrapsychic dimension of self are limited, by contrast to the expanding capacity for awareness at the interpersonal boundary. The early adolescent often identifies, sometimes stridently and uncompromisingly, with a relatively limited portion of the field of self experience. From the broad array of involvements and activities, from the entire allocation of time, interest, and energy, some discrete portion or portions are likely to stand out as more important, more interesting to the self. At the same time, other portions of experience are actively relegated to ground, disassociated from the self, and frequently projected onto the environment.

Thirteen-year-olds, as a group, have begun to generate their own culture, laced with sexual tension and strivings for autonomy. The new self may well be rooted in these interests. At the same time, however, thirteen-year-olds remain rather involved in adult and childhood culture. They spend time in classrooms, time with their siblings and parents, and time involved in activities that the adult world organizes for them. The distinctions between what they want to do and what is expected of them become much sharper than in preadolescence. The particular configuration of self that emerges as figural at this time is not, typically, viable for eventual adult living. For one thing, it is highly changeable. For another, it is characteristically short on practical living skills. And, most important, as a structure for containing experience, it does not tolerate much internal conflict. Consequently, as we have seen so often, the early-adolescent self characteristically manages psychological conflict by deflecting it away from intrapsychic boundaries and onto interpersonal boundaries. And, as we have seen, polar tensions typically emerge in early adolescence not as *owned ambivalence* but rather as *tensions across the interpersonal contact boundary*, as themes that organize the adolescent's interactions with others. From the full field of potential experience of self, which contains both aspects of any emergent polarity, the adolescent typically identifies with one pole and relies on the environment to carry the other.

Polarities may be mapped across any combination of interpersonal fields—the family field, the field of peer relationships, or the field of real-world adults. Thus a thirteen-year-old boy struggling with his own emotional dependency may distance himself from his parents, denying that he cares about their approval, but at the same time he may become sensitized to other children who seem emotionally attached to and dependent on adults. He may chide his younger siblings for running to Mom when they are hurt, and he may scorn agemates who "suck up" to teachers, displaying their need for adult approval. Or, to take an opposite example, another boy may identify himself as responsible and criticize agemates who act out their impulses to challenge and evade adult authority. In both cases, we find that a budding polarity—the need for adult support versus the need to disengage from adult influence—has become a thematic organizer of interpersonal contact. One side of the polarity is identified as belonging to the self, and the other is encountered in the environment. The interpersonal contact boundary is where the dynamics of this polarity begin to get worked out, where contact between the opposing tendencies is initiated, and where the ground for their eventual integration is prepared.

To take yet another example, a young teenager is able to let go of his childhood inhibitions and fears precisely because his environment contains others, usually adults, who represent these for him: he projects the introjects of his child self onto the adults in his life. Recently, in a therapy group for thirteen- and fourteen-year-old boys, the subject of prostitution came up. Several of the boys complained about the difficulty of finding and picking up prostitutes. The fact that none of them had ever met a prostitute or perhaps ever even seen one was not the issue, as far as they were concerned. The only thing getting in the way of their indulging their sexual impulses, they claimed, was that their parents would kill them if they found out.

A common example of interpersonal dynamics in this phase has to do with the ownership of schoolwork. An eighth-grade girl has a history of academic success and reasonably good work habits, but now her interests have turned to peer relationships and boys, and her grades begin to drop. She used to value the approval of her teachers and parents, but she now discovers a mildly polar position and begins to "detest" schoolwork. Her parents become concerned. They begin to supervise her homework time, set limits on her use of the telephone, and so on. She complains, especially to her friends, but essentially complies with the structure laid down by her parents because she has "no choice." This is a garden-variety example of how a polarity emerges in experience as a property of the wider self-environment field. Because her parents are willing and able to hold up the "responsibility" end of this polarity, she is able to take up the "rebellious" end. She can inhabit this pole with relatively little intrapsychic conflict, and by doing so she learns what it is like to oppose authority and set her own priorities.

The same girl is likely to map the same emergent polarity across her contact boundary with peers. She may maintain a friendship with a peer who is more studious and responsible than she is, and together they may play out a friendlier version of the dynamic that she has with her parents. Her friend may remind her of important assignments, offer to help her study, and so on. At the same time, she may choose to link up with someone even more rebellious than herself, and in this relationship she may play out the responsible end of the polarity. The variations are endless and will change from one adolescent to another and from one time to another. What is common is the fact that the emergent polar tension, however the individual wrestles with it, is initially mediated by the adolescent's interpersonal world.

Mapping of emergent polarities is also evident in those behavioral themes that have more significant clinical implications. For example, I have often had adolescent patients who would engage in therapy but would not openly admit to needing help and would come only as long as some adult insisted. This frequently occurs with depressed teenagers who are struggling with the emergent polarity of neediness and self-sufficiency. Even though they are miserable to the point of considering suicide, these adolescents are sometimes not ready to own their need for help and will accept help only as long as someone else in the environment adopts ownership of their neediness. It is important for them, in the service of their fledgling self-integrity, to claim, "I can do it myself."

Another phenomenon well known to clinicians is the youth who asks for help by acting out. A boy who passionately argues with his parents that he can stay out of trouble on his own turns around and acts out in such a way that the adults are forced to intervene. One patient of mine was caught drinking on school property while cutting classes. He insisted that it was a one-time offense and managed to convince a chemical dependency counselor that this was the case. The counselor advised against further professional intervention and established a no-use contract with the parents and school officials. Having succeeded in getting people off his back, my patient promptly cut a full day of school with a friend, and together they got thoroughly drunk at the friend's house. In intrapsychic language, we could say that he was asking for help, but it would be somewhat more accurate to say that he arranged for his interpersonal environment to ask for help on his behalf.

The value of this phase of ownership is often lost to adults, lay and professional alike. It is important to remember that interpersonal conflicts are, in many instances, natural precursors of owned intrapsychic polarities. This is a principle of growth perhaps best understood (although in a very different developmental context) by practitioners of Gestalt therapy. Fritz Perls, for example, introduced the method of two-chair work to help adult psychotherapy patients own and integrate polar aspects of their experience of self. In the framework of a single session, a Gestalt therapist may ask the patient to actively segregate competing aspects of his experience, placing them in separate chairs. While dissociating from one pole, the patient is urged to identify with the other pole and feel it as congruently as possible. "Put your 'kind self' in the other chair, and let your 'aggressive self' speak to him," he might be instructed. The purpose of the exercise is to heighten the individual's awareness and ownership of his aggressiveness—to allow him (for a few moments, at least) to embrace it without internal conflict. The conflict is mapped interpersonally, as it were, so that the patient's aggressiveness can emerge with integrity. His aggressive self might say, "You're always getting walked on. You never stand up for yourself, and it makes me furious." The patient may be surprised at the inherent wisdom and self-support that underlies his aggressiveness, and this realization may lead him to own and integrate this aspect of experience.

The adolescent is doing a protracted developmental version of two-chair work. The process may require months, even years, but the potential for movement toward eventual growth is essentially the same as it is in Gestalt two-chair work.

The critical psychological needs at this stage are essentially organizational. The youth needs to establish, for his parents and for himself, that he can maintain his separateness and integrity. His focus in doing so is on the contact boundary of self with environment, especially with parents and other important adults.

In therapy with disembedding adolescents, the primary considerations are the family field as a whole and how that field is managing (supporting or interrupting) the disembedding process. Our focus may be the adolescent's development, but the entire family field is what is developing or failing to develop. Parents often continue in modes of contact that were appropriate and supportive for a younger child but that fail to recognize and confirm the adolescent's process of disembedding an authored self from the family milieu. It is also common to encounter clinical difficulties, particularly acting out, that reflect a family's understructured management of development. Individual therapy with disembedding adolescents is nearly pointless unless it is integrated with family movement that supports this developmental process.

Interiority

Once psychological boundaries and a sense of the self's integrity have been established, contact processes, both within the self and with others, begin to undergo change. There is at this time, *in the adolescent's own experience*, a differentiation of the intrapsychic and the interpersonal as salient and distinguishable fields of experience. That is, the individual begins to develop a heightened sense of the divergencies of inner, private experience from the outer world of social relatedness.

Simultaneously, as relationships become more complex and enriching, the subjective experience of the adolescent opens onto a richer inner world of poignant feelings, interesting and frightening awarenesses, and intriguing abstract thought. Now that the processes of defining boundaries and identifying the self have become established and operational, there is a decided movement toward exploration, both outwardly and inwardly, of these differentiated fields of self experience

Interpersonally, in the middle-phase adolescent, we see the beginnings of a relatedness that resembles mature contact. Relationships become more reality-based. Others are perceived and valued more in terms of their own attributes and less in terms of their service to the integrity needs of the emergent adolescent self. There is now more give-and-take, more interpenetration at the contact boundary, more genuine transaction between self and other. Relationships lose their decidedly narcissistic quality as friends are chosen less because they agree on important matters or provide a confirming audience and more because they appeal to the self's innate capacity for expanding its horizons.

Polarity themes may continue to play a significant role in the organization of interpersonal contact boundaries, but in a somewhat different fashion than is true for early-phase adolescents. Polarity friendships become common. The "straight" kid seeks out association with someone who is considered wild. The shy girl pairs up with someone who is outgoing and confident. The athlete develops a friendship with someone from the chess club. Personal qualities that were previously scorned now become interesting as the self seeks to expand its own internal repertoire.

Romantic interests and attachments burgeon at this time and have a quality distinctly different from the more generic and less personal flirting and probing that characterize earlier adolescence. This is the time of the first real boyfriend or girlfriend for many adolescents as attachment and dependency longings are taken out of storage, as it were, and experienced anew in a framework of ownership and identification. These relationships represent a sort of voluntary vulnerability: the self experiments with relaxing its boundaries and merging with another person.

The extent of this vulnerability, as the newly claimed self literally offers itself to another for acceptance and confirmation, is beyond the recollection and comprehension of most adults, who have a tendency to dismiss these interests as puppy love, downplaying the significance of the narcissistic damage and identity disintegration that can accompany a romantic failure. Adolescents who have experienced significant loss or rejection during childhood (for example, the death of a parent) are particularly vulnerable to serious psychological crisis when a romance breaks up. This event ranks high on the list of precipitators of adolescent suicide attempts. Psychoanalysis has taught us to view these effects as transference, the reawakening of earlier feelings of loss. And, indeed, it is as true for adolescents as it is for all of us that current loss reawakens former losses. But it is also more than that in the case of an adolescent. Adolescent love is a daring experiment in learning to become vulnerable and attached in a nonchildlike way. It is an experiment in psychological chemistry, where attachment and dependency are commingled with sexuality. The results can be spectacular, but the new composition is volatile and unstable. The failure and breakup of an attachment signals a sort of failure of the self, a disintegration of its new gestalt.

The interiority-stage adolescent's relationships with adults also take on a different cast as dependence and counterdependence become less the issue. The adolescent now becomes more *interested* in adults; that is, he or she finds certain adults interesting not just because they are nice or cool, but also for what they have to say or what they represent. And what adults find interesting about a given adolescent—his or her ideas, humor, appearance, cleverness—is also paid careful attention as the individual begins the process of synthesizing an identity for the real world.

Respect or its absence becomes a highly salient aspect of the adolescent's experience of being with adults. Youths in this phase become acutely attuned to whether or not they are taken seriously, whether their experimental sense of authorship is implicitly confirmed or disconfirmed in their interactions with adults. By the same token, sensitivity to adults who see past the public face, who "call" them on childish or irresponsible behavior, becomes painfully acute for middle-phase teenagers. The upsurge in self-reflective awareness and the loosening of the projective framework make this a stage typified more by internal pain than by projected anger.

The developmental work of this stage is to expand the boundaries of the self to include aspects of experience previously relegated to ground, or projected onto the environment. In this way, the adolescent becomes more interior, more reflective, and more conflicted within himself. Issues previously wrestled out with parents or peers now become struggles within the boundaries of the self. This is the phase when polarities, previously mapped across the self-environment contact boundary, emerge as inner divergences that the self recognizes as its own.

This change typically occurs tentatively and intermittently at first. Therapy patients in this phase will often, within a single session, shift back and forth between projecting their issues onto the environment and expressing issues of owned ambivalence. A girl may begin a therapy session by telling of a classmate who cheats on exams or flirts outrageously. By the end of the session, she may well be telling of her own temptations to cheat, or her own frustrated attempts to attract the attention of a romantic interest.

Dana, the fifteen-year-old described in Chapter Five, typifies this level of boundary functioning. Dana came to therapy intent on making her father's behavior the issue, but she readily accepted my gentle challenge to focus on herself instead. As she did, her outwardly focused frustration and anger melted to an inwardly focused confusion and sadness. Dana now found it easier to be aware of how her father had changed since switching his career from social work to business. Her experience of her own duality, and of the change she was in the process of making from child to young adult, was harder for her to grasp. Her inner experience had become both problematic and fascinating to her: painful enough to warrant avoidance but interesting enough to warrant exploration.

This middle phase of boundary development is characteristically the stage when adolescent inner life intensifies, when reflective journals are kept, poetry is written, moral dilemmas are raised and discussed—in short, when adolescence begins to resemble the dreamy stage of self discovery so commonly represented in literature about this age group. The experienced differentiation of the intrapsychic from the interpersonal leads to a heightened awareness of the segregation of the self from its context. This is manifested in various ways, among them the adolescent's vulnerability to feelings of alienation and the adolescent's sensitivity to phoniness.

Teenagers often report acute feelings of alienation and aloneness. It is not at all uncommon for adolescents to virtually sink into the newly discovered intrapsychic field, to find themselves swimming in a sea of private affect and intuition that segregates them from others in their environment, and to feel trapped as if in a whirlpool from which there is no escape. The intrapsychic world, once it opens up, can seem cavernous to the middle-phase adolescent. There may be a sense of despair at the idea that it may never be possible to link this dense inner world to the outer world of interpersonal contact.

As for the adolescent's acute sensitivity to phoniness, it represents precisely the segregation of outer from inner wherein outward behavior is experienced as disengaged from a richer and more genuine inner world. The adolescent's critical appraisal of phoniness in others is represented by Salinger's *Catcher in the Rye*. Holden Caulfield, Salinger's protagonist, rails against the phoniness he finds all around him. His real issue, of course, is with himself, and specifically with his own struggle for authenticity. In a larger sense, the adolescent's sensitivity to phoniness represents a new and painful awareness of the divergence between inner and outer, and of the boundary that is beginning to segregate the two. This is a development that is at once liberating and isolating, growth-promoting and pain-inducing. It makes possible a richer sort of connectednesss and sharing with others, but it simultaneously opens up an inner world that accentuates loneliness and isolation.

Individual therapy work is often profitable with interiority-stage adolescents. The general challenges include providing a relationship that supports the exploration and ownership of this newly enlivened inner landscape. The work requires the therapist to manage the adolescent's shuttling toward and away from experience of self. The therapist must respect the periodic need for deflection and avoidance but must also challenge and support the growth of awareness and ownership.

Integration

In later adolescence, we find evidence of the general trend for the identified, owned self to move away from the fragmentary and partial and toward the more comprehensive and inclusive. As the adolescent self matures, it becomes literally more of a *con-figuration*, an assemblage of figures, a gestalt formation that assumes into its structure the fragments and partial organizations—impulses, prohibitions, introjects, attributions, wants, polarities, and partial self gestalts—of childhood and earlier adolescence. In this way, the self emerges progressively through adolescent development as a *higher-order gestalt* that integrates increasingly diverse aspects of self and promotes an ever-growing sense of ownership of experience. Therefore, older adolescents become truly complex beings in their own experience and can identify not just with a specific impulse or want in a given situation but also with the need to literally *be* a framework sufficiently broad to encompass and integrate discordant shards of experience.

By the latter part of adolescence, the boundaries of the psychological self have attained enough resilience and sturdiness to support mature contact (interchange with others that allows mutual influence without risking disintegration). Older teenagers often "return" to their parents at this stage, becoming more engaging while maintaining a sense of themselves as sufficiently free-standing and centered to withstand the field forces of the family milieu. Likewise, parents are aware of this change in status and sometimes describe their role as being more like that of a consultant than that of a parent.

The goal of adolescent development is not *in*dependence but rather *inter*dependence. New kinds of interactions emerge at the boundary between the later adolescent and parents. He or she may now be able to ask for assistance (with how to buy a car, apply for a loan, bake lasagna, and so on) without feeling the undertow of earlier organizations of the field. Negotiation, in the true sense of the word, becomes possible as the later adolescent and parents engage more on a horizontal plane and less according to a vertical hierarchy of power and control.

The later adolescent's perceptions and judgments of external and interpersonal reality become more accurate as they become unharnessed from the needs of self-development. He or she no longer needs to see parents as obstructive or abandoning or as unforgivably failed and fallible. The field of the later adolescent's experience is much less a projective field, one appropriated for developmental purposes, and much more a field that exposes others (including parents) as who they are in their own right.

The energy and work of development undergo a significant transformation in later adolescence. The processes that were so much the issue before—synthesizing experience and identifying the self—have now been won, and can begin to be taken for granted. It becomes time to put these processes to use. Now that the task of laying claim to the self has been accomplished in principle, the older adolescent begins to lay claim to a *life*; that is, he now feels the weight of responsibility for managing what he has won. The organizing developmental theme switches from "Am I in charge?" to "Now that I am in charge, what am I going to do with myself?" In general, we see energies shifted away from the contact boundary of self and family, away from the temporal boundary of self and childhood, and directed more toward the business of living—into choices about relationships, career direction, values, and the like. There is, in other words, a shift from the developmental task of establishing self processes and toward the existential task of living them out.

This is the age when identity formation comes front and center as the measure of developmental accomplishment. Does this individual have a consistent sense of who he or she is becoming? Does he or she have a sense of sexual identity? Does he or she have a sense of educational or occupational orientation? Does the world seem like a hospitable and manageable enough place in which to find his or her way? These are questions raised to measure the successful navigation of adolescent development in the emergent young adult. Implicitly, they boil down to something more fundamental: Has this individual succeeded in gaining ownership of self, and has he or she become a choice maker in the existential sense of authoring a personal life?

The latter part of adolescence is a period when developmental trends and projects come together, and we begin to see what sort of contact process has been in the making all these years. Successful adolescence is defined by a reorganization of the field as a whole, in which we include the individual's experience of body and of self, his or her relationships with family, peers, and extrafamilial adults, and his or her relationship with society as a whole. The expectations that we have, quite unreflectively, of people between seventeen and twenty are significantly different from those that organize our perceptions and interactions with them at fifteen and sixteen. When I see my eighteen-year-old nephew at Christmas, I no longer ask, "How's school going?" I ask him, "What are your plans?" The developmental-societal field of the later adolescent evinces a paradigm shift characterized by a pervasive sense of existential responsibility. This means that the adolescent, and society, expect a more future-oriented outlook, a more centered version of selfhood, and the ownership of a life for which the individual is uniquely responsible.

PART II

Adolescents and Psychotherapy: Application of the Tasks Model

CHAPTER SEVEN

The Structure
of Adolescent Psychotherapy

What does psychotherapy with an adolescent client look like? If we had to construct a "snapshot" that reflected the essential quality of psychotherapeutic work with adolescent clients, what image would we settle on?

For many therapists, something fairly specific comes to mind. It may be an image of client and therapist working together one to one. It may be of the adolescent in a group setting with peers; or of the adolescent in family therapy. The image may have the look of a friendly conversation or of a pointed confrontation. It may have the tight focus of structured, goal-directed problem solving or the looser focus of a rambling chat about a favorite topic or hobby. It may conjure up the formality of the fifty-minute hour or the happenstance of a brief, impromptu interaction in the middle of some other activity. The variations are nearly endless.

This variety is not accidental, and it certainly does not reflect any sort of problematic inconsistency in the field of adolescent psychotherapy. To be sure, there is nothing approaching unanimity of method among professionals who work with adolescents. One writer describes the delicate business of building a one-to-one therapeutic alliance with the adolescent's fledgling ego functions. Another describes the reordering of the family's communication patterns. Still another stresses methods of organizing the adolescent's environment so that he or she will learn the relationship between choices and consequences. One approach may emphasize the importance of the client's learning to attend to and articulate the inner world of feelings, urges, and fantasies. Another may stress the importance of learning to assess external reality accurately and of acquiring practical skills for living in the real world.

Adolescent psychotherapy is all these things, and necessarily so.

Adolescents, as a cohort, constitute a population as diverse as all humanity. The adolescent therapist's caseload may include future scholars, laborers, sociopaths, spouse abusers, clerics, alcoholics, schizophrenics, police officers, and psychotherapists, and yet all are adolescents. The only truly unifying theme is that they are all engaged in the process, with varying degrees of success, of *developing*, of working through the transition from childhood to adulthood and designing and enacting a self.

The organizing theme of psychotherapeutic work with adolescent clients is the facilitation of the natural developmental process. Adolescents who enter psychotherapy have become stuck in their developmental progress. In some fashion, the process has become snagged or hung up. In some way, the adolescent has found his way into a pattern of routinized experience and behavior, a fixed gestalt, that short-circuits the vibrancy and learning that is inherent in adolescence.

The psychotherapist is a visitor in the life of his client. As such, his or her task is to stay no longer than necessary. In the lives of adolescents, extrafamilial real-world adults play important roles in shaping and fostering the developmental process. They provide advice, perspective, and support, which the adolescent is free to take or leave. By taking him seriously, they confirm the legitimacy and viability of the adolescent's experimentation with self. By listening, they provide the sounding board for the adolescent's growing mastery of inner life. These adults, unwittingly perhaps, are all "therapists" to their adolescent charges. Psychotherapists become these real-world adults for those youths who are unable to mine this sort of important adult involvement from their own developmental landscapes. Not uncommonly, adolescents who come for psychotherapy are lacking the capacity for healthy contact with real-world adults, perhaps because they are frightened of it, or perhaps because it has been unavailable.

The tasks of psychotherapy are organized by the ultimate objective of moving the adolescent along the developmental path. The roles that the therapist assumes in the service of this objective are varied. At different times, he or she must be case manager, parent educator, school consultant, family therapist, and individual therapist. This last role includes being friend, advocate, teacher, guide, confirming witness, wise adviser, challenger of assumptions and ideas, confronter of behavior, representative of reality, and voice of sanity. The profile of roles appropriate to therapy with one individual may not be appropriate or therapeutic with another, and a style that is genuine and grounded for one therapist may be awkward and artificial for another.

I find it useful to think of the overall project of psychotherapy as possessing a certain structure, an internal or underlying logos that organizes the encounter and the work of therapist and client. I find two organizing frameworks particularly helpful in therapeutic work with adolescents and their families. One is the contextual structure of the concrete psychotherapeutic tasks. The other is the developmental structure that situates clients and helps to define the feel and the objectives of the work.

The Contextual Structure of Therapeutic Tasks

I have found it useful to think of effective psychotherapy with adolescent clients as possessing a sort of "boxes within boxes" arrangement of therapeutic projects, a sequence of concerns and tasks, each of which builds on and emerges within the context of what precedes it. The last of these tasks is what we generally call the figural work of therapy. This is what we tend to think of as the productive moments of psychotherapy, those sessions when work gets done: an unexpressed emotion comes forth, a new understanding of some old problem is achieved, an important decision is made, a problem gets solved, and so on. These are the moments when client or therapist thinks or says, "Something was accomplished today."

But the work may also be more protracted. A piece of therapeutic work may span several sessions—or, indeed, the whole of therapy. It may entail the gradual raising of self-esteem, or the process of learning to challenge long-standing habits or beliefs. For an adolescent, it may involve learning to think ahead and anticipate consequences, or learning to identify affective states and verbalize them rather then act them out.

The figural work of therapy, however, always takes place in the context of a certain therapeutic relationship. This relationship can be characterized by some degree of trust, familiarity, and understanding. Without a therapeutic relationship of some description, there is no therapy. With many adult clients, the building of a therapeutic relationship is a relatively straightforward process, an unpremeditated

function of the client's distress and the therapist's attention and interest. The good faith of both parties is more a given condition of the
ground than a figure that must be constructed. In many textbooks on
adult psychotherapy, the business of establishing rapport is given little more than perfunctory attention.

With adolescent clients, however, the likelihood that a therapeutic relationship will take root and flower can hardly be taken for
granted. The very fact that there is typically an age difference of anywhere from ten to fifty years offers some perspective on the difficulties intrinsic to creating a therapeutic relationship with adolescent
clients. Many adolescents who come to therapy do so against their
will or, at best, with considerable ambivalence. Even those who seek
out professional help have usually had negative experiences in their
earlier relationships with purportedly helpful adults, and they typically do a fair amount of checking out before getting down to what is
really on their minds. The truth is that a high percentage of referrals
for adolescent psychotherapy never yield anything like therapeutic
work, because no viable working relationship between client and
therapist is ever established. Therefore, it could be argued that the
real work of therapy with an adolescent client is getting the adolescent to become a client in the first place. In fact, it has been my
experience that this is where the real challenge lies, and that adolescents, if and when they become clients, tend to profit from the work
of psychotherapy much more readily and dramatically than most
adult clients do. Thus the creation of a therapeutic relationship is the
platform on which the work rests, the context in which it proceeds.

But we are still nowhere near the starting point of adolescent
therapy, nowhere near the foundational layer of the structure of this
undertaking. This relationship in which the work takes place has its
own context: the developmental process itself, and the psychological
environment provided by the family milieu. The adolescent would-
be client who comes to my office is part of a family and a developmental history, and any relationship that we may establish must be
evaluated in terms of its impact on this larger context. In turn, the
potential value of our relationship will be very much determined by
what is going on in this larger context. Most therapists have had the
experience (I know I certainly have) of building a good relationship
and doing good therapeutic work with an adolescent client, only to
find that the benefits accrue about as quickly as water fills a sieve. A

youngster comes faithfully, takes therapy seriously, and seems to be learning a lot but continues with the same dysfunctional or symptomatic behavior because of some entanglement with parental or family dynamics. How many times do we find ourselves wondering, after the fact, whether we should have been doing family therapy instead? This is not to say that we should do family therapy in every case before we initiate individual therapy with an adolescent, but only that individual therapy takes place in the larger context of the individual's embeddedness in or disembedding from a family milieu, and that we should attend to that milieu in whatever way we can—learning about it, accommodating it, perhaps attempting to influence it—before blithely wandering down the path of individual psychotherapy with an adolescent.

Some professionals who work directly with adolescents—in schools, at drop-in centers, in residential treatment facilities—do not have direct access to the adolescent's family milieu. In other situations, one or both parents refuse or are unable to cooperate with or participate in the psychotherapeutic process. (And there are professionals and agencies that wrongly, to my mind, dismiss family context as extraneous to the adolescent's "personality functioning.") But in all these instances it is still important to know what is being missed, if for no other reason than to understand the field forces that have influenced and continue to influence the adolescent's experience and contact style.

There are three nested projects in the psychotherapy of adolescent clients, as I am conceiving it. These three projects—assessing the family context, building a therapeutic relationship, and doing the figural work of self-exploration, expanding awareness, problem solving, behavior change, and so on—together constitute the whole of adolescent psychotherapy. In ideal circumstances, we see this tripartite structure unfold. As therapist and client initiate a relationship, the family background and contact processes are explored—perhaps directly with the adolescent, perhaps collaterally in family sessions. As this adolescent's embeddedness and disembedding dilemmas become clearer, and as the working relationship between therapist and client begins to take hold, some objectives for therapy begin to announce themselves—some goal to be reached, some skills to be acquired, some pain to be articulated and digested.

In fact, however, therapy with adolescents sometimes takes place on the high wire, or on the run, where all these components cannot unfold so gracefully. We work with families whose kids will not have anything to do with individual therapy, and with kids whose families are unavailable for family work. We are thrust into crisis situations where the work of grounding someone who is out of control, or of securing someone who is suicidal, must proceed without any preliminary relationship-building work. But this structure of psychotherapy applies even to these circumstances in so far as it gives us a map for assessing the disadvantages under which we are operating.

The Developmental Structure of the Therapeutic Work

The point of psychotherapy with adolescent clients, at least with most adolescent clients, is the support and promotion of the developmental process. It follows that our map of developmental unfolding is also a framework for organizing the work of psychotherapy. The difficulties that clients present, and the styles and objectives of therapeutic work, can be charted within the developmental schema presented in Chapter Six. Some clients present difficulties expressive primarily of disembedding-stage issues. For others, the issues are centered more on developing interiority. For still others, the focus may be dilemmas related to the emerging integration of their developmental accomplishments. The nature of therapy, in other words, is contingent on the unresolved and emergent developmental work of the individual client and the family. This is important because the objectives of therapy are different for clients at different levels of development, and because the look and feel of the therapy work itself can be quite different according to the developmental issues being addressed.

Disembedding-stage work is certainly the most difficult, and teenagers at this level are the ones most often dismissed as "unworkable," particularly in individual therapy. Disembedding-stage clients are tangled up in their families, sometimes in the passive role of "good child," but more often in the unsuccessful struggle to move the family's (and their own) paradigm forward developmentally. These clients are often stuck or frustrated in their efforts to find confirmation of their separateness and their right to self-authorship. Therapeutic intervention with a disembedding-stage client is most effective when it includes some component of working with the family system and helping the parents in particular to organize their energies construc-tively. Individual therapy is also valuable with many disembedding-stage adolescents, particularly for confirming their reorganization of boundaries and ownership of self functions.

Interiority-stage clients are those who seem on the verge of deep-ening self-awareness, who seem poised to discover and explore the expanding inner world but need support in order to do so. They are also those clients who have already discovered this world but are very nearly drowning in it and desperately need a guide to find them and lead them back to the world of human sharing. These adolescents are often the ones who seem to benefit the most (or, at least, the most ob-viously) from individual psychotherapy. For many therapists, interiority-stage clients provide the most palpable rewards of working with an adolescent.

Finally, there are clients who arrive at therapy having already established themselves in their own right, with a grasp of their own internal horizons, but who need help (and usually are not afraid to ask for it) integrating these accomplishments into the fabric of their lives and their relationships. These integration-stage clients are the ones who seek assistance with choices and commitments that are difficult precisely because they are authentic and personal. They are wrestling with dilemmas or learning to act and to interact in the world with integrity.

In general, adolescents move through these developmental levels as they get older. Twelve-, thirteen-, and fourteen-year-olds are more likely to require the sort of therapy work that addresses disembed-ding. Seventeen- and eighteen-year-olds are more likely to present integration-stage issues. We must remember, however, that at any point during adolescence all three tasks are being dealt with in some way, even if the emphasis does shift gradually throughout the teenage years. Many clients, over the course of therapy, will indeed shift from one emphasis to another (and the point of therapy is to facilitate the shift to the next stage of development). Some will do this gradually. Others will shuttle back and forth, moving ahead and then backfill-ing with some developmental work that supports and reinforces the new accomplishments.

Those therapists who work with a broad range of adolescents will certainly identify some clients who fit neatly into each of these de-velopmental levels, as well as others whose functioning spans multiple developmental levels and tasks. But some treatment settings primarily serve clients who fall into only one of these stages. College counseling services, for example, are likely to see a great many integration-stage adolescents, whereas residential schools and treatment facilities are likely to see a great many youths mired in unresolved disembedding-stage difficulties. The work of therapeutic intervention at each of these developmental stages can vary widely, so that professionals in residential schools and college counseling services may be practicing entirely different arts. It is important to recognize this fact, so that the literature on adolescent psychotherapy can be applied more usefully to the practical needs of the individual professional.

In the four chapters that follow, I will focus primarily on the stages of disembedding and interiority, and on the therapeutic projects of promoting the developmental work of each stage. This is the work that is most characteristic of therapy with adolescents, and which has received the least attention in the literature on psychotherapy. Integration-stage work will not receive the same emphasis here, since its technical challenges are similar to the challenges of work with adults.

Clinical work with integration-stage clients, like therapeutic work with adult clients of all ages (who, after all, are recapitulating their adolescence in the self-defining work of adult psychotherapy), will necessarily involve revisiting and reconfiguring the work of disembedding and interiority. It is crucial to understand that all three stages are best conceived as embodying *tasks*. These tasks are urgent at a particular phase of adolescence but continue as recurrent developmental themes throughout life.

CHAPTER EIGHT

Addressing Family Process

I have spoken of disembedding as a stage and a task in the development of the adolescent, but in reality it is a stage and a task of the entire family field. We may be presented initially with an individual child who has concerns, complaints, symptoms, or troublesome behavior but it is imperative to look beyond this child and assess the evolving contact boundary, or boundaries, within the family field. In the process of adolescent disembedding, *everyone* is changed, parent as well as child. As the family field is reorganized, both parent and child will acquire new contact skills for the relationship. Along the way, parents are likely to confront much of their own unfinished business related to themes of dependency, loss, control, confirmation, autonomy, and authority. When adolescence has finally passed, they will be different people. And as will be true of their post adolescent child, their capacity for contact is likely to be broader and deeper in some significant way.

Sometimes.

As clinicians, we are regularly confronted with situations where this sort of system adaptation and individual growth does not readily occur, where it becomes blocked in some way, or where it is achieved at considerable cost. In these families, disembedding adolescents encounter significant difficulties. They may stir up their own childhood pain, for which there was and is insufficient support. They may struggle violently (acting in or acting out) against rigid and inflexible control. They may become entangled in their parents' marital problems or feel trapped in binding role relationships with their troubled parents, as confidants, companions, caretakers, or scapegoats.

In general, when we encounter disembedding-stage issues in therapy, we encounter an adolescent who is struggling (or *failing* to struggle) with the paradigm of child-self experience. These are clients who have still not resolved the questions of their littleness, neediness, or relative powerlessness, and who are continuing to struggle with the bigness, influence, power, and control of the adult world.

When we encounter these clients later in chronological adolescence, we find them still fighting earlier battles, still trying to *prove* that they are independent or capable of resisting external control. We find them not yet having begun to own and cultivate a center of themselves, not yet able to accept responsibility or generate well-grounded wants and choices. One of the hallmarks of disembedding-stage issues is the client's focus of both awareness and energy on the troubled boundaries of relationships with adults. A corollary is the avoidance of inner life and the tendency to use projection as a means of organizing experience. With many younger adolescents, these struggles will strike us as developmentally appropriate. With many older ones, they will reflect an incomplete or frustrated process of reorganizing the family field.

What characterizes families that effectively disembed their adolescent children? What are we to look for, and how are we to intervene when disembedding-stage issues present themselves clinically? Our best answers to these questions lie in an assessment of the fundamental contact repertoire and style of the family field. As a way of focusing on this issue, we need to look at the developmental contact needs of the adolescent and the ways in which parenting styles meet or fail to meet these needs.

Contact Needs of Adolescent Development

Contact, as we have seen, is the meeting at the boundary of organism and environment, and this meeting involves complementary dimensions of joining, merging, or connecting and of separating, or differentiating. There is no contact if there is not some sense in which the organism is connected to its surrounding field. By the same token, there is no contact if there is not some degree to which the organism is defined and bounded in the process of discovering this connection. Contact gives us our connectedness, but it also defines our differences.

If adolescence in general and disembedding in particular are a matter of more fully developing the capacity for contact, then it follows that this development can be tracked specifically along the lines of connecting and differentiating. Adolescents present complementary sets of developmental needs that derive from the fundamental nature of contact—needs for connectedness, and needs for differentiation.

Adolescents need to feel a sense of belonging to something larger than themselves: to belong to a family, to be part of a group, to participate in a tradition, to be anchored in enduring relationships. In this way, the adolescent self emerges from a ground of connection and commitment, of taking in and giving out, of caring and being cared about. With this sort of ground, the adolescent inherits a capacity to *manage the continuity of self and other* and to *integrate an essential interdependency* into the self's evolving structure.

It is just as important for adolescents to develop the capacity for relative independence and self-support, to develop internal resources and an experience of relative autonomy, and to cultivate a sense of identity and ownership of self functions. In other words, the adolescent must also learn to *manage the discontinuity of self and other* and develop a beginning capacity for *centered autonomy* in the field of contact.

In order for the disembedding process of adolescence to occur organically, without undue stress or difficulty, the adolescent needs to experience both of these dimensions palpably in the context of family interaction. When these needs are met, the disembedding process is likely to proceed and lead to growth of the adolescent's capacity for satisfying contact. When we encounter adolescents with difficulties related to disembedding—prolonged attachment, seemingly pointless rebellion, intensely conflicted dependency, and the like—we usually find one or both of these contact needs not being met.

Parenting as Contact Style

Parenting can be understood and assessed along the same lines. How are parents providing (or failing to provide) for their adolescent's need for connectedness? How are they supporting (or failing to support) the development of differentiation? Parenting is not a matter of technique and strategy, as some popular literature would have us believe; it is itself an expression of parents' fundamental contact skills and style. It is the way in which parents manage the contact boundary with their children, and so parenting can be thought of as encompassing the same fundamental dimensions of contact. Adolescent development in particular is influenced by how parents make contact with the individual child's emergent adolescent self, and thrives when the parents can respond to the adolescent's full range of contact needs.

Ideally, parents respond to their child's emergent adolescence in a fashion that implicitly conveys their ongoing connectedness—with support, acceptance, interest, validation, and a willingness to accommodate the child's ever-widening arc of wants and interests. By the same token, however, parents will respond with certain forms of differentiating contact, which heightens the separateness of parent and child and which requires the child to accommodate his own burgeoning wants and interests to the wants and interests of others. This aspect may come through in parental communication of expectations, and in parents' willingness to stand their ground when certain values and principles are at issue. As I recently heard one parent say, simply and elegantly, at a parents' discussion group, "My son and I were good friends all through his childhood, and I expect we will be good friends again when he's a little older. But right now he doesn't need me to be a friend. He needs me to be a parent."

In the final analysis, what adolescents need from their parents is *confirmation* of their developmental process of authoring a self. I use the term here in the same sense that we find in religions that confirm their believers when they reach adult status, or in the same sense expressed by certain cultures that confirm their members through rites of passage into adulthood (perhaps with tattoos or by other indelible marks). In our culture, confirmation is less formalized, but the meaning I have in mind here is essentially the same. It is the process whereby the perceptions and expectations of adults and of the adolescent himself are transformed and indelibly mark the individual's passage from childhood. Parents, and adults in general, confirm adolescents by conceding their *separateness*, their ownership of self, but within the unmistakable context of their *belonging* to the tribe.

Thus confirmation signals the fruition of this evolution of contact potentials, which I have cited as the central theme of adolescent development. It represents an integration, or resolution, of the inevitable tensions that develop between connecting and differentiating during adolescence. The confirmed adolescent is one who no longer fears his inclusion in the adult community comes at the expense of his individual selfhood. And, for adults, confirmation means an acceptance of the adolescent's right to differentiated selfhood, and a resolution of the fear that his differentiation comes at the price of enduring connectedness. For the field as a whole, confirmation means a successful redrawing of the boundary in such a way that both the relative independence of the adolescent and his enduring connectedness to the community are ensured.

When the adolescent and his parents succeed in balancing and integrating the complementary processes of joining and differentiating, their contact boundary is characterized by their relative ease in maintaining their connectedness as separate selves. When they fail to achieve this reorganization of the family field, we typically find some form of enduring tension that reflects an imbalance of contact skills. Some individuals, well into chronological adulthood, maintain their sense of belonging to their reference group, perhaps even to their family of origin, but at the expense of their creative individuality. Others seem virtually isolated by their independence, having given up their connectedness to a family of origin and lost the contact skills that could connect them to new relationships. In assessing families with adolescent clients, this is what we must pay attention to: How is this family managing the processes of contact, the joining and the separating, particularly as they are related to the adolescent's developmental work of taking ownership of and responsibility for a self?

Imbalances of Contact Process

Many families favor one or the other of the complementary dimensions of contact process, tending either to connect or to differentiate more easily. In their more extreme forms, these imbalances are quite capable of impeding or interrupting the process of disembedding.

Families that promote a sense of connection and merging at the expense of differentiation can be thought of as *underbounded* in their contact process. Families that foster separateness at the expense of connectedness can be described as *overbounded*. It is helpful, for the sake of clarity, to think of these styles as opposing alternatives and, in that sense, as providing us with a typology of contact disturbance in families. In clinical reality, however, underbounded and overbounded phenomena do not often present themselves in pure forms, characterizing a family's or an individual's contact style in all situations. More often, we find that a family is under- or overbounded only in certain critical respects, or underbounded in one area and overbounded in another. For example, an adolescent may be overly involved with one parent, lacking a sufficient sense of differentiation in that relationship, while feeling distant from and unconnected to the other parent. Or the adolescent may go through a period of vacillating between contact episodes in which boundaries are highly permeable and episodes dominated by a sense of isolation and alienation from parents. As adolescents evolve from an earlier, childhood organization of self to a more recent adolescent organization of self, we often find earlier modes of underbounded contact with parents replaced by compensatory overbounding.

Underbounded Family Process

In underbounded families, we regularly observe interactions in which the boundaries separating and defining individual selves become confused. Parents tend to be unclear about what is the child's business and what is their own business. They seem to have difficulty accepting that the adolescent's sphere of ownership and responsibility will constantly be expanding.

In more balanced, clearly bounded families, parents seem to accept that the adolescent's intrapsychic life (that is, his thoughts and feelings) are increasingly his own turf, even if his outward behavior is still very much the family's business. In such families, we are likely to find parents exerting their guidance and influence in a manner that implicitly affirms boundaries. These parents, especially when they are providing discipline and structure, tend to confirm that the adolescent has an "inside" that is more or less his own business and an "outside" that the parents have a greater right to concern themselves with. These parents say, in so many words, "Your thoughts and feelings are your own, but we have definite expectations and limits where your behavior is concerned." Such "clean-boundary parenting" generates an experience of differentiation within the family field, promotes disembedding, and cultivates experiences of choice, dilemma, and ownership.

Underbounded parenting, by contrast, is characterized by the parents' overinvestment in, and sometimes fixation on, the intrapsychic life of their adolescent children. These parents will tell the therapist, for example, that it is not so much the child's *behavior* that concerns them as his *attitude*: "It's not the *fact* that he doesn't help out around the house that bothers us, it's that he doesn't *want* to help out. That's what really gets to us." In these families, parents are inclined to obsess about their adolescent's inner life, worrying about it and trying unduly to influence it or change it according to their own designs.

One expression of these boundary conditions is that parents in underbounded families tend implicity not to see their children as choice makers who must accept the consequences of their own behavior. And children in these circumstances tend to introject these implicit parental perceptions and regard themselves in like manner. This kind of "muddy-boundary parenting" has the predictable effect of promoting projection and overidentification, with resulting confusion over ownership of and responsibility for the experience of self. Since the existential posture of self as responsible choice maker represents an intrinsically painful and difficult learning, children in underbounded families become experts at sidestepping this experience.

In underbounded families, where the self-domain of individual members is not clearly delineated, there is an uncanny way in which people take on and "carry" experience that belongs organically to other family members. With younger or disabled children, of course, parents rightfully carry certain self functions that are not yet sufficiently developed—maintenance of safety, or planning for the future, or anticipation of natural consequences. But in underbounded families, we commonly find this style lasting into the adolescent years, beyond the age when a child might be expected to have begun to manage these things himself.

I am reminded of a sixteen-year-old boy, Joey, whom I evaluated recently, shortly after he had been thrown out of high school for an accumulation of misdemeanors. Joey was a classic adolescent goof-off. He was not malicious. He simply had not developed the elementary ego skills that most adolescents use for keeping themselves out of trouble, or for cutting their losses once they get into trouble, or for sensing the limit that signals when adults have had enough. Joey had not developed the ability to manage his consequences in the way that most reasonably bright, socially astute, high school goof-offs do. Joey's father, it turned out, carried these self functions for him. He had made a regular practice of interceding with school officials whenever Joey stirred things up. Joey's father admitted that he had been much like Joey as a teenager, and his identification with his son had led him to carry out this function on his son's behalf. This is a common observation in underbounded families: a parent carries some self function (motivation, self-discipline, anticipation of the future, guilt, worry) that is correspondingly underdeveloped in the adolescent's emerging repertoire of capabilities.

Overbounded Family Process

At the other end of the continuum we encounter families whose boundaries are rigid and relatively impenetrable, and where the capacities for connecting and joining are correspondingly underdeveloped. In these overbounded families, we sometimes find that parents do a good job of setting expectations and establishing limits on behavior, but we typically find that relationships are missing a dimension of distinctly *personal* interest and involvement. Children may know how to behave, but often they do not feel truly known by their parents. The inner world of adolescent experience, which seems so threatening to parents in underbounded families, does not seem to stir much interest in these families. Indeed, parents in an overbounded family may be quite oblivious to the existence of inner-world experience—their children's or, for that matter, their own. In certain rigid but otherwise functioning families, adolescents report that their parents "only care about what I *do*, but not about what I *think* or *feel*."

In other overbounded family systems, the boundaries that separate and isolate children from their parents have more to do with the parents' absorption in their own private lives and problems. The father who is wrapped up in his business, to the point of not knowing his children, is a stereotype that all too often comes to life in clinical work with children. Parents going through personal turmoil—a divorce, the loss of their own parents, the loss of a career—are often experienced by their children as unavailable and distant. Depressed adolescents are frequently found to have parents who are themselves depressed or otherwise disengaged and unavailable.

Parents whose own contact style curtails their ability to loosen their boundaries, engage with more personal parts of themselves, and empathically get inside someone else's skin are likely to generate a corresponding sense of isolation and alienation in their children. It is no mystery that children who grow up in communities where parents are absent or absorbed in poverty and despair seek instinctively to join gangs, doing their best to provide themselves with the experience of inclusion and connection that development requires and that their families are unable to provide.

Specific Contact Styles

There are occasional families that present a clear picture of one-dimensional over- or underbounded parenting. And anyone who works with the families of adolescents certainly spends a good bit of time and energy with fairly straightforward intervention designs—getting parents more involved, or getting them less involved. We might ask a mother to be more available to talk or even fight with her daughter. We might ask a father to consider stepping back from certain superficial matters of dress and appearance, supporting him in letting go of his investment in these badges of the child's differentiation. We might counsel a parent to be less disclosing to a child, supporting her in finding adult resources of companionship and understanding. We might suggest to parents that they allow their child to take more ownership of schoolwork, making his or her own mistakes and learning to live with the consequences. Or we might do just the opposite, urging parents to step in and provide structure for a teenager who is seriously floundering or out of control. The point is that there are myriad ways in which our therapeutic interventions with disembedding systems pivot around the simple but critical axis of under- and overinvolvement. In each case, we are effectively coaching and supporting parents to broaden and balance their own repertoire, not in the spirit of correcting mistakes but in the interest of increasing their range of contact skills. But in the majority of families in clinical treatment, the forms and combinations of over- and underinvolvement are more subtle and complex, sometimes difficult to identify, and frequently more challenging when it comes to designing interventions.

If the underbounded and overbounded extremes give us a crude demarcation of the range of the family's contact process, a number of common individual contact styles allow us to describe more specifically the influence of family process on adolescent development. In Gestalt therapy, specific modulations of contact traditionally have been referred to as *resistances*. The catalogue of specific resistances includes introjection, projection, retroflection, deflection, confluence, and desensitization. Resistances were initially conceptualized as neurotic interferences with the organism's contact with its environment. Wheeler (1991), however, has interpreted these resistances more as stylistic modulations of the contact process, modulations that tend to emphasize certain aspects of the process while deemphasizing others. Wheeler suggests that the creative adjustment of an organism to its environment requires not the absence of but a full repertoire of resistances, so that the organism is capable of modulating its contact process in a flexible and adaptive manner.

In families that we see in clinical situations, it is fairly common to find contact styles that lack this adaptive flexibility. Instead, we frequently are presented with families that lean not only toward the under- or overbounded end of the continuum but also toward a particular style of over- or underboundedness, or toward some characteristic combination of the two. Let us examine a variety of these specific styles in terms of their developmental and clinical relevance to adolescent clients and to the developmental business of disembedding.

The Introjecting Family

Introjection, of course, is a generic component of any family's child-rearing. It is the necessary means by which parents organize the child's internal and external reality—crystallizing meaning, creating values and guidelines, defining the acceptable and the unacceptable—before the child is capable of doing this for himself. But the emergence of the adolescent self's synthesizing function stands in developmental counterpoint to introjected views and beliefs. To the extent that any family struggles with this transition, we might expect its members to exhibit some of the characteristics of the introjecting family.

In this family, there is an expectation that children will accept what parents have to teach, and a corresponding undervaluation of the adolescent's need to learn by experience. Introjecting families are often quite controlling, especially of the child's intrapsychic process and particularly of ideas, values, beliefs, and ways of looking at the world. The child is often expected to deny his or her own sensory and cognitive processes and define reality in the same way his or her parents do.

Seventeen-year-old Glenda came from such a family. Glenda's parents were strict Catholics (of "the old school," as Glenda liked to say) who were rigidly insistent that their children share their religious beliefs and values. Theirs was not the garden-variety conflict over whether the adolescent child should continue to attend religious services with the family. It reflected their uncompromising insistence that she think as they did. Glenda, however, had other pressing concerns; for example, she wondered whether she might be homosexual. Her mother, catching hints of her daughter's struggle, could only speak of it as a betrayal of her "good Catholic upbringing." For her mother, whose own introjects were rigidly powerful regulators of intrapsychic life, the notion of sexual feelings and gender identity as spontaneous regions of experience, to be discovered, accepted, and integrated, was foreign indeed.

Many introjecting families, Glenda's included, can be thought of as simultaneously underbounded and overbounded. Glenda's parents fought for control of her heart and mind, radically disconfirming her boundaries as an emerging self. In this sense, they were underbounded (too invested in Glenda's intrapsychic business). But they were also overbounded: insofar as Glenda was able to carve out a circle of differentiated experience of self, and a self that struggled to know and define itself, she felt distant and disengaged from her parents, alienated and unknown in her own family.

By the time I met Glenda, she had already done much of the later developmental work of adolescence. She had opened up a rich inner life, which she cultivated through several important peer relationships and with a counselor at school whom she trusted. But she was only months away from leaving for college. She seemed now to be returning to the unfinished business of disembedding. She had become her own person, almost in underground fashion, playing the role of good Catholic girl for her parents' benefit as long as she could but eventually losing the will for such duplicity. What she needed now—and this is the essence of disembedding work—was some recognition, however implicit, that her own boundaries did indeed belong to her.

That she could neither get this recognition *nor let go of her need for it* is a characteristic dilemma of adolescents in introjecting family systems. The more dedicatedly introjecting a system is (any system, whether a family, a religion, an individual psyche), the more it tends to produce the dramatically opposed polarities of true believer and rebel. Several of Glenda's siblings were true believers, children who accepted the family's culture unquestioningly. Glenda was the rebel, at least for now. But before she could battle with her introjects as a part of herself, she needed to battle with them as part of the family system.

Introjecting families present certain specific characteristics and dilemmas in psychotherapy. One of these is that they often screen therapists in order to find one who they hope will ally with their introjected belief system, and they often have very pointed expectations that therapy will serve to reinforce specific family ideals and views. The therapist often finds himself or herself in the same position as the disembedding adolescent: needing to establish and maintain a connection while preserving the integrity and authenticity of individual personhood in the field. The challenge is to manage that bind in a way that is different from the current resolution of the family field. The therapist, in other words, must find a way to avoid the polar dichotomization of true believer and rebel, must resist the field forces that exert pressure to take sides one way or the other. The therapist's task is to change the believing-rebelling boundary into an *interactive contact* boundary.

This was an issue with Glenda's family from the outset. Her mother initially contacted me because I was recommended by some mutual Catholic friends. She presumed on this basis that I was sufficiently like-minded to share her values and beliefs. Her daughter agreed to see a therapist (actually, she had already been confiding in a teacher at school, but her parents put an end to this because they feared it was only "making things worse"). I was the person their daughter would see, they decided.

The trouble was that Glenda did not want to see me, and she said so. I complimented Glenda on her ability to know and speak her mind in this way and assured her that I didn't take it personally.

"This is your God-given right," I said, and I told her I was bound to respect it. "But," I added, "your parents also have a right to feel comfortable with your therapist, especially if they're paying for therapy."

I suggested and described several people for them to consider. Once Glenda found a therapist she liked, and whom her parents could live with (even though she was *Jewish*, of all things), I worked with the parents on issues of parent education and guidance. I empathized and commiserated with them about the trials of raising and *releasing* adolescent children. My hope was to help them stretch their understanding of adolescent development. We also talked about Catholicism, about the history of the Church, and about the Catholic education their children were receiving. The mother complained that her son, who was attending a Jesuit high school, seemed to be getting a better education than Glenda was. I talked about how the Jesuits had become renowned educators because they had been intellectual rebels throughout Church history, and about how both the Church and the Jesuits had survived their past turmoil. In particular, though, I tried to educate them about the nature of adolescent development in the modern world. Here, we often came up against our different points of view. It really did not matter whether they agreed with me. What mattered was that they listened to my foreign ideas without firing me. They accepted, perhaps even appreciated, that we had a different way of looking at these things, and that in spite of this (or *because* of it, I would say), our conversations proved helpful in getting them through this very frightening period of their lives.

In the end, Glenda stuck with therapy and then went off to college. As is true with most introjecting families whose children succeed in disembedding, her leavetaking was more an unimpeded escape than a heartily supported send-off. But escape is usually good enough, and the last I heard, Glenda was faring well in college.

The Confluent Family

If the introjecting family seeks to establish like-mindedness by parental force-feeding of children, the confluent family seeks like-mindedness by emphasizing agreement and cooperation. Confluent families value "getting along" above all else, and they often consciously pride themselves on how pleasantly family members interact (or *used to* interact) with each other. Parents in these families often preach the gospel of "cooperation," elevating above other forms of contact the fluid, joined-at-the-boundary style of sharing and agreement.

One hallmark of confluent families is their failure to integrate conflict as an acceptable dimension of relationship. In these families, conflict reveals, usually abruptly and in flashes of anger, the differences that the family conspires to diminish. The underlying feeling is usually that security requires togetherness, and that togetherness requires sameness.

The presence of conflict does not counterindicate a confluent style. In fact, many confluent families fall into an uncomfortable state of regular conflict. What characterizes the conflict, however, is that it is *unintegrated*. It is not accepted as part of family life. It leads neither to the assimilation of individual differences as part of the family palate nor, ultimately, to a strengthening of the connectedness that people feel with one another. Instead, it tends to leave people feeling some degree of despair that they have failed at the business of being a family.

Helen's family was classically confluent. After her divorce, Helen basically raised her two boys by herself, with little help or involvement from her ex-husband. Conflict in their marriage, once it surfaced, had led to their splitting up, and they had remained bitter and angry with one another ever since. Both of them had established new households characterized by confluent togetherness: Helen with the two boys, and her ex-husband with his new wife. Both households were "blessed" with an absence of conflict—that is, until Helen's elder son, Peter, turned fifteen. Confluent families often work smoothly until the children enter adolescence, when differentiation is abetted, literally, by the forces of nature. These are the parents who, during the very first interview, lament an earlier time when the family functioned organically, warmly, and smoothly as a unit. Helen lamented in just this fashion, describing how she and her boys had banded together, becoming a tight and synchronous unit, in order to survive. She was an exceptionally warm and positive woman, and she had developed close, attentive, richly involved relationships with both children. It is important to remember that confluence, as a contact style, is not a pathology but an attenuation. Its clinical significance is not the closeness that develops but the corresponding underdevelopment of contact skills for dealing with difference. In this family, as in most confluent families, difficulties emerged around the issue of discipline.

Helen approached disciplinary issues in the manner of most underbounded, confluent parents. She asked, indeed begged and pleaded, for *cooperation*. She desperately wanted a household where people helped out because they *cared about* each other and about the common good. When these expectations were frustrated, as they almost inevitably are with adolescent children, she lectured and lobbied her children, pulling out all stops to *persuade* them to share her wants and goals. The art of *insisting*, which reflects a parent's own well-centered resolve about the nonnegotiables of family life, conveyed with understated power, was simply not part of Helen's repertoire. As a result, discussions turned to arguments, arguments turned to fights, and the fights sometimes got out of control. Helen's heart was broken that her Peter was abandoning her to his own selfish indulgence. He was becoming, she confided to me in tears, his father.

Peter's behavior in recent months had become increasingly contentious and impulsive. He was neglecting his schoolwork, had occasionally become severely abusive of his younger brother, and was sometimes frighteningly hostile and defiant when even minor demands were placed on him. But what distressed Helen most was not Peter's behavior, even when it became impulsive and uncontrolled. It was his *not wanting* to cooperate the way he had when he was younger, and this is what had prompted her to seek help.

When Peter and Helen were not battling, they were very much like peers, more like good friends than like parent and child. Once, when I opened the waiting-room door to greet them, they were jointly crooning along to an old Beatles tune on the radio, both bouncing in their seats in time with the music. They had many good times like this, they said, but more in the past than recently. Their underbounded closeness, once an important source of support for each of them in their development, was more and more a source of conflict and confusion. They had a way of tangling themselves up in each other's business, and even minor expressions of this tendency were sometimes the occasion for major fights. Peter would doodle on his mother's calendar when he was on the telephone with friends, and this irritated her. She in turn would come into his bedroom unannounced, and on one recent occasion this invasion had triggered an abusive explosion of rage from Peter.

What Peter and his mother were both unable to manage were transactions that required them to experience their fundamental separateness from each other. Helen had great difficulty making unilateral parenting decisions that did not have Peter's collaboration and approval. A critical part of the therapy work was to tap into other sources of support for Helen, people other than Peter, who could ratify her parenting decisions and encourage her to stand her ground. It was a long time before she could truly take a stand with Peter, presenting him with a decision, or following through on a consequence, in a manner that said, "This is the way it is!"

Peter was similarly uncomfortable with interactions that heightened his separateness and differentiation from his mother. When Helen was able, later on, to turn to her ex-husband for support and consultation, Peter would sometimes literally step between them and say to her, "Don't talk to him. Talk to me!"

It was the same for both of them: connectedness felt natural, even if it did not always feel good; separateness felt unnatural and frightening. The work of therapy centered around broadening their contact repertoire so that they could tolerate the necessary transactions between a parent and a teenager that required them to occupy different positions and allow the gap between them to stand.

Two specific interventions, neither of them unusual, helped them to accomplish this reorganization. The first was the use of a contract for household chores, a topic that almost daily got them tangled up with one another and almost daily triggered screaming and sometimes shoving matches. Contracts, verbal or written agreements specifying each party's commitments and responsibilities, are a familiar and useful tool for anyone who works with adolescents and their parents. This contract was a fairly ordinary one, but it had several noteworthy twists. For one thing, the impetus for the contract came from Peter rather than from his mother. Too frequently, a therapeutic contract is introduced by the adults in the situation, and the adolescent is cajoled or sometimes bullied into accepting and signing it. Set up in this way, a contract will often fail because it rests on the very foundation that adolescent development is striving to reorganize—namely, the skewing of power and initiative toward the adult side of the relationship.

When proposing a therapeutic contract, I always begin at the adolescent end of the field, and that is what I did with Peter.

"I have an idea for getting your mother off your back," I told Peter in private, and I presented the idea of approaching her with a contract for regulating both his chores and her nagging. It could be quite simple: he would agree to complete certain chores by a specified deadline, and she would agree to forgo reminding and nagging.

"It'll never work," he answered. "She loves to nag, and she'll never keep her end of the agreement."

I conceded that he knew his mother better than I did, and we let it drop for the time being. At our next individual session, I added a new idea.

"What if we attached a penalty for any reminding or nagging that your mother does?" I asked. "What if each word she says to you about the chore earns you a one-hour extension on the deadline for completing that chore?"

The idea of double-binding his mother in this way intrigued Peter. He agreed to bring the contract up, with my assistance, at our next joint session with his mother.

Helen accepted the offer and rounded out the negotiation by asking what provision would be made if Peter did not complete the chore by the deadline. They eventually agreed that if this happened, Helen would be entitled to nag to her heart's content, and that Peter would forfeit his right to object to the nagging.

Did the contract work? In my experience, contracts never work in the magical way they are designed to, since humans are not the logico-legal beings that contracts presuppose. Both Peter and Helen kept the agreement sometimes, and both of them broke it sometimes. But it worked in the sense of providing them with an exercise and an opportunity for remapping their relationship, for standing separately in an arrangement where each was expected to stay out of the other's business. Like most therapeutic contracts, this one worked by laying down a template for a new sort of relating.

The second intervention, and the one that certainly went more powerfully to the heart of the difficulty, was bringing other players into the field in such a way as to change the way the game was being played. I tried at the very outset to involve Peter's father. Helen agreed that this was a good idea (although she stated flatly that he would not comply; he was simply "too selfish," she assured me). Peter, however, flatly refused to interact with his father, and that seemed to settle the question, at least for the time being. What I learned later on was that Peter, as had become his custom, was shutting his father out as an act of loyalty to his mother. His father seemed to be doing quite well in his new marriage, but his mother had still not recovered from the shame and blame of the divorce, and Peter's refusal to have anything to do with his father was a remnant of his childhood resolution to stand by his mother's side.

This state of affairs changed only when Helen met a very solid and eligible man and entered the first serious relationship in the six years since her divorce. Once it became apparent that this relationship was going somewhere, and that Peter was no longer the man in

Helen's life, he did an abrupt about-face and expressed an interest in bringing his father into the therapy. His father, I should add, although somewhat self-absorbed, as Helen had implied, involved himself willingly and constructively and brought his new wife along, too.

The field changed. In one session we had Peter, Helen, Greg (soon to become her fiancé), Phil (Peter's father), and his wife, Hanna. I could easily observe how this family's boundary functioning interfered with Peter's adolescent development. As underbounded as he was with his mother, his relationship with his father could only be described as overbounded. He and his father had barely spoken to each other in almost four years. Their interaction was awkward, cautious, and somewhat formal.

As a general rule, when a parent-child pair needs to learn to differentiate, it helps to bring other adults into the field and work at building or strengthening the supportive relationships among the adults. When adults come together, it is much easier for them to maintain differences and distance at the contact boundary with their children. The general rule is this: When you want to separate an underbounded family, get the adults to function and experience themselves as a team. This firms the boundary. When you want to break down the barriers in an overbounded family, the strategy is the reverse: separate the adults as a unified subsystem, and promote more intimate, one-to-one relationships between parents and children.

We did two things in our therapy sessions. First we brought the family together (without Phil's wife, who was not very involved with Peter and opted not to participate), and we worked to separate Helen and Peter while building a stronger collaborative bond between Helen and the other adults in Peter's life. As issues came up, Helen would instinctively turn to Peter with a question or a comment. When Peter did not like the direction of the conversation among the adults, he would take hold of his mother's arm and turn her toward him. They were like two magnets clapping together and arraying the field around them. I had Peter sit next to me, and I taught Helen to attend to the physical magnetism she felt whenever Peter spoke. She began to slow her process down and make more choices about where she looked for support during the session. Both Greg and Phil were eager and available, and once she slowed down enough to notice this, she engaged them, asking for opinions or advice, or just for ratification of something she was saying. Deciding on a consequence for

Peter's breaking curfew, she would no longer turn reflexively to Peter and ask, "Does this sound fair?" Now she turned to Greg or Phil and asked, "What do you think?" Initially, Peter was furious and scared about his mother's developing independence, and he and I did some individual work together to support him through this change.

The second thing we did was to arrange several sessions with just Peter and his father, and we used this time to begin the process of their learning how to be connected to each other. This work had the simple and straightforward quality of conversation. I began by asking the two of them, "How do you want this relationship to grow?" Both agreed that it needed to become less formal and more friendly. I asked Phil to tell Peter about his own teenage years. I suggested to Peter that he let his father in on his problems with girlfriends, and I coached his father on the art of just listening. They found this easy enough to do, and they agreed to make time for their relationship to develop.

The net effect was to broaden the range of contact skills in Peter's relationship with each parent. His father and he already knew how to keep their distance, but they needed to learn the simple mechanics of getting interested and getting to know each other. I am not suggesting that they became best friends; they did not. But they each sensed an openness, an availability of the other, and when they did intersect once or twice a month, they did so as friends rather than strangers. The learning for Peter and Helen was to broaden the repertoire of contact skills beyond the confluence that came so easily to them. They learned how to be in conflict, how each could take a position, define a difference, and stand by it. Their arguments changed and were no longer escalated by the panic of their disagreement. No longer did Peter and Helen privately anguish about standing apart from each other, each obsessing about how to get the other to come around. They both learned to stand their ground without needing the other's support for doing so. Their disagreements came and went the way disagreements between parents and children do: like thunderstorms passing through a fertile landscape.

The Projecting Family

Projection, as an organization of contact, involves a disowning of some aspect of the experience of self and its attribution to the environment.

"I'm not interested in other women," says the projecting, jealous husband. "You are interested in other men!" Projection has the character of accurately identifying the experience in question but locating it somewhere else in the field, outside the boundary of the self. I remember anxiously taking my puppy to the vet to be spayed and repeatedly taking her from the waiting room to the lawn outside, certain that she needed to urinate. When the vet came and took her from me for her surgery, and I returned nervously to my car, I found myself overcome with the urgent need to urinate. I knew there was a full bladder *somewhere* in the field but got confused as to exactly where. This is projection.

As a generic psychological mechanism, projection is an important contributor to the richness and vitality of contact process, serving as the basis of empathy and identification with others. But when projection comes to dominate the contact style of any system, there are certain problematic outcomes for the relationships involved. For one thing, highly projective families systematically and inadvertently promote a characteristic disownership of the experience of self. Family members tend to focus their awareness on what others are thinking and doing, and they tend correspondingly to underdevelop awareness of their own inner experience. Conflict is generally accompanied by blame of others, and individuals typically experience each other as unavailable for disclosing or discussing inner thoughts and feelings.

In my clinical experience, projecting families may be decidedly overbounded or underbounded. Sixteen-year-old Shawna and her parents typified an underbounded projecting family. Shawna's parent's brought her to see me because she had clearly become depressed. A normally upbeat and successful girl, she had become progressively moody and irritable, was sleeping more than usual, complained of fatigue and loss of energy, and was acknowledging difficulties with concentration at school. Her usually good grades were beginning to show the effects.

Shawna had "silently" undergone a similar period of depression three years earlier. Her parents learned about it after the fact, when an English teacher contacted them to share an essay that Shawna had submitted, in which she described a suicide attempt (an overdose of Tylenol) of several months before. At that time, her parents had insisted that Shawna see a therapist, which she did, begrudgingly, for almost a year. Her parents reported that the therapy had helped considerably; Shawna conceded that it had helped "a little." The therapist had not involved Shawna's parents in the treatment in any way.

"Not this time," Shawna insisted firmly but courteously. Her parents, she stated, were as much a part of the problem as she was, and she was not going to take the rap all by herself. Their response was condescendingly strategic: "Yes, honey, we know we all have problems, but we're just very worried about you right now."

During our first meeting, with Shawna and parents together, I was interested in all points of view and encouraged Shawna to make her case.

"You guys are fighting more than usual," Shawna told her parents, "and it's driving me crazy. That's the reason I get depressed sometimes. I can't stand what you're doing to each other."

With the parents' permission (I always ask permission when I shift the focus unexpectedly to something more personal than people had intended), I asked them about their relationship and about the fighting that Shawna had referred to. They acknowledged that they had been fighting, but they said that they often fought in times of stress: "We've been married twenty-five years, and fighting doesn't threaten our relationship."

I believed they were right. Their relationship did seem deeply rooted and sturdy. But I pressed on, in deference to Shawna's reality.

"When you fight," I asked, "do you hurt each other?"

Here, the picture began to change. Yes, they both admitted, checking with each other as they did so, they were hurting each other.

"Is that what gets to you?" I asked, turning to Shawna.

Bingo, she nearly said. She couldn't stand to see them wound each other the way they sometimes did. And, indeed, she resonated with their pain, took it inside and made it her own. This she claimed, was the source of her "so-called depression."

I proposed the following compromise: since each side felt that the other was the real "patient," I would meet with Shawna and with her parents separately, three or four times each, in alternate weeks. I would explore with Shawna and her parents, separately, their own experience of pain and discomfort.

Shawna agreed that under this arrangement she would be willing to discuss candidly with me how she had been feeling. Her parents also agreed, although I suspected that they were doing so mostly to play along with my "plan" to "get Shawna to open up."

This was a deeply caring family, where people were very tuned in to one another, so much that they were far more aware of each other's painful struggles than they were of their own. My first session with Shawna's parents alone, during which I asked about their family history, was illuminating, to say the least. They revealed that several years before, when Shawna was about eight years old, a series of awful things had happened. A very dear grandparent had died. The father's younger sister had committed suicide. Shawna had been diagnosed with diabetes. Her mother spoke of having grown up in a highly dysfunctional family and related how these recent awful events had shattered her image of a "happy, healthy family life," which she had always envisioned for her adulthood. The diabetes in particular overwhelmed her, leaving her anxious and, yes, depressed.

She had begun to drink, and her drinking quickly got out of control. The marital relationship faltered, and it took everything they had to stay together. But then things began to improve, and Shawna's mother stopped drinking as abruptly as she had begun.

Then, just as life began to feel almost normal again, her younger son "came apart at the seams," developing a host of accentuated behavioral and learning problems, which they found themselves completely at a loss to manage. There was a "year of hell" before he was eventually diagnosed with a severe case of attention deficit hyperactivity disorder and treated successfully with medication.

This was a time of nearly unbearable stress and strain for both parents. And as if this were not enough, they moved at about this time into a new house, an event that is always stressful to family life. During this entire sequence of events, they "bucked up" like good soldiers and managed matters as best they could. They were resilient people, survivors, and they were determined to claim the stable and idyllic family scene that they had always planned for themselves.

"What happened next?" I asked.

That was when Shawna had written her suicide essay. And, as we already know, the suicide essay was what had crystallized her parents' perception that something was emotionally awry. Like me at the animal hospital, they knew that emotional pain was going on *somewhere* in this system. They just were not exactly sure where. Shawna's behavior gave them a focus for what was going on, not only with

Shawna but also, by way of projection, with themselves as well. And if this had been the state of things three years before, it seemed likely to me that something similar was going on now.

This story is characteristic of close families where projection becomes a ruling function of the parent-child contact boundary. Its effect is that individuals develop a tendency to disown their own psychological process. In the case of an adolescent in particular, this tendency interrupts the disembedding of the self.

Shawna certainly struggled with issues of ownership. For example, she battled constantly with her mother over the management of her diabetes. She complained that her mother needed to butt out and trust her to test her own blood-sugar levels and monitor her own insulin. But, left to her own supervision, Shawna regularly "forgot" to check and would often fake the entries she made in her weekly medical log. Her blood sugar would get out of control, and many of her depressive symptoms emerged or were exacerbated as a result.

Like her parents, Shawna was very invested in maintaining a "face" of competent self-management, so that her needs for support and assistance were often disowned and projected.

"Would you like me to help you negotiate your parents' noninvolvement in your diabetes?" I asked her.

No, she said; she would have to continue checking in with her mother because *her mother* needed this procedure to continue.

With some pushing on my part, and with my assurance that I was making her parents look squarely at their own emotional distress (which I was), Shawna began to develop a more clearly bounded self-awareness. What made this difficult in the context of the family field was that whenever Shawna opened up to her own experience, whenever she acknowledged her emotional distress or need for support, she felt the weight of her parents' (well-intentioned) projections come crashing down on her. She did not know how to be honest with herself without becoming the "family patient," a role she had occupied once before and was determined never to take on again. Supported by my willingness to take her seriously, and to insist along with her that this was indeed a family matter and that others in the family needed to take responsibility for their own inner lives, Shawna, as it turned out, was willing and quite able to begin taking responsibility for hers.

Projecting families are not always this amenable to shifting from their projective focus and accepting responsibility for their own experience. I am reminded of fifteen-year-old Maurice, an angry, defiant boy who refused to give therapy any more than a cursory trial, and then only to get his parents off his back for a few weeks. His parents had brought him to see me after he was caught shoplifting, the most recent in a series of acting-out episodes. Maurice's mother informed me on the phone that his father would probably not participate.

"Our last experience in therapy really turned him off," she said.

"I can't possibly do an adequate assessment of an adolescent boy without his father's perspective," I informed her, wondering what had happened the last time around.

I quickly found out. Maurice's father wasted no time in telling me how thoroughly disgusted he was with his son's behavior, how inconceivable it was that a son of his could have broken the law. He himself had been no angel during his own adolescence, he assured me, but he had never done anything illegal. Furthermore, to add insult to injury, the previous therapist, a year before, had targeted *him* as the focus of her intervention. (Listen carefully to the tales of previous therapists' failings. They often hold the key to entering a family's boundary. And hope that the next therapist, who hears the gory details of your own therapy failures, will have the good sense to do the same.)

Maurice's father was an impressively accomplished man. He held two postgraduate professional degrees and had attained (in his professional life, at least) a reasonable approximation of the perfection to which he unabashedly aspired. His son seemed to represent to him all the things that he himself had successfully deleted from his own life history. Maurice was willful, impulsive, hedonistic, irreverent, and antiestablishment. Maurice's acting out was projection of a different order, a projection of his father's dark side, the irruption into the light of those qualities that his father had so successfully held in check in the developmental organization of his own self gestalt. And the tragedy of all this was that Maurice's father also distanced himself from his son, which is to say that he overbounded, just as desperately as he had dissociated from these potentials in his own personality.

The difficulty in working with overbounded projecting families is that it is often almost impossible to get the warring parties to participate in therapy. Both Maurice and his father, the two people who most needed to be in the room together, refused or nearly refused to come to my office. Maurice came twice, and I felt by the end of our second visit that I had almost succeeded in presenting myself as an appealing opportunity for support—but not quite. In the end, he refused to come back because, like Shawna, he felt that his participation in therapy amounted to a guilty plea to the projections heaped on him.

Families like Maurice's have been described in the clinical literature as scapegoating families. In scapegoating families, a child becomes the direct object or movie screen, so to speak, for parental projections. As a rule, these are parents who come to therapy with a strong investment in having the adolescent labeled "the problem." It is often as if the family needs a repository for what is "bad"—what is too angry, too sexy, too selfish, too disruptive—and as long as the scapegoat fulfills this role, other family members are relieved of any potential responsibility for such characteristics.

The scapegoated adolescent typically responds in kind, which means to disown, project, and blame—in short, to struggle to escape the shameful responsibility and the implicit alienation of being the family problem. These adolescents, when they are organized and mature enough to resist carrying the family badness disproportionately, will do anything rather than enter individual psychotherapy, where their "patient" status constitutes an admission of responsibility.

With Maurice's father, I was slightly more successful than I was with Maurice himself. I saw his demanding perfectionism toward his son for precisely what it was—an offering of parental love—and I told him so. Likewise, his disengagement from his son was something that I saw as his only solution to *caring too much* about a boy who was not about to listen.

Once I listened to him—not with my "therapist" self gestalt but with the part of myself that is, like him, a loving-controlling father—he began to make sense, and the overbounding, projective quality of our own boundary, at least, began to change. He decided that maybe I had "something worth listening to," and he opened himself to my comments.

For the most part, I tried to teach him about fathers and sons, and about the enormous anxiety that many sons feel when it comes to living up to a father's legacy (especially a father as successful as Maurice's was). He softened slightly; and while his conflict with Maurice persisted for a time, I am still hopeful that his softening portended the future of their relationship.

The Retroflected Family

Retroflection, in Gestalt theory, refers to a sort of *acting in* on the self of impulses originally intended to be acted out on the environment. A great many psychosomatic symptoms serve this function, yielding physical tension and pain where otherwise conflict and contact with the environment might occur. In retroflected families, there is a great deal of holding back. What might otherwise become a field of lively interaction and growth-inducing contact becomes instead a field of insulated individuals with closed-off body postures and uncomfortably clenched jaw muscles.

Tim's family fit this description. In the office, there was a visible stiffness to family members, an air of reserve, almost of formality, and a palpable carefulness in the way they spoke to one another. Tim came to therapy as a seventeen-year-old because he was depressed, having been referred by a counselor at his school. Tim's family consisted of himself, his fifteen-year-old sister, and his parents. They were unmistakably "close," as families go, but their closeness did not include the quality of straight talk, of family members speaking from the heart and saying exactly what they meant, especially when differences of feeling and opinion were concerned. Stylistically, they were also confluent in this sense, and their spontaneous dialogue in family sessions was characterized by their nodding heads and their gravitation toward agreement but also by their uncomfortable pauses, by their shifting in their chairs, by their pursed, restraining lips, and by their messages felt but not spoken.

Conflict was not managed through contact in Tim's family. Instead, it was swallowed and internalized. Tim's father had a history of stomach problems, and his mother had back tension that often made it difficult for her to sleep. It is safe to say that confluent retroflected families like Tim's produce more than their share of depressed offspring. This makes particular sense if we keep in mind the traditional psychoanalytic vision of depression as anger turned back on the self.

Tim's more acute depressive episodes were accompanied by cutting, a behavior not uncommon among depressed adolescents. In a semidissociated state, Tim would take a razor blade and make a series of straight-line cuts down his forearm. Cutting, as a form of self-mutilation, can usually be understood as anger retroflected against the self.

Tim was not able to express even garden-variety adolescent anger toward his parents without leaving them feeling deeply wounded and himself feeling horribly guilty. And yet, like most teenagers, Tim experienced a host of frustrations with his parents, mostly the outcome of simple unresolved differences having to do with issues of privacy, curfew, privileges, and restrictions. None of these were earth-shattering, but virtually none were resolved at the contact boundary of Tim and his parents; the unresolved tension accumulated and found expression only at the boundary of Tim's relationship to himself. When he felt like cutting them down, he cut himself instead.

But cutting behavior, as a retroflection, at least in Tim's case, carried much more complex meaning than the simple impulse to confront his parents with his anger. In Tim's family, as in many families where retroflection becomes a contact style, it was not only anger that was retroflected but also other heartfelt impulses for contact. Tim's depression represented an accumulation of psychic pain related to a host of developmental issues—his fear of the future, his social awkwardness, his early disappointments in romance. This was pain that Tim bore alone, retroflecting his desire to reach out to others, parents as well as peers, for understanding, comfort, and support.

In Tim's family, interpersonal support, comfortably sought and comfortably given, was not the rule. His family had more of a "bootstrap psychology" tradition. Individuals were expected to pick themselves up and dust themselves off when life dealt out some disappointment. Tim's mother told the tale of his having had a mysterious, protracted, recurring illness as a young boy, and of her having turned, after months of frustrated doctoring, to her own parents for solace and direction. Her parents, as she told the story, provided scant sympathy, implying that if only she would stop obsessing, Tim's "psychosomatic" symptoms would go away. And while she did her level best not to repeat her own parents' policies of nonsupport, she was clearly uncomfortable in the presence of Tim's emotional pain (perhaps she felt responsible for it) and unwittingly conveyed her desire that he pick himself up and get on with life. This family had not worked out the mechanics of interpersonal support.

Tim's cutting reflected and played out this complex interpersonal style. For Tim, it was a way of revealing his experience of pain, expressing it, and making it real in such a way that he could stand apart from it and confirm its reality. In cutting himself, he found a way to do all of this within the boundary of his private relationship with himself—literally on the surface of his skin—and in lieu of the connecting and supporting that he so desperately needed and wanted from his parents. For all the members of Tim's family, there was a lot going on. Their feelings for one another were complex and intense but, as in Tim's self-cutting, they were transacted intrapsychically rather than interpersonally. These individuals crumpled under the weight of their own retroflections, and the family system was deprived of its vital energy. In Tim's family, what was interpersonal by design became intrapsychic by default.

In retroflected families, adolescent disembedding suffers because the ordinary contact episodes of supporting and differentiating are damped down or suppressed. What needs to be said—words of understanding, and words of challenge and disagreement—is held back and internalized. The family's sense of relationship is accordingly diminished. Encouraging words, statements of empathy, "when I was your age" wisdom—all are held back. So are differences of interest, delineations of deeper values, arguments, and even air-clearing temper tantrums.

As an expected component of the child's developmental evolution, retroflection is part and parcel of the middle-adolescence shift away from battling with parents and toward interiority, when the adolescent begins to contain his impulses for engaging parents and engages himself instead. But earlier, during the disembedding stage, retroflection curtails the important boundary engagements that serve as leverage for lifting the adolescent up and out of the family field of childhood. In retroflected families with chronologically older adolescents, it is not uncommon to find clients who are very much tangled up in their private worlds of inner experience but who, like Tim, have arrived there without resolving fundamental issues of boundary and ownership. It is probably also safe to say that many of the most dedicated adult "neurotic" clients come to us with foreshortened disembedding and retroflected-family backgrounds.

The simplest guide to working with retroflected families is that the therapist must, sooner or later, get the members speaking more authentically to one another. The result is almost always to make things "worse," from the family's point of view, and it behooves the therapist to provide the necessary support when this happens. With these families, I have found it invaluable to predict, in no uncertain terms, that things are going to get worse before they can get better. In this situation, an ounce of prediction is worth a ton of after-the-fact explanation.

But this is exactly what I did not do with Tim's family. We began with whole-family sessions, but these terminated when Tim's mother withdrew, saying that she found them too unsettling. By default, I continued with Tim in individual therapy, where the bulk of our work together involved his finding the words for important encounters with his parents, and then my supporting both him and them in the aftermath of their gradually deretroflected interaction. I have often looked back on my work with Tim, which continued for over a year and a half, and regretted that I did not work more carefully to estab-lish support for everyone involved and properly warn them of the difficult work that lay ahead.

The Deflecting Family

Deflection, in Gestalt therapy, refers to a diluting of contact that makes it less direct, less frontal, and less to the point (Polster and Polster, 1973). Humor, for example, is a deflection when it is used to water down the intensity of a contact episode. Excessive talking, ab-straction, or politeness may also be instances of deflection. Deflec-tion has the quality of glancing contact, a meeting of selves that diverts away from deeper concerns, away from content that might deepen intimacy or heighten an appreciation of differences. In fami-lies, in some circumstances, anger can also serve as a deflection, par-ticularly when it is blustery and quick and has the effect of drawing attention away from more centered concerns and interactions.

In families with adolescent children, deflection sometimes serves to overbound the contact boundary of parent and child, diverting away from themes that might otherwise deepen and "fatten" the in-timacy and connectedness of family members. Parents and teenagers may, for example, rivet their attention on the concrete particulars of control—matters of curfew, forbidden activities, "bad" friends, and so on—as a deflection from sharing deeper, heartfelt fears and feel-ings. One family that came to see me was embroiled in a conflict over whether the sixteen-year-old son would be allowed to attend a Grate-ful Dead concert. The parents flatly refused permission, and he threatened, in a manner quite uncharacteristic of him, to defy their ruling. It seemed odd to me that this family, which up to this point had proved itself quite capable of negotiating the business of freedom and constraint, was so totally gridlocked on this particular issue.

With families that deflectively overfocus on details of behavior, appearance, and so on, it is worth the effort to push for increased awareness and expression of bottom-line issues. I usually say something like this to parents: "This (concert, earring, new boyfriend) is clearly very important to you. I'd like permission to push you a little on this. I'm not trying to get you to change your mind, but I'm interested in getting the real importance of this more into words. Is this okay?" Then, with their permission, I might give them a thought experiment: "I want you to stretch your imagination a little; imagine that this behavior were to go unchecked and then get *really* out of hand. What's your nightmare fantasy about where it could lead?"

While the parents ponder this question, I turn to the adolescent and say something like this: "I'm not suggesting that anything like this is going to happen, but all parents have disaster fantasies about their children. It's one of the crazy ways they love them. I'm just trying to find out what worries your parents, deep down. Is this okay with you?"

This exercise most often manages to drop the discussion down to a different level, where the unspoken and avoided issues can be dealt with more directly. Occasionally parents discover that there really is no deeper issue, that they are making an issue of something for no particular reason. But often, the deeper organizing context of awareness may come to light.

Once my Grateful Dead family began to explore the ground of this conflict, the avoided issues emerged. Grateful Dead concerts, at least by reputation, are notorious for the amount of drug use among attendees, and this belief triggered some powerful but hitherto undiscussed fears and feelings. The mother's younger brother, it turned out, had involved himself in smoking marijuana around the age of sixteen, and eight years later, after a tumultuous increase in drug use and the accompanying family turmoil, he had committed suicide. This chapter of the mother's life had never been shared by her in anything more than a cursory allusion. She had certainly never shared the overwhelming fears that the episode had bequeathed her for her own children.

This is a common overbounding pattern in families with adolescent children—that concerns deeply and tenderly felt will somehow go undiscussed, and in their place will be family fights about superficial aspects of behavior and control that deflect attention away from the unspoken heart of the matter.

Deflection can also have the impact of underbounding the parent–child relationship, particularly when it takes the form of avoiding differences and conflict through the use of humor. I recall David, a fifteen-year-old boy with a facile mind and a delightful sense of humor, whose family members prided themselves on the general tenor of hilarity that characterized their time together. In our very first meeting—even as they told me of David's diagnosis with diabetes six months earlier, his maternal grandmother's death two years before, his maternal grandfather's death four months before, and David's own "inexplicably" plummeting school performance in the current semester—they had themselves nearly in stitches. These were indeed funny and friendly people, whose style for coping with the pain of life was to "keep it all in perspective" and retain their ability to laugh.

The more essential deflection in David's family was the collective attention to David's adjustment difficulties, all the while his mother, having lost both her parents and having been extremely close to them throughout her adult life, was struggling against an overwhelming but unarticulated sense of sadness and loneliness. Her marriage, for all its playful bantering, provided for virtually none of her intimacy needs. Beneath the laughter, she and her husband felt distant and unconnected. David's father had what amounted to a long-standing affair with his boat, a preoccupation that absorbed the greater part of his leisure time and energy. It had been that way "forever," his mother confided in me, and she had compensated over the years by maintaining her intimate ties with her parents, particularly her mother. After her mother's death, she had leaned on David as a source of support and sympathy. Now that adolescence was pulling him away from her, they were both showing signs of stress. But to get to all this feeling, to make it available for awareness and interchange, they first had to decide to get to the point, and to let pass the constant temptation to paint their pain with humor.

Some therapists are inclined to meet deflection with fairly straightforward confrontation, pointing out its incompatibility with the objectives of therapy. Since I am something of a deflector myself, my style is a little different. I typically join the family members in the deflection, particularly if it is engaging or humorous. And, once having joined them—in other words, from *within* the deflective contact—I pose the dilemma for *all of us* (not just for them) of getting down more directly to the business at hand.

David's family was able to do this, at least enough to release him from his role as family entertainer and companion-supporter to his mother. She agreed to see an associate of mine briefly, to work through her unfinished grieving and her need for support, but she chose not to pursue the issues of her marriage. "It works well enough," she concluded, and she decided to leave well enough alone. David, for his part, worked with me in therapy, also briefly, and quite competently opened up and began to integrate his own emotional interiority.

The Desensitized Family

The role of desensitization as a contact process has been explored by Kepner (1987), a Gestalt therapist who emphasizes body-oriented psychotherapy. Kepner points out that desensitization, which involves dulling or numbing of the organism's capacity for perception, is an adaptation response when escape from or avoidance of the environmental disturbance is not possible. In the family milieu, which to some degree always functions as a closed system, desensitization is an invaluable way of firming up the contact boundary and insulating the self from threatening or invasive input. As common currency of adolescent development, desensitization is probably most familiar in the "I don't care" posture that so many teenagers assume when caring (especially caring about what others feel) threatens to disintegrate the newly organized adolescent sense of self.

Desensitization is also a useful adaptation for parents when they begin stepping back to allow their children to encounter the consequences of their own behavior. In this circumstance, desensitization helps them manage the pain of watching their children "learn the hard way."

In families characterized by desensitization, there is a general deadening of contact boundaries and a corresponding tendency for interactions to become stereotyped and empty. There may be a lot of anger, or constant bickering and arguing, but it does not generally lead to anything other than more of the same. In other desensitized families, there is more an atmosphere of deadness and withdrawal, as if family members have lost interest in one another or given up all hope of any nurturing connectedness. This is often the case in families that have experienced a death or other traumatic loss but where the family members have been unable to mobilize themselves to provide support for one another. The loss heightens their need for connectedness and inclusion, and when these needs go unmet, family members tend to retreat from one another.

Kate's family was like this. When Kate was nine years old, her mother entered college as a full-time student and boarded at the school, about thirty miles from home. Kate stepped in to fill some of her mother's role, supervising her younger brothers and preparing many of the family meals. Kate made these adjustments "like a good soldier," to quote her mother, and complained about it only in retrospect, at age fourteen, about the time she began to act up. Within months after her mother completed her degree, her parents announced to the children that they were getting a divorce. In hindsight, they confided to me that the marriage had been dying for years.

I first met Kate and her mother about a year after the divorce became final. They were referred by another therapist, who had attempted unsuccessfully to work with them on their rapidly deteriorating and increasingly stormy relationship. Kate had shifted gears out of the "helpful eldest child" mode of her preadolescent years and had become—overnight, it seemed—despondent, angry, and argumentative. She picked on her younger siblings, and in a recent incident she had pushed her mother down the basement stairs. She was becoming unmanageable.

Emotionally, Kate's parents were unavailable to her. Her father had become embroiled in two concurrent romantic relationships, one of which produced an out-of-wedlock pregnancy and both of which drained him of his time, energy, and emotional resources. He gave Kate lip service but little else.

Kate's mother was unavailable for different reasons. She was really quite a remarkable woman. She had grown up in a family that afforded her little in the way of guidance and support, and she had more or less raised herself, by her account. She had married Kate's father and soon found herself burdened by a very needy husband and three small children. It was then, having decided that she must do something with her life, that she enrolled in college. She saw college and, after that, divorce as the only way she could make a real future for herself and her children. She was a survivor, someone who drew on inner resources when her environment left her taxed and unsupported.

But, by the same token, she was hardnosed. In my first session with them, Kate complained about the years of her mother's absence, and she mentioned how much she now objected when she was required to supervise the younger children. "We've been through all that already," her mother stated flatly, making it clear that she was not about to offer sympathy. She believed Kate needed to toughen up and get on with life, just as she herself had done so many times.

Kate's mood swings, her volatility, and her deep currents of sadness and emptiness all pointed to her need for support and connection. The previous therapist had urged Kate to be open and share her feelings with her mother, but her mother tended to see this as a manipulation and was not very interested.

From Kate's point of view, her family had died, but she found little in the way of confirmation and support for her emotional loss. Her mother immersed herself in productive activity, as she had done throughout her life whenever emotional pain became a possibility. Her father buried himself in the knot of new relationships that kept his life exciting enough to distract him from the emotional business of the divorce. Many adolescents in Kate's shoes do something similar. They ratchet up the excitement level of their lives in a hundred different ways—becoming sexually promiscuous, driving one hundred miles per hour, shoplifting, using drugs—and obscure the deeper and slower current of emotional loss that threatens to engulf them. Kate had not begun to do this sort of dangerous acting out at the time I met her, although she seemed to be inching toward it. Her argumentativeness, which kept the household in a state of high tension, seemed to take the edge off the deadness that she felt most of the time at home. She was beginning to cultivate the only strategy that seemed to work: desensitizing herself, callusing over her psychic skin.

Kate's mother was willing to participate in therapy briefly, so long as it had a practical focus and offered the promise of bringing Kate's behavior under control. My initial efforts were to sensitize the boundary of their interaction, which I attempted in several ways. First and foremost, I sensitized myself to the situation, especially to the mother's story of the long hard row she had hoed. I asked them both to listen to each other, and I encouraged them to talk about what they felt.

But Kate's mother was not interested, and she said so. I was reminded that desensitized families, in the absence of a crisis, are difficult to pull into therapy, or at least into the sensitizing mode of therapy that I was prescribing. Therefore, we worked briefly in the problem-solving mode that made more sense to Kate's mother. We identified some objectives, clarified responsibilities, and did some negotiating. And all of it helped, to a point.

During this time, Kate and I also began to meet occasionally for individual sessions. It quickly became clear to me that these meetings had a steadying effect on her, presumably for the adult support and interest that I made available to her. Her mother also noticed that Kate "was better" once we began these sessions, and Kate herself expressed a strong interest in continuing.

It is often the case in working with adolescents and their families that a therapist must take what he or she can get. My preference had been to work directly with the relationship of Kate and her mother. But it was not to be, and so I did what I could. As it turned out, that was enough. Kate and I met every few weeks or so for a little over a year, and I made myself available by telephone whenever she felt the need to call (which was quite often, although, like most adolescents, she called only often enough to make sure my offer was genuine). Our relationship was valuable to her, and it got her through a tricky stretch of development, to a time when her own legs felt more sturdy. She stopped calling and moved on.

Conclusion

If we work with disembedding adolescents, we will be rewarded for getting interested in and getting involved in their families' process. The goals of such involvements are modest. It is not necessary to change the family system, although it is difficult *not* to once you get involved, since adolescence itself changes the way families operate. The point is to abet the process, to nudge it along or untangle the snag that braces the adolescent against the current of development. I think that almost any school or approach to family work can accomplish this goal, although my own preference is a Gestalt approach, which aims to fill out the family's repertoire of contact process.

Not every clinical situation allows a clean shot at the family's developmental or contact process. Circumstances often conspire to prevent the degree of involvement that we might recommend. However much families may *operate* as systems, they do not always *think of* themselves as systems, and so they may not avail themselves of the kind of work that family therapists prefer. Thus we as therapists, like our adolescent clients, are left to tend to the developmental process with insufficient support. And we take what we can get.

CHAPTER NINE

Initiating
the Therapeutic Relationship

When an adult or an older adolescent elects to come to therapy, there is a certain straightforwardness to the meaning of the enterprise, at least at the level of social reality and interpersonal contracting. By contrast, when a disembedding adolescent comes to a therapist's office, it is a complex event in an unfolding family history. And, precisely to the extent that disembedding is still a developmental issue, the meaning of therapy will be conferred by the nature and nuances of this still unfolding history.

The Meanings of Coming to Therapy

Given the adolescent's entanglement in the larger family field, the whole business of therapy may represent some unresolved aspects of the family's drama. In one bitterly divorced family, for example, "therapy" had become part of the mother's domain, and the decision to bring children to therapy became a regularly disputed issue whenever one of the children began to falter. I was the third therapist for the thirteen-year-old boy, each of the earlier ones having been chewed up in the meat grinder of the parents' antagonistic relationship. Each time, the boy would begin to open up to his therapist, who in turn would buy into the mother's version of how all the family's problems expressed the pain induced by the boy's awful father. The father would then begin to pick up the drift of things. He would stall or refuse to pay the therapist's bill, undermining the therapy. Then, off mom would go to find her son a new therapist. For my young client, once I got to know him, the internal conflict about therapy was virtually unresolvable. If he went, he involuntarily testified to his father's badness. If he refused, he involuntarily negated his mother's version of reality.

From another family came a seventeen-year-old haunted by the specter of his mentally ill older brother. He feared that his referral to "therapy" meant that his parents had given up on him, and that he was following in his brother's footsteps. This fear surfaced only after months of therapy, during which he was intensely conflicted about coming.

In addition to this sort of "tainted meaning" that derives from the adolescent's entanglement in family dynamics and history, there is also the matter of determining just what sort of contact the client is capable of establishing with real-world adults (which is another way of asking how disembedded the client is). What is common to disembedding-stage clients is that they do not know how to use extrafamilial adults to support their growth and development. Consequently, they arrive at therapy as something other than ready, willing, and reasonably able "therapy clients." Instead, their interaction style is likely to reflect the status of their development—perhaps too attached and submerged, perhaps battling to disengage—and this makes them, as a group, among the most difficult of all psychotherapy clients to engage productively. They may be passive, hostile, dubious, paranoid, indifferent, utterly compliant, skillfully manipulative, excessively polite, or they may use any of a host of other styles that render the interaction less than therapeutic.

As therapists, we may find ourselves construed as something other than the supportive, objective, helping adults we take ourselves to be. Instead, we may find ourselves cast in the role of parent surrogate or stand-in for the entire adult world, and we may find our client braced for the judgment, criticism, lack of interest, control, or propaganda that he is certain lies in store. All of this is usually unspoken and, for most disembedding-stage clients, largely unaware. If it is spoken, it is easier to deal with. When it is not, it is capable of gripping the therapeutic field with a silent, choking sort of power.

Client Entry Styles

Each adolescent organizes the relational field of self and therapist in some characteristic, meaningful fashion. As a broad generalization, this style will reflect the client's history of experience with important adults, as well as his or her current progress with the developmental business of disembedding and constructing a stable sense of self. The children who are referred for psychotherapy are, generally speaking, those for whom this developmental process is not going well or smoothly. For them, as we have seen, the business of owning and reworking the contact boundary between self and others, particularly adults, is often difficult or problematic. We commonly see children whose response to the developmental task of disembedding is skewed either toward connectedness and joining or toward bounding and differentiating. At the one extreme, we encounter the youth whose deference, politeness, or eagerness to win our approval makes him difficult to engage in the work of therapy. At the other extreme, we encounter the youth whose determination to keep us at a distance makes a working relationship nearly impossible to conceive. These two stylistic extremes, of underboundedness and overboundedness, bracket the range of client entry styles. We will look at each of them in turn.

Underbounded Entry Style

The underbounded adolescent typically comes to therapy coopera-tively, in a spirit of complying with adult expectations and accepting that adults know what is best and will provide guidance on what to do. These teenagers tend to get along well with adults, or at least not to cause much trouble. Referral problems generally reflect more in-ternalized than acted-out distress and may include such complaints as psychosomatic disturbances, sleep difficulties, depression, and anxiety-related symptoms. If underbounded adolescents are battling with adults, it is usually in passive ways—underachieving in school, appearing "lazy" or irresponsible, complying superficially while act-ing out their private intentions, and so on.

Passivity is often characteristic of underbounded adolescents. It may be the florid passivity of the client who extends a limp hand to shake and awaits permission before entering your office or taking a seat. Or it may be the much more subtle passivity of the client who engages readily in animated conversation, but with keen attunement to adult expectations, in the hope of being found pleasing and accept-able. Both of these clients will leave a therapist with the experience of driving the interaction more than he or she would like to. At the extreme, therapy with a passive, underbounded client can be like dancing with a ragdoll.

For the underbounded adolescent, the relationship of self and adult is a powerful force field that influences immediate, ongoing experience in a fashion analogous to the effect of a magnet on iron filings. I had the good fortune recently of meeting with an articulate thirteen-year-old girl who helped me to understand this experience.

Sarah was referred to me for assessment of what appeared to be obsessive-compulsive symptoms. She had confided in her mother that she had certain rituals that governed her movements in certain situations, and her mother arranged for a consultation. She was a model client, being cooperative and frank in every way possible. After a session spent exploring her symptoms, in which Sarah thoughtfully answered questions that I put to her, I shifted my focus to a less structured exploration of Sarah's life and experience. As my queries became more open-ended and required more of Sarah's initiative, our interaction became more stilted and awkward, and silences crept more and more into our conversation.

I shifted my focus to what was going on with Sarah in the moment. She looked perplexed, as if to say that she herself did not quite understand.

"Is there something you want to say?" I asked.

"No."

"What happens to you in the moments when we just sit, when I'm not asking a question and you're not figuring out the answer?"

"It's like I just go blank," she finally offered.

"How come?" I asked. She shook her head slowly. "Ever happen in other situations?" I asked, and after a minute of squinting pensively, she slowly nodded.

"With my mother, sometimes," she added after another pensive minute.

Sarah went on to describe her experience of conversation with her mother, which for the most part occurred easily and pleasantly. Occasionally, however, Sarah would see things a little differently from her mother, and although these moments clearly proceeded as conversations and not as arguments, Sarah felt overwhelmed in these interactions. Her mother, she observed, just seemed so sure of herself, and Sarah usually found herself conceding that her mother knew more and probably was right. Sarah's mother, in my experience, was a bright and confident woman who made a genuine effort to listen to and support her children's ideas when conversing with them. She was not some ogre who would not permit any difference of opinion, but merely a bright and articulate adult whose opinions carried weight and authority in their intrinsic merit. In Sarah's experience, most often discussions of contended issues moved toward her mother's meaning, and Sarah would find herself (in the subtlest and most diplomatic way possible, I imagine) overruled or, even worse, persuaded of her mother's rightness.

What is it like to be thirteen years old, a "good kid," and engaged in contact with such an adult? The experience for most, I believe, is similar to Sarah's. And one common response to this experience of being in an interactive field with people smarter and better informed is to cognitively fade out, to become vacuous and inarticulate. Being with someone more clear and certain than oneself often induces a sort of cognitive drying up. This happens to adults as well. I typically become blank-minded and dumb when someone begins to talk knowledgeably about economics or politics. And if this happens to adults now and again, we can be certain that it happens to young adolescents routinely, particularly when speaking with unfamiliar adults. The inarticulate vacuity that often characterizes disembedding-stage clients is not necessarily defensiveness or passive aggression. More often, it is the natural expression of the unbalanced interpersonal field of an underbounded individual.

In therapy work with these clients, the overriding objective is to create a therapeutic field that supports the child's here-and-now disembedding. With these adolescents, authored experience in the form of "I feel . . . " and "I think . . . " does not flow spontaneously. In general, underbounded clients respond well to interviews where there is a format (a task, such as constructing a time line or a genogram, or an exercise, such as imagining oneself three years from now) that satisfies their need to know what is expected of them. The trick, of course, is that the format supports a more active role, rather than inadvertently reinforcing the client's passivity. It also helps if the therapist is willing to drop the structure at any point and digress in the direction of whatever spontaneous interest or energy the client may display. In this way, clients come to experience spontaneous self-expression as *relevant* to the field, and themselves as potent enough to influence the direction of the contact.

The central focus for the therapist in this sort of work is on the *form* of the contact process, not on its content. The initial objective with these clients is to create a disembedded field of interaction; becoming too interested or invested in content areas (focusing too insistently on "problems") only reinforces the embedded passivity of the child's contact style. It is important to remember, with underbounded adolescents especially, that it is the *field* we are working on, not the client. And the objective is to cultivate this field so that it can become a milieu where cognitive and perceptual figure formation can occur spontaneously. With many underbounded, introjecting adolescents, this is like cultivating a fragile organism in a petri dish. Ideas and observations may emerge only tentatively at first and will flourish and develop only if initial experiences are safe and nurturing.

The Overbounded Entry Style

The overbounded (read "unwilling and uncooperative") adolescent is the bane of most adolescent therapists' professional existence—the supreme challenge, and the reason why so many competent therapists decline to work with this age group. The first step in building relationships with these youths is to understand, as well as we can, what their overbounding is all about.

These are the youngsters who come to the first appointment against their own wishes, typically because some authority—parents, school, or court—has insisted on it. Their unwillingness may be played out loudly, with angry protest, or softly, behind superficial compliance, passive resistance, or staged indifference. For them, the contact boundary of self and therapist is purposefully hardened, or deadened, so as to make the self as impermeable as possible to adult impact and influence. Their presentation of self in the therapy situation communicates a clear message: "You're not going to get to *me!*"

It is an easy and largely accurate inference that these adolescents are not so unlike their underbounded counterparts. Their public refusal to engage obscures a deeper sense of powerlessness and malleability, a feeling that adults can all too readily get to them and affect how they feel about themselves. Anger and projection, as we have seen, are tailor-made for diminishing the contact surface of a tentative and vulnerable self gestalt.

Todd was one such adolescent, although at age sixteen, when I saw him, he had mellowed considerably from his earlier self. At age fourteen, his parents had taken him to see a therapist, with disastrous results. He had angrily refused even to look at the therapist, raged loudly at his parents, and stormed from the therapist's office. They had given up the endeavor as not worth the trouble. Now, he entered the situation with an attitude of disdain and indifference. Like Sarah's, Todd's case is valuable because of his eventual willingness and ability to put his experience into words.

Todd's parents had a variety of complaints, none of them overwhelming, but in aggregate describing an extremely passive-aggressive boy with a penchant for infuriating adults and avoiding responsibility. His primary target for this sort of battling was his stepmother, whom he had regularly reduced to tears of frustration and displays of impotent rage. He affected several of his teachers in similar fashion, being an extremely bright and moderately successful student who took undisguised pleasure in getting by with as little work as possible.

His parents offered a telling story during their first visit to my office. On his way to a recent soccer tournament, Todd had traveled with a teammate, whose mother drove. She telephoned Todd's parents upon returning from the tournament, which was in another city, to report that she had felt insulted and demeaned by Todd's behavior, and that he was the rudest youngster she had ever met. Todd answered these charges with a shrug and a wry smile, casually dismissing them as the unfounded ravings of a woman "with a broom up her ass." *She* was the one who needed professional help, he suggested.

What had happened on the trip to so severely distress this woman? Only weeks later, once Todd and I had negotiated an initial relationship, did an accurate description come forth. Todd had essentially ignored the woman, treating her as if she were not there. At one point, by his own description, he had leaned over from the back seat to the front seat to change the station on the radio, without saying a word.

"Why did you make such a point of not interacting with her?" I asked.

"Because she held back and didn't speak to me first," he answered. "She wasn't friendly to me, so I wasn't friendly to her."

"Why not take the initiative?" I suggested. "A friendly hello from you might have loosened things up."

"Too risky," he replied summarily. "You never know when an adult might blow you off."

Todd went on to elaborate this explanation by giving me a

related example of the same behavior. When hunting for a job recently, he had made the rounds of the stores in neighboring shopping centers that might employ teenagers. He reported that he spoke only to those managers who took the initiative to engage him in conversation. In those stores where the managers did not engage him in some fashion (for example, handing him an application with a perfunctory "Here, fill this out"), he disengaged, usually walking out without a word as soon as he had completed the application.

Todd confided in me that he found adults scary. "Not like kids my own age," he elaborated. "Teenagers, I know I can handle. I can say something to humiliate them if they try to make me look stupid. I don't worry about kids my own age." Indeed, around peers, Todd was outgoing and confident, if occasionally acerbic and critical. Around adults, however, he sometimes felt overmatched, unable to adequately defend himself should a given adult decide to diminish him. "You can never tell when an adult is going to blow you off," he reiterated. "And when they do, there's nothing you can do, because they don't care what you think of them." In other words, Todd was telling me, with adults he felt little control of the contact boundary. Adults had enough interpersonal centeredness and power to define an interaction, to confirm him as worthy or disconfirm him as unworthy of their time and attention.

This experience is similar to Sarah's. But Todd's strategy for dealing with his vulnerability was stylistically different from Sarah's friendly, cooperative complacency. Todd's solution was to hold back and watch, to behave as if he were invisible while waiting for adults to show their hand, revealing something of their underlying attitude and deportment. Once he got a reading on adults, he could mobilize himself to interact with them—graciously, cleverly, defensively, congenially, whatever the situation demanded. But until he could read the adult in question and determine whether this was friend or foe, he would lie low, even if this entailed behavior that ordinary folks might find quite rude, as his friend's mother had done.

When Todd sensed indifference, he determined that it was *he* who would do the "blowing off," and he did so in a manner that typically left adults feeling inadequate and angry. When Todd sensed hostility or authoritarian control, he adjusted his response accordingly by always making a preemptive strike that settled the issue of who was controlling the interaction. When he sensed friendliness and acceptance, he put forward his socially comfortable, playful, conversational side, but not without caution.

What Todd's story illustrates is the subtler phenomenology of the overbounded adolescent, the nuances of experience that lead to the characteristic hardening of the contact boundary. Todd was atypical precisely because he could share his experience so descriptively. More commonly, overbounded adolescents have a less developed capacity for articulating, which is precisely why they act out their self-protective and integrity-preserving intentions with such determination. Even when they are engaged in a working therapy relationship, they often retain their projective focus and their sensitivity to the dangers of trusting adults.

The most interesting questions concerning Todd's story remain to be addressed: how he came to the decision to trust me in the first place, and what I did as a therapist to solicit and support that decision. The answers to these questions, as they are related to adolescent clients in general, will occupy the remainder of this chapter.

Initial Pragmatic Considerations

By contrast with adult therapy, as I have pointed out, adolescent therapy is often not initiated by the client but rather by concerned adults. Most often, the adolescent's response to this event ranges between ambivalence and outright resistance. The specific management of the business of referral can greatly affect how this resistance gets played out early on and, accordingly, whether individual therapy is to become an option at all. A number of practical considerations bear on the eventual matter of building a viable therapeutic relationship with an adolescent client.

Getting the Adolescent to Come to Therapy

Frequently, in the first telephone contact with a concerned parent, the therapist is asked "How do I get him to come?" There are no magic words, to be sure, but there are things that help and things that hurt the odds of getting off on the right foot. Parents who ask this question are usually expressing their own experience of having lost control of their child, or their fears of confronting him with the need for action on some existing problem. Sometimes the parents will suggest some ruse for getting the adolescent to the therapist, in the hope that the therapist's consummate skill can somehow take over from there. But this maneuver amounts to therapeutic suicide. No one, adolescent or adult, is likely to proceed willingly in a relationship whose opening move has been deceit and manipulation. Parents also sometimes wait and spring the news of the appointment on their unsuspecting adolescent at the last possible minute, again in the hope of evading a negative reaction. If we find ourselves confronted with an intensely resistant, angry youngster in the initial meeting, it is always a good idea for us to ask when the appointment was announced, and whether there has been any opportunity for discussion among family members.

I always, when asked, recommend an approach that is straightforward, wherein parents present their concerns frankly and allow time for the adolescent's reactions, discussion, and psychological preparation. It also helps, in many cases, to coach the parents on how to present family and relationship concerns as such, rather than as problems belonging solely to the adolescent. "We have not been able to get along lately" is easier to accept, and always more accurate, than "You've had problems controlling your temper."

When Todd's parents brought him to my office, they had been battling at home for several months over matters related to his behavior. In their eyes, he was out of control, and they had told him so. He in turn had reminded them of the futile attempt at therapy two years earlier, and he scoffed at the prospect this time around. At my suggestion, his parents informed him that the initial few visits with me were a trial, for them *and him* to decide whether I could be of help. If Todd felt uncomfortable with me, they assured him, they would move on to someone else.

Presenting the matter to Todd in a manner that affirmed Todd's opinion as relevant was an important part of defusing the power struggle. The fact remains, however, that his parents did insist on a trial with somebody, and this part was nonnegotiable. The inability of some parents to exert even this much authority is always symptomatic of significant problems at the level of the family system. Suffice it to say that when parents are not able to get their adolescent to a first meeting, the initial critical work is not with the child, anyway. It is with the parents.

Whom to See Initially

The question of whom to see initially is one that is open to discussion and opinion on all sides. In some situations, it is rendered moot by the unavailability of one party or another. In my career as an adolescent therapist, I have tried just about every combination I can think of. Here are some of the factors that I have come to consider important.

Seeing the Adolescent Alone.

For many years, I chose to see adolescents initially without their parents, believing that this helped to establish initial rapport. Today, therapists with theoretical approaches that stress the individual psyche, apart from its contextual field, tend to prefer this approach. What I discovered about this approach, however, was a host of minor complications that retarded subsequent relationship-building and therapeutic work. Seen initially alone, adolescents often express some degree of mystification, sometimes purely face-saving and sometimes entirely genuine, about the reasons for their referral. Particularly if an adolescent views the therapist as a potential ally, he is motivated to present himself in the best possible light. This is an understandable inclination, but it can have the effect of placing the therapist almost immediately in a no-win dilemma. Do we support the adolescent in his skewed version of reality? Or do we risk premature confrontation about his evasion of the real issues? If we tell the client what we have been told by the referring adults, how do we convey our neutrality and avoid being construed as agents or spokespersons for the absent adults? By leaving the referring persons out of the interview situation, the therapist can unwittingly place himself or herself in a triangulated position, where any approach may be construed by the adolescent as either "for me" or "against me."

The rule of thumb, then, is "don't see adolescent clients alone in an initial contact." There are two common exceptions to this guideline. The first is when the presenting adolescent has requested the consultation himself, and when it seems reasonable to expect that he is willing and able to present facts and concerns in a reasonably objective manner. The second is when the adolescent is developmentally at a point where it seems important and useful to underscore the premise that this problem is the adolescent's business and responsibility and would best be dealt with independently. Older adolescents, reasonably mature but still struggling with differentiation issues, are candidates for this way of setting up an initial contact.

Meeting with Parents or Other Referring Adults Alone. This approach to initial contact is attractive, to me at least, because it offers the promise of getting an adult's-eye view of the presenting problem. Furthermore, referring adults are generally more apt to be candid and thorough when meeting with a therapist privately, without the child. The liability of this approach is that it establishes an alliance among the adults in the situation, something most adolescents are prone to suspect and construe even when it is not present. I have often heard adolescent clients describe an earlier "failed" therapy, where this kind of beginning prevented them from ever accepting the therapist's stated intention of working on their behalf. The rule of thumb, then, is "Don't meet with parents alone." But this rule also has its occasional exceptions—for example, when parent guidance seems the most promising therapeutic intervention.

Meeting with Adolescent and Parents Together. I have learned that it is easiest to set the stage for a positive working relationship with an adolescent when the individuals making the referral—usually the parents—accompany her to the initial visit. This allows the therapist to listen to all sides of the presenting issue while maintaining a posture of interested neutrality. In some instances, the parents may be only weakly representing the referral intentions of a third party—a probation officer, for example, or a school guidance counselor. I have had parents and teenagers come to my office for an initial visit and collectively shrug their shoulders about the reasons for being there, claiming, "The school told us we should come" but not being clear about the reasons for the school's concerns, or at least not disposed to present them objectively. "You call the school, and find out why they sent us here," they may suggest when pushed about the referral problem. These are tricky situations, which usually involve unfinished and unclear contact between the family and the referring party. In such situations, rather than approach the referring party myself (and doing the family's work), I offer to help the family sort out the issue, perhaps by inviting the referring party to the next visit or by arranging a speakerphone conference with the referring party.

Over the years, I have found that the most workable format for the initial contact is a meeting that includes the adolescent and the parents. When the parents begin to give me information over the telephone, before our first meeting, I ask them to hold off discussing their concerns in any detail until the first visit, when I can give them the proper attention.

The Initial Meeting

In an initial meeting with an adolescent and her parent(s), I have four fairly specific objectives, things I want to make sure get attended to or accomplished: getting referral issues and circumstances on the table, establishing safety, arriving at an assessment contract, and establishing ground rules for confidentiality and feedback.

Getting Referral Issues on the Table.
Something has prompted these people to call me and make this appointment, and finding out that something is the best contact I can make with people in an initial visit. Background, history, previous experiences in therapy, theories and suppositions about underlying causes—these are all important, but they are usually deflections from the immediate life experience that has prompted this family to take this step at this time. If parents cite long-standing difficulties, I ask, "Why now?" I want to hear about the conversations, dilemmas, arguments, disagreements, discoveries, and thought processes that have congealed to produce the family's arrival on my doorstep. This typically includes a recitation of "problems" or complaints by parents, and often a counterrecitation by the adolescent. If the parents are vague or noticeably delicate in their presentation, I respectfully push for more specifics. My intention is to make sure that I offer all the encouragement, receptivity, interest, respect, and inquisitiveness necessary for each individual to say out loud the things that he or she came to say in this first meeting.

As the parents begin to recite their concerns about the child, I adopt an interview style modeled by Oaklander (1978). With each new chunk of information, each new concern or complaint, I stop them and turn to the adolescent with several questions, respectfully proffered: "Are you tracking what your father is saying?" "Do you see it the same way?" "Are there parts you see differently?" One of the very first things I convey to families is that I am interested in all points of view, and I try to convey that their ability to disagree at this point is a good sign and makes my job of understanding their situation easier. I am especially interested at this point in hearing and registering the adolescent's individual voice, particularly if there has not been sufficient space made for it in the family field.

Establishing a Sense of Safety.

The first visit to a therapist's office—something a good many of us have experienced ourselves—is an anxiety-fraught occasion for most individuals. We therapists have a way of forgetting this, just as the expert swimmer forgets how terrifying it was to first jump into the water unattended. But it is extremely important that we not forget it, because new clients are often using considerable energy to contain and manage their anxiety. The adolescent's trepidation is usually the most obvious and the easiest to understand. After all, he has been made the issue. This stranger-therapist is an *adult*, and if real-world adults had proved helpful in the past, this meeting probably would not have been scheduled in the first place.

What may be a little less obvious to us is how much the parents often feel at risk when they bring themselves and their child to a mental health professional. Parents often find it far more threatening to expose their children, and their parenting, to the objective eye of a third party than to discuss their own personal secrets and insecurities. Anyone who has raised children knows that parents are invested in their children to a greater degree than any nonparent can imagine, and every parent carries the awful secret that he or she has done an inadequate job of parenting, scarring each child for life. These feelings express a truth, for each parent knows, at some level of intuition, that he or she *is* part of the environment to which this child has adapted.

It is not unusual in a first meeting, where individuals feel exposed and tensions sometimes run high, to be faced with behavior that is indeed provocative in some way. An adolescent mutters, "Fuck you" under his breath. A father lectures pompously about his son's "inexcusable selfishness." A mother woundedly refuses to listen to her daughter's side of a disagreement. For every therapist, I suspect, there are trigger behaviors that call out our judgmentalism, or our need to rescue, or an impulse to angrily confront. I know that it nearly drives me up the wall when I hear a parent plead with an adolescent to speak his or her mind, to "just let us know what's bothering you," and who then proceeds to defend, criticize, deny, or overrule once the reticent teenager has taken the risk of putting feelings and perceptions into words.

But in a first meeting, as I have said, the essential condition is safety. And to prematurely or ungracefully enter the foray, to take sides, to confront (and thus probably to shame), is likely to be experienced as a breach of safety *by all family members*, not just the offending party. It is absolutely critical, in other words, that *all* behavior, even the most provocative or offensive, be met by the therapist's empathy for what motivates it (which is almost always some degree of caring or concern) and by his or her respect for the individual who displays it. (Of course, like all rules, this one has its exceptions, as when we are dealing with individuals whose abusive behavior inflicts damage upon others in the room. In such an instance, direct and forceful confrontation may be necessary to approximate the condition of safety I am interested in here.) We are on trial from the opening handshake, and it is important for us to realize that each family member attends to how we treat everyone in the room.

Another safety issue for many families and individuals has to do with the structure of the initial meeting—the "what's expected" of the situation. I believe it is imperative for the therapist to take the initiative in some fashion. This can be done simply by speaking first and laying out a concrete suggestion for how the session might proceed. This need not be detailed or rigid. It might be as simple as "I'd like to hear first from each of you, one at a time, about why you're here." This sort of introduction may seem like a belaboring of the obvious, but it can be greatly reassuring to a family entering a new and unfamiliar situation to sense that the therapist has a game plan for what is about to happen.

Some years ago, when my children were preteenagers, I made the mistake of volunteering my family as a client-system for a training program in Gestalt family therapy. I thought it would be a wonderful learning experience for all of us, and my family reluctantly agreed to go along. The initial session opened in classic Gestalt fashion, with the cotherapists waiting calmly and receptively for "something to emerge." What emerged for all of us, myself included, was an overwhelming sense of disorientation and anxiety, from which we never recovered in our four-session tour of volunteer duty. It was months before my children forgave me. The moral of the story is that we need to remember that families, even when they include individuals who are "therapy wise," need at least a minimal structure in order to feel safe in such an unfamiliar situation as an initial interview.

The adolescent in a first session is particularly vulnerable, and she frequently enters the session armed and guarded for the criticism that seems certain to come. The therapist's management of this vulnerability, and the conveyance of an air of safety for the adolescent, is often a delicate business. Two things help. The first is obvious: listening carefully and with respect to whatever the adolescent has to say, sidestepping the temptation either to agree with or to challenge his or her views. This sort of respectful neutrality is a shock to many adolescents entering a therapy situation, who have managed so often to polarize the adults in their lives. The second important strategy for making safety a palpable experience in the first interview is to affirm the adolescent's control over how involved or uninvolved to become during the session.

In my initial meeting with Todd's family, I began by addressing Todd:

> Todd, your father made this appointment, so I'm assuming this was your parents' idea. Am I right? So I want to find out what prompted them to call me. I'll probably check out what they say with you, just to find out where you agree and disagree; but I want to start with them. Whatever you have to say, I'm definitely interested. But if you prefer to sit back and let them do the talking, that's okay, too.

It is my objective to make the initial contact as nontraumatic for the adolescent as possible. To this end, I give as much leeway as I can regarding the extent of the adolescent's direct participation. Many teenagers expect to be put in the hot seat in a therapist's office, interrogated and asked to explain their behavior. The explicit permission to sit back and watch puts many adolescents at ease who would otherwise be defensive and uncooperative right from the start.

Occasionally, an adolescent will enter an initial meeting in a therapist's office with a steely resolve to resist the whole business, having vowed not to participate. If the therapist works too hard to engage an adolescent who assumes this posture, it can easily become a messy situation, with the teenager feeling no face-saving option but to make good his or her vow of noncooperation. The more invested the therapist is in undoing this vow, the more likely a polarized situation will develop. A standoff in the first meeting means the certain miscarriage of therapy. Responding to this posture of refusing involvement by endorsing it, essentially conceding the adolescent's power to make these choices, avoids a standoff and initiates the relationship in a spirit of respect.

There is another reason for allowing the adolescent to sit back during the initial contact. The adolescent is sizing the therapist up from the very first moment of meeting. She wants to know if you are open-minded, whether you side with her parents, whether you listen and are respectful, whether you jump to conclusions, whether you are smart or easily fooled, and a host of other things. This is precisely as it should be, and it is easier to evaluate a therapist from an observer's position, watching him or her interact with parents, than it is when interacting directly. Conversely, it is much easier to demonstrate these qualities for an adolescent by acting them out, auditioning them as it were, while the adolescent sits back and decides whether the therapist is safe to approach.

As I interact with parents in the opening moments of a first session, I am aware of being scrutinized carefully by the adolescent, and that every aspect of my demeanor and behavior is a statement about myself, my interest level, my integrity, my neutrality, and so on. Parents are usually willing to give a therapist the benefit of the doubt, to accept on faith (for a while, at least) that I am there to do my best to help. The adolescent typically grants no such grace and is much more empirical in his assessment of a therapist's potential to help the situation.

Another reason for opening in this way is that it helps in avoiding the sort of triangulation that inevitably occurs if I hear the referral information from the parents, without the adolescent present, which tends to generate dilemmas about how to bring up issues with the adolescent without slipping into the role of speaking as the parents' mouthpiece. When the adolescent is present, then everything that parents say is read into the record, as it were, and can easily enough be raised for clarification and discussion with the adolescent at a time that I feel is opportune and appropriate.

There are several other things I try to do to promote overall safety in the therapy situation. I ask the family members, after their initial concerns have been presented, to tell me how they operate when things are going well. I want them to have an opportunity to present the whole range of their functioning, not just the part that pains them. I also look, whenever possible, for an opportunity to focus for a time on each parent individually (drawing the focus away from the adolescent), perhaps asking the parent about his or her background. The point of all this, apart from what I learn at the content level, is to challenge the adolescent's assumptions about the danger of the therapy situation. I want him to know that he will be heard, that there will be no adult power play, no scapegoating, no pathologizing, no hot-seat interrogation. And I want this first meeting to afford him the opportunity to sit back, if he chooses, and make his own observations.

Establishing an Assessment Contract.

An assessment contract is an understanding or explicit agreement with the adolescent and her parents that there will follow some number of visits or series of sessions devoted to getting acquainted and arriving at recommendations. The contract may be spelled out formally or understood loosely. To some extent, this will be determined by the therapist's style of professional practice. Of course, youngsters who come to an initial meeting with some degree of openness, or who decide by the end of that meeting that they are willing to continue, present no particular challenge to an assessment contract.

If I sense that an adolescent has begun to drop his defensiveness, I will propose that I be given the opportunity of several sessions to "get to learn more about who you are, apart from your family and parents." I then outline a short-term plan, which usually includes several individual sessions with the adolescent and at least one additional family-assessment session. If this proposal is made somewhat matter-of-factly, and with a genuine interest in learning what the adolescent has to say, it is most often accepted.

Some adolescents, however, even at the end of the opening session, remain unwilling or ambivalent. They may still feel unsafe and threatened by the uncertainty of the situation, and by the potential for judgment and blame. They may feel required to retain their uncooperative posture in order to save face. It is important to offer the assessment contract in a manner that fully takes account of the adolescent's experience of the situation. Adolescents who are not particularly ambivalent, but who are singlemindedly and adamantly opposed to spending individual time with a therapist, are the ones who most often construe therapy as an allocation of blame. It is a mistake, in my opinion, to begin seeing the adolescent in this case without first doing some work with the family system. With a family that is offering its adolescent as a scapegoat, I will almost certainly refuse to see the adolescent alone and will ask instead for an opportunity to get more acquainted with the family before making a judgment about individual therapy.

With the more genuinely ambivalent adolescent client, her outward words and behavior may shout no to the therapy situation, while more subtle cues—a willingness to engage, a smile, humor, responsiveness to the therapist—may signal an underlying receptivity. Herein lies the challenge for the therapist: how do we respond respectfully to this youth's no while creating an opportunity for yes without a loss of face?

Todd presented just this sort of dilemma. His parents were sufficiently in charge to bring about this first meeting, but he was committed to maintaining his integrity. He was not about to cave in at this point. Still, his acerbic edge melted noticeably during the first hour, and there had been moments when he had let me in. (I remember a smile leaking from the corner of his mouth when I commented—quite seriously—on his impressive expertise at reading and frustrating adults.) I turned to him toward the end of the visit and stated, matter-of-factly:

> Look, I think your parents probably understand that at your age, no one can *make* you do anything, as far as counseling is concerned, any more than anyone could force your parents, or me, for that matter, to go along with something we didn't agree to. But still, I would like very much to have a chance to meet you and learn something about who you are in your own right, apart from your parents.

Then, without awaiting a reply, I turned to his parents and said:

> What I'd like is a chance to talk to Todd a couple of times confidentially, without you here.

And then I turned back to Todd:

> Can you live with that?

My sense of Todd at this point was that he was open to our meeting but needed an easy way of saying yes. If face saving had been less of an issue, I might have simply said, "Would you be willing to come back by yourself?" If Todd had seemed more invested in remaining dug in, I would have suggested that they all return again as a family, thereby avoiding a premature confrontation around the issue of Todd's collaboration. As it was, Todd was one of those adolescents who broadcast an air of "Yes, if you *insist*," and the trick was insisting just enough (and respectfully enough) that he was free to take the next step.

Establishing Ground Rules for Confidentiality and Feedback.
Confidentiality is so fundamental to the therapeutic situation that it generally receives only passing commentary in discussions of therapeutic practice. But confidentiality with adolescents is a different issue than it is with adults. It is far more complicated, much more discretionary, and much more of a factor in the therapeutic process than many therapists realize.

In my training workshops for adolescent therapists, I regularly bring in a group of adolescents who have current or former experience as clients in various treatment modalities, and I have them discuss their experiences in a fishbowl discussion-group format. Inevitably, the issue of confidentiality emerges as a salient aspect of their experience. What has amazed me most is the high percentage of client discussants who report violations of confidentiality, in most instances accompanied by a sense of betrayal and anger. Frequent outcomes are loss of trust in adults and a renewed resolve to work out problems without adult assistance.

This is genuinely tragic, because I believe that the majority of these breaches of confidentiality were outcomes of well-intentioned adults acting with their clients' health and well-being at heart. In fact, some of the breaches cited by our discussants were probably not breaches at all, since they were only able to report vague suspicions or unsupported conclusions about their therapists or counselors colluding with their parents or other adults in authority. Sometimes a "breach" is actually a misunderstanding of what is meant by confidentiality.

One client of mine reported being betrayed by his pediatrician, and he vowed never to go back to her again. What had happened? In mutually agreed-upon confidence, he told her how difficult things had been at home in recent months, and how unhappy he had become. True to her understanding of confidentiality, she reported not a word of what he had said to his parents, but at the end of the visit she called his mother into the examining room and recommended that the family see a counselor. To his mind, this represented an outrageous breach of their agreement. Their respective versions of confidentiality were equally valid but nevertheless discrepant.

The inverse of these stories reflects the enormous therapeutic power of a relationship where the adolescent finds confidentiality honored, where confidentiality amounts to an implicit confirmation of personal integrity, boundaries, and responsibility. The word *confidentiality* may have relatively little meaning at the outset of therapy, since most children have not experienced a relationship where such ground rules would be appropriate. But the *process* of confidentiality, as it comes to take on meaning and substance over time, can be transformative of the adolescent's experience of self.

What constitutes confidentiality with an adolescent client? There is no single right answer, other than that the ground rules must be made clear and adhered to religiously and demonstrably. Some therapists operate according to the letter of the law, maintaining confidentiality on all matters except those that are life-endangering or involve child abuse. Some include issues related to chemical use and abuse in the list of exceptional circumstances, while others keep these matters confidential unless they become physically life-threatening. The bottom line is that it is risky business to announce confidentiality as a blanket guideline and then be forced to work out the specific exceptions later. What must be reported to parents, when and how feedback will be given to parents, how parents' phone calls will be handled—these all need to be spelled out explicitly at the outset. Doing so is not just a matter of covering the ethical bases; it is also an important means of inviting the adolescent into a relationship.

As with other issues where I expect a certain measure of skepticism from the teenager, particularly at the first meeting, I address my remarks about confidentiality to the parents and allow the adolescent to eavesdrop. There is greater credibility, I think, when confidentiality matters are presented to parents as boundary issues, as ground rules that they must be prepared to accept if I am going to proceed with therapy. In this day of therapeutic sophistication, most parents understand and readily accept the need for confidentiality between therapist and client, but it is important to enact the ritual of explaining this to them, so that my adolescent client can see that I take this issue seriously.

Conclusion

The business of initiating therapeutic contact with potential adolescent clients is probably the aspect of therapy most neglected in the clinical literature. Practitioners seem to segregate themselves unconsciously into those who "have the knack" for engaging adolescents in the therapeutic project and those who do not, as if it were a gift or an occult science. The initial moments of clinical contact are the delicate microsurgery of adolescent psychotherapy. Accordingly, they warrant the most careful and thoughtful attention. In this chapter, it has not been my intention to say, "This is how you do it" but to say, "Attend carefully to how you do it." The thirteen-year-old entering a therapist's office for the first time is a little like a newborn duckling waiting to imprint on the world of psychotherapy. The subtle nuances of respect, confirmation, directness, and trustworthiness that unfold in the opening moments set the stage for what can be expected to follow. I have tried to describe some of the practices that I have developed over the years in light of the adolescent client's phenomenology. My hope in presenting my own research and conclusions is that other therapists will be supported in proceeding with their own.

CHAPTER TEN

From the Family to the Self: The Psychotherapy of Disembedding

In the natural history of development, most adolescents find their way into meaningful relationships with real-world adults. They may be coaches, neighbors, youth ministers, or employers. The relationship may be personal and friendly. It may be functional and even impersonal, experienced as only an incidental involvement outside the family orbit. There may be one such relationship, cherished deeply, or there may be many, none of which stands out as singularly important. The point is that these relationships, these contacts with real-world adults, are a critical part of the process of disembedding from the family field of childhood. This has generally been the case historically and in primitive cultures, where it has been the adult members of the tribe, *not the parents*, who initiate and carry out the rites of passage and transformation. Through these relationships, the individual learns how to tap the world beyond the family for resources of guidance, modeling, and confirmation and, in the process, to stand differently in the world, to take the self seriously and become a citizen beyond the family. When the adolescent is disembedding *from* the family, in other words, he is also moving *into* a wider world of potential involvements and support.

The adolescents who arrive for psychotherapy are very often the ones who have not learned, for whatever reason, to mine the resources of the adult world that surrounds them. They may have peer supporters, but these prove insufficient to the task of finding a way in the modern world. The function of psychotherapy for these adolescents is precisely to arrange for them an experience, a relationship, that accomplishes in an intentional way what happens incidentally in the natural course of ordinary development.

The primary therapy work at this stage is to build a relationship that supports, both directly and indirectly, the disembedding process. This happens at several levels. Most obviously, the therapist becomes an ally and a consultant to the adolescent as she goes about the business of reworking relationship boundaries "out there" in her life. The therapist will teach, coach, sympathize, and challenge as the adolescent wrestles with the shifting stresses and demands of her parents, siblings, school, and peers. The therapist will raise questions, give answers, pose dilemmas, help to solve problems, make suggestions, and generally support the emergence of self-ownership and responsibility.

And in the process of providing these "obvious" things, the therapeutic relationship will implicitly create (or reinforce) a *new form* of contact with the adult world, contact wherein the adolescent is recognized precisely as a self, an author, a center of experience and synthesis that legitimately holds its own place in the field. The therapist will help the client identify and articulate sensory experience and nascent perceptions. The therapist will become interested in and take seriously what the adolescent observes and opines, and promote and confirm the adolescent's self-authored synthesis of meanings. In carrying out these functions, the therapist creates in the therapeutic field itself a new form of relating, a new style of being in contact.

All psychotherapy with adolescent clients has this dimension—this implicit soliciting and confirming of the disembedding status of the adolescent self. Even in work with more mature clients, where therapy moves gracefully into the issues of interiority and integration, there still exists the underground project of confirming this more differentiated and contact-rich *form* of the interpersonal field. The ultimate goal of psychotherapy with disembedding-stage clients (or perhaps with all adolescent clients) is to return them to their lives with contact skills that will enable them, outside the special world of psychotherapy, to seek out and utilize the support they need for their development.

In this chapter, we will concentrate on those clients for whom disembedding is problematic, or at least insufficient, and for whom the essential skills of entering a therapeutic relationship are more the goal of the work than its foundation. Disembedding-stage adolescents are most often the ones who resist the prospect of therapy, or at least who begin with no notion of how one might go about using such a relationship constructively. In the pages to follow, I will address this dimension of psychotherapy, where the rudiments of connecting and collaborating are the essence of the therapeutic work.

Therapy as Ordinary Conversation

Therapeutic interaction involves, in large part, the use of *words*, simple conversation. Gestalt therapy has traditionally eschewed psychotherapy's traditional emphasis on words ("talking therapy," as psychoanalysis came to be called) in favor of more immediate and expressive enactment. But Gestalt therapy was born of the need to loosen up adult clients who had become encased in words, to the point of losing their spontaneity. Spontaneity is not really the problem with many adolescent clients, and so the work is quite different in flavor and emphasis from work with neurotically constricted adults. I think that there is a tendency for professional therapists, products of an educational system that fills us up with words, to underestimate, at least at the level of theory, the enormous power of words in healing pain and organizing experience.

My wish is to instill a proper respect for the therapeutic power of ordinary conversation with adolescent clients. For the adolescent in the process of learning anew to *see* the environment (and, in learning to see, to become a centered self), finding the right words can make all the difference. The linguist Benjamin Whorf (1956) has demonstrated convincingly that language is the powerfully contextualizing ground that determines which figures will emerge perceptually in a given culture. Language, according to Whorf, teaches us to see. Annie Dillard (1974) underscores this idea when she reveals how she came to see such incredible detail and activity in the ordinary surroundings of Tinker Creek: she used words. She would walk to the creek daily and force herself to describe what was there, in nuance and detail, and as she did so, the creek opened up to her an enormously rich and articulated perceptual world. This is the same principle that phenomenological psychologists (for example, Giorgi, 1970) use as the very basis of qualitative scientific research: they *describe* the obvious in detail, and in so doing they arrive in time at its deeper meaning and implicit structure. Thus the so-called ordinary conversation of adolescent psychotherapy is actually much more than it may appear to be. In its attention to the obvious, it accomplishes a gradual elucidation of what, for the client, is the deeper meaning and implicit structure of the world.

Connecting with the Disembedding-Stage Client

An integral part of a Gestalt approach to psychotherapy is the therapist's use of self as an instrument of the therapeutic process. This has somewhat different meanings in adolescent therapy and in therapy with adults, particularly in light of the generational difference between therapist and client. It is important to look carefully at what aspects of the experience of self get stirred up and brought by the therapist to the therapeutic field. Ultimately, when an adolescent or young adult looks back on a successful experience in therapy, it is not specific interventions or conversations that he remembers, but rather the "who" of the therapist. He feels better off for having had this person in his life, even if it is not possible to label the specific learnings and experiences that made the therapy worthwhile.

What the Therapist Brings to the Field

Most therapists can readily identify the types of adolescent clients they find easy or difficult to work with—those who bring out empathic support, those who trigger an impulse to judge or parent, and those who generate boredom or indifference. What are these stirrings about? The answer for any individual therapist is an intensely personal matter, but several general factors seem to play an important role.

One such factor is the therapist's own developmental distance from adolescence. Another is the presence of real adolescents in the therapist's own life. When I was newly out of graduate school and adjusting to the rather rigid authority structures of an old-style Catholic hospital, I was inclined to overidentify with my clients in their struggles against the controlling adults in their lives. Some years later, when my own children were going through adolescence, I more often found myself sympathetic to the parental side of family conflict and less tolerant of seemingly pointless campaigns of rebellion. As my children passed into young adulthood, I found myself more readily able to see these struggles more clearly as field phenomena. The ground we bring to this work, the ground that shapes our perception and judgment, is reflective of our own movement through the life cycle.

Another powerful dimension of the therapist's ground is the legacy of his or her own adolescence—the wonderful and the painful experiences, the unfinished business, the unique resolutions of various developmental issues. Our own histories influence the way we respond to themes of acting out, sexual experimentation, peer relationships, rebellion against authority, and so on.

Another, somewhat less obvious, way in which our own unfinished adolescent issues enter into our work as psychotherapists involves our gut-level reactions and responses to the adults in the adolescent client's life. How am I affected by adults who are overinvested and intrusive? narcissistically preoccupied? authoritarian and demanding? Do I find myself impatient and intolerant with certain types of parents? Or do I tend to feel the pressure of parental expectations for behavioral change and feel obliged to produce the results that the parents are expecting and paying for? The answer here, as in all countertransference issues in psychotherapy, is awareness—stopping, noticing, becoming curious, appreciating my own process as it is stirred up by the therapeutic field. Since every one of us has had parents and lived through adolescence; and since many of us are parents ourselves, some of us with adolescent children, it is virtually impossible for us to come to the therapy situation without having our perceptions organized to some degree by our personal histories. The idea is not to override these tendencies but to *open up* to them, become aware of them, become interested in their role in our therapy work.

The Therapist as a Self

Meeks (1971) writes about the "fragile alliance" of therapist and adolescent client. There is always, he states, the danger of forming an "unholy" alliance with the adolescent. Specifically, he describes "id alliances" and "superego alliances." An id alliance is a relationship in which the therapist overidentifies with the adolescent's propensity to act out and indulge his wants and wishes. The therapist in an id alliance plays more the role of an adult buddy and implicitly supports the adolescent's indulgence of impulses and his challenges to structure and authority. A superego alliance is a relationship in which the therapist tacitly aligns with the forces of judgment and restraint within the adolescent's own life. The therapist in such a relationship plays more the role of representative of the adult world or, even more narrowly, representative of the adolescent's parents. Meeks's advice is that the therapist work diligently to establish an "ego alliance," a relationship based on the principles of observing, getting curious about experience, and investigating deeper motives, a relationship joined to the psychoanalytic project of analysis and understanding. I have no criticism of Meeks's recommendations; his map of the therapeutic relationship is useful, and his advice is consistent with the psychoanalytic notion of how therapy works.

But, speaking for myself, I must admit that my connections with adolescent clients are not as pure as psychoanalytic psychotherapy would recommend. The therapist essentially brings his or her own person, or self, to the therapeutic encounter, and this necessarily encompasses a broader range of functioning than neutral cognitive ego functioning alone. Therapy is a real relationship between two human beings, and this is no less true with adolescent clients than with adult clients. And, just as he or she does with adult clients, a therapist working with an adolescent bears the responsibility of shepherding the relationship so that it serves the growth of the client.

To do this, I must bring the whole depth and range of my humanness to the encounter. I bring my wisdom about growing up and making it in the world, to be sure, but I also bring my willingness to be influenced, my irreverent sense of humor, my sympathy for the underdog, and my recollections of the excitement, pain, and confusion of adolescence. I am not, I must admit, especially motivated to share much of this with a stranger who is thirty years my junior. In fact, my natural inclination is to keep my more personal, livelier side to myself, just as it is my inclination to keep my advice-giving, parental, protective tendencies to myself. But in the course of therapy, as a relationship takes root, my contact with my client usually takes on greater dimensionality, a richness that allows joining and sharing as well as disagreeing and debating. The relationship becomes livelier and more faceted. It becomes the sort of contact that both brings us together and allows us our differences. In the end, if I am successful in helping my client become a more authentic and genuine self, it is inevitable that I, too, do something very similar in the context of our relationship.

Attending to the Therapeutic Field

We have all experienced having an immediate and strong reaction upon first meeting another person. Perhaps we felt attraction, repulsion, intimidation, confidence, or any of a number of interpersonal "chemical reactions." The interpersonal chemistry of an anxious and angry teenager meeting an adult therapist for the first time is particularly unstable, given the precariousness of the adolescent's sense of self, the provocative nature of overbounding strategies, and the absence of historical ground for the relationship. With relatively little cause, these fields are readily disrupted, particularly when the adolescent construes the situation as dangerous or hostile and behaves accordingly, usually with silence, anger, or defensiveness.

If there is going to be any possibility of an eventual working relationship with a client whose opening posture is angry, defensive, and uncooperative, we must begin by understanding the integrity of this behavior. There is a tendency, I think, for therapists to focus their attention on what is being "defended," and on how the behavior may be a "manipulation." If a teenager is suspected of drug use, for example, his angry reaction to an initial interview is seen as part of his disorder. There is a tendency, in other words, to discredit the adolescent's experience when it makes our job more difficult.

But if some sort of collaborative working relationship is what we are hoping to establish, then it is essential to place ourselves in the adolescent's shoes, at least as a starting point. It makes sense, and it reflects a degree of organismic integrity, for the adolescent to object to an imposed meeting with a stranger when the expectation seems to be that the adolescent will let down his guard. If he senses danger or is uncertain about the intentions of the people involved, it would be insane for him not to object. To be uncooperative in these circumstances reflects the self gestalt's natural tendency to preserve itself, and it is important that we understand it as such. Many a prospective adolescent client, finding himself in an uncertain and anxiety-provoking interview situation, will manage this discomfort by doing his best to take control of the interaction. Some adolescents do this by attempting to polarize the field in such a way that it becomes familiar and predictable—and this usually means provoking an adult to become angry, argumentative, judgmental, indifferent, and so on. To provoke this response, the adolescent may become sullen and silent, or he may become angry and insulting. The point of these postures is to organize the contact boundary as a place of separation rather than a place of connection, thereby diminishing vulnerability and the risks of exposure. Such provocative postures often mystify adults, who are inclined to judge them as excessive and unnecessary, but who, by so judging them, fail to see their effectiveness in resolving the considerable ambiguity of encountering a new adult, with uncertain intentions, in an unfamiliar situation.

Avoiding Land Mines

Most adolescent therapists have spent ample time with teenagers whose ability to frustrate and anger adults can only be described as masterful. With such youngsters, however, it is equally masterful for the therapist to get through the interview without allowing the nascent relationship to become irredeemably polarized. The initial objective with such a client is nothing so lofty as to build rapport or initiate a working alliance. It is simply to prevent a spontaneous miscarriage of the potential relationship. A colleague of mine has described the first several sessions with such clients as "walking through a minefield." The object is not grace or speed or style; the object is to get through with the therapeutic field undamaged. The most commonly encountered polarizing strategies of adolescent clients are anger, silence, and provocation. Each deserves consideration.

Anger.   Anger can be a way of making contact with another human being; and, as a general rule, the more the adolescent displays his anger in a therapy situation, the easier it is to establish a working connection. Anger is more of a potential land mine when its presence is felt but it is not openly acknowledged and owned by the client. With a cold-angry adolescent, nothing very constructive can happen in an interview situation until the anger is flushed out into the open and acknowledged. I believe that it is best not to "interpret" anger; few things intensify an adolescent's anger as much as being told by an adult what he or she is thinking or feeling. Simple, nonpresumptive, straightforward questions generally suffice: "How do you feel about coming here today?" "It seems like you don't want to talk. How come?" The longer the anger is unexpressed, the greater its power for polarizing the therapeutic field. Once anger is on the table, respectful interaction becomes possible. Almost always, the unwilling client's anger makes phenomenological sense. Who would not be angry about being coerced to talk to a stranger? Becoming interested in what the client says and acknowledging that the feelings make sense will usually diffuse the potential for polarizing the interaction.

It is not necessary or even important that the anger disappear. Angry contact is still contact. What is important is that the adolescent have an opportunity to speak his anger, and that he experience the therapist as someone willing to be affected, informed, and enlightened. In these conversations, I make a genuine effort to be as simpleminded as I can. I do not want to anticipate the adolescent's anger, and I do not want to dismiss his unique experience by saying, "Of course you're angry." I want to be so naïve that it has not occurred to me that he might be angry, and I want to hear what he says and be enlightened in the moment of his putting his experience into words. I want to experience, and I want my client to experience, the power of our connection, right now, in this moment. Anger, once heard and validated by the other, is a powerful bonding agent.

Silence. Silence is more difficult to deal with because it offers less opportunity for engagement and contact. Many therapists adopt one of two opposing strategies. Some announce, early on, "If you won't participate, there's nothing I can do. Come back if you change your mind." Others sit silently for minutes, hours, and even months, waiting for the patient to come forth. The key to managing silence in the early stages of therapy is to avoid its becoming a power struggle between therapist and client. The unwilling client often perceives therapy as adults' attempt to manipulate and control him, and silence may be his best effort to preserve a sense of integrity in the face of such a challenge. If a therapeutic relationship is to become a possibility, power struggles must be avoided at all costs. Once such a struggle develops, therapy is over, even when it has not yet begun. For the adolescent who has decided not to talk, therapy is possible only if he is given an opportunity to change his mind without losing face. This can happen if the therapist creates a situation in which the client is permitted his silence while taking in more data about the therapist and the situation. As we have already seen, including parents in initial interviews and granting the adolescent latitude for sitting back and witnessing the interaction will often accomplish this objective.

In a one-to-one interview situation, silence is more dangerous to the maintenance of the field. The rule of thumb when the therapist is confronted with a cold-silent adolescent is simple: anything but silence. For a while, the therapist may have to do all the talking—asking and answering questions, carrying the conversation, telling stories, explaining therapy, discussing background, and so on. I find that it is often helpful to take this sort of client through a detailed, structured interview composed of nonthreatening, factual questions—names, dates, educational and medical history, family background. The formal nature of such data gathering makes it less personally threatening, and the client may feel less compromised for participating. The point of any such exercise is to avoid the land mine of the silent power struggle while buying time for the adolescent to check out and acclimate to the interview situation. The longer the therapist can manage to stay in the field without its becoming polarized, the greater the chance that something will begin to happen. It is like actuarial statistics: the longer you stay alive, the longer your life expectancy. The same is true in the therapy of a resistant adolescent.

The effects of cold silence on most therapists (certainly on me) are powerful and painful. There is something intrinsically dehumanizing about another's refusal to acknowledge or respond, and even the most centered therapist is bound to feel its lethal effects in time. Our most natural tendency, I suppose, is that of Br'er Fox confronted with the silent tarbaby: to get worked up into a rage, demanding that the other at least acknowledge our existence.

If I feel polarization beginning to occur in an interview, I end the interview rather than permit this to occur, even if the interview began only a few minutes ago. I might say, "This was a good beginning. It's understandable how you feel about being here today. We can meet again in a few days." Then I proceed as if twenty-minute interviews were quite common. With one silent and uncooperative client, I had two such interviews within a week. Each was brief and superficially cordial on my part. More important, each one ended with our interactive field intact rather than polarized. At the beginning of the next session, I asked my client if he would like to meet longer this time. "If it means I don't have to come here so often, okay," he replied, and we were able to move on to something resembling an interview at this meeting.

This sort of beginning can be enormously important for the business of building rapport, especially with a youngster who is accustomed to adults who take the bait of his silent brooding by becoming annoyed, judgmental, or indifferent. Remaining interested and centered, while seeming to need no more from the client than is available at the moment, goes a long way toward establishing a field where contact can develop.

Provocation. Provocations are behaviors that seem to call for a pointed response on the part of the therapist, one that would structure the field in such a way that therapeutic contact would become unlikely or impossible. The adolescent makes a statement, or asks a question, or reports some behavior that seems to put the therapist on the spot. The most common provocations are designed to put the therapist in a parental or power position. The client who asks, "Do I have to come back?" or "Can I go now?" is organizing the field as an entrapment. If the therapist accepts this construction of the field and unwittingly steps into the role of warden, the adolescent will most certainly play out the complementary role of prisoner.

If the client is going to insist that someone play out that polarity with him or her, it is wise to arrange that someone other than the therapist fill the part—parents, court officials, school officials, or even another therapist. But if the primary therapist takes the role, he or she forfeits control of the therapeutic field to the adolescent's provocative manipulation.

Another provocation that is standard fare in the early phase of therapy is the one whereby the client places the therapist in a position to play out the role of judging adult. This usually entails acting out or relating some behavior that violates adult mores—using provocative language, lighting up a cigarette, and the like. One boy asked me at the end of our first individual session together if he could use my telephone, and then he made a show of calling a friend whom his parents, the week before in my office, had proclaimed off limits. The internal logic of such provocations is to draw the therapist into a parent–child conflict, getting the therapist to declare an alliance with one side or the other.

The therapeutic artistry lies in addressing the provocation without being drawn into it—for example, by expressing curiosity about the client's intentions or expectations, or by verbalizing my own experience of being pulled into an authority role. I am not suggesting that a therapist does not have to support limits sometimes. After all, limits are a part of life, and challenges to the client's acting out are an important aspect of therapy. But in these opening moments of the relationship, it is important not to let a provocative behavior become the determining force that organizes the relationship field.

The Work of Liking, Respecting, and Valuing

One way to look at adolescent behavior is to see it as a testing of hypotheses about the self: "Am I likable?" "Am I to be taken seriously?" "Will I have anything to offer when I enter the adult world?" In a therapy situation, the experience of being liked, being confirmed and acknowledged, and having one's value and potential confirmed amount to experiencing support. The therapist's task becomes clear when we realize that many adolescents who come for therapy go about the business of testing hypotheses in a manner different from that of their better-adjusted counterparts.

Their sense of vulnerability and the relative fragility of their self-esteem lead them to adopt a more conservative strategy as they wrestle with all these important issues of the self's acceptability. As research scientists will tell you, the most conservative test of any hypothesis is to assume the opposite of what you really want to hear and then look to see if the evidence proves your assumption wrong. This is called *testing the null hypothesis*. Troubled adolescents often adopt a strategy of testing the null hypothesis by conservatively assuming that they will *not* be liked, taken seriously, or valued by adults in their environment. Their behavior then betrays these assumptions and is designed, unconsciously, to test them for confirmation.

The unwilling client may behave in a manner that is manifestly designed to provoke rejection. He may propose views that strain the credulity of the most open-minded adult, or he may disdainfully dismiss any suggestion that he is interested in participating in the adult-run "real world." Rather than approaching a new encounter with the vulnerability of wondering whether they will be accepted, these adolescents adopt a behavioral style that states, "You don't accept me, do you?" The behavior may be frankly rude, patently silly, or absurd. Its intention is to resolve the ambiguity of the relational field, to establish quickly where people stand with each other.

In school consultations, I have often had the experience of meeting with a group of teachers in a conference about some child who has become a troublemaker and has managed to alienate just about everybody. Sooner or later, I get around to asking, "Does anyone here *like* this child?" More often than not, a lone hand will tentatively rise from some previously silent corner of the room. (After all, it is not popular to admit that you are fond of the student who is driving everyone else up the wall.) That teacher, the one who has mysteriously managed to cut through the negativity, who is able to see the child so effectively camouflaged to others, often becomes the key player in any plan to help the student. This teacher is invariably the one individual who has passed the test of the troublemaker's null hypothesis, and who accordingly makes contact with the student on an entirely different level than the other adults do. There are schools of therapy that suggest that liking clients is irrelevant to the essential work of psychotherapy. I believe that nothing could be further from the truth. Most adolescents have antennae that are sensitively attuned to the subtle valences of the interpersonal field, and the experience of finding themselves accepted or appreciated in some unexpected way by a therapist can spell the entire difference between therapy that succeeds and therapy that fails.

The point, of course, is that certain clients make an art of being unlikable, and with these clients the therapist has to work. The work most often takes the form of letting go of conventional frames of reference and pushing oneself to see behavior in a more phenomenological (and necessarily more empathic and compassionate) light. The boy who flips off his English teacher as he storms from the classroom is also the boy who struggles to hide his frustration as a learner and who has felt singled out and shamed whenever his teacher commented publicly on his failure to arrive in class prepared. The girl we are interviewing who at every opportunity rolls her eyes and mutters, "God, these questions are so stupid!" is the same one who feels coerced and manipulated by most of the adults in her life, and she feels certain that our questions are a trap for exposing her shortcomings.

Since difficult clients typically hide those aspects of self that might be appealing and engaging, offering in their stead behaviors designed to discourage adults, a peculiar combination of presence, perceptiveness, imperturbability, and determination is required of an adolescent therapist. The therapist must be able to see, or at least imagine, who the client is behind his or her veneer. This requires faith as much as a knowledge of adolescent personality formation and dynamics. It means being present not only to the client's behavior but also to the *meaning* of that behavior. Perhaps most of all, it means being able to sidestep the highly valenced force field of ordinary social interaction.

The work required to approximate these skills is primarily work on oneself. When interviewing unwilling adolescents, I occasionally find myself feeling irritated, annoyed, insulted, or summarily dismissed. I may feel pulled to challenge prematurely and am almost always surprised at what has been stirred up in me. The work in these moments is to reengage a certain way of looking, a certain way of organizing my perceptual field. It is analogous to the hovering attention one gives to an ambiguous-figure drawing while scanning the background waiting for the hidden rabbit to emerge from the bushes. With the difficult adolescent client, I presume there exists a "hidden figure," a scared and uncertain child who is struggling to establish believable boundaries and preserve a precarious sense of integrity. And my faith that this figure will emerge from the tangle of provocations and defenses is what allows me to hang around long enough to begin the work of establishing a connection.

Confrontation and Contact

Much of the connecting work described so far has emphasized, implicitly at least, the supportive dimensions of the therapeutic relationship. We have seen the critical importance of the adolescent's experience of this field, this relationship, as one where trust and respect support the development of an emergent self. But this is only part of the story of therapeutic growth.

In adolescent development generally, much growth is prompted by the experience of limits and boundaries, and by the frustrations and accommodations that inevitably follow. We have seen that this experience is most directly mediated by the parents' range of contact skills. Articulating expectations, holding to values, saying no, all within a context of caring and belonging, teach the developing child the rudiments of differentiated contact. This learning is highly contextual, which means that it is absorbed simply as a matter of course, in the way life arranges itself around the developing child. Adolescents learn that parental expectations must be taken into account, that wants must often be compromised, that love and support have their terms and limits, and that there is always another side to a story.

Youngsters who find their way into therapy are often precisely those adolescents who have not had the benefit of competent limit setting or enough exposure to caring and well-bounded adults, or who, for any of a host of reasons, have not been able to profit from such exposure. When the family's resources are insufficient to the adolescent's task of accepting limits and tolerating differences, the adolescent often ends up in a residential treatment facility. There, the context of day-to-day life is managed in such a way as to promote this sort of learning. Typically in residential settings, challenge and confrontation are viewed as essential components of the treatment process. It is usually a straightforward matter of pointing out some piece of behavior as unreasonable, defensive, provocative, or headed for trouble. Glasser's (1965) reality therapy, probably the most dominant therapeutic model in residential treatment facilities, is based on this straightforward and powerful practice.

In individual psychotherapy, however, it is important to understand the differences between confrontation as limit setting, which is a task for parents and residential workers (and for other adults whose job it is to manage the adolescent's life situation or context) and confrontation as a contact skill, which touches on the role of the psychotherapist. Confrontation, as a component of psychotherapy, amounts essentially to fostering the client's capacity for differentiating contact skills. Healthy contact includes the potential for relaxing boundaries and joining the other and the potential for firming and sharpening boundaries, highlighting difference and individuality. With disembedding-stage clients, this range of contact skills is characteristically underdeveloped, and it is the primary task of the therapist to generate a field where both these dimensions will be cultivated.

The psychotherapist who works with adolescents needs to become skilled at the art of confrontation—the knack of bringing up and talking about difficult things *without compromising the quality of the contact*—that is, without provoking either superficial confluence or angry polarization. When an adolescent responds to a therapist in either manner, it effectively dulls the contact between them, and their interactions from that point on are likely to become stereotyped, predictable, and often lifeless. Thus the work of therapeutic confrontation is really the work of introducing *differences* into the relational field and teaching the adolescent first to tolerate them and, in time, to grow from them. It is an axiom of human relationships that when individuals manage their differences with awareness, respect, and tolerance—that is, through authentic contact—they cannot help influencing each other. They cannot help accommodating their differences, learning from them, and, in that process, beginning to change and be changed by the other.

How is this done with a touchy and disagreeable adolescent? How does it look and sound? By way of illustration, let me describe my work with a generally negative and uncooperative teenage girl. Amy was an obese, headstrong fifteen-year-old from an intact but extremely dysfunctional family. Home was an intensely charged place, where explosive conflict occurred on a regular basis. Her mother was in therapy. She was on medication for depression and anxiety and had been for years. A brittle woman, she cared deeply about her children, but her involvement with them was punctuated by explosive arguments, followed by periods of hurt and withdrawal. Most of the trouble started with Amy's twelve-year-old brother, who had just been placed in a hospital school at the time I first saw Amy, and who came home only on weekends. He was described by everyone as out of control, unable to accept limits or discipline with any sort of grace.

Amy's father was a mild-mannered, accommodating man who tried to calm the home front by pleasing everyone. Financially successful, he often attempted to appease family members and calm the waters with expensive gifts, vacations, and the like. The net effect was painful to witness—a very indulged and very unhappy family of four.

In the middle of all this, Amy had emerged in early adolescence as a bossy, angry, highly defiant young woman. She had begun to use the family car when her parents were out of town (she was too young for a license), and she insisted that she would do so again if she felt like it. She was extremely and relentlessly critical of the way her parents managed the family (especially her younger brother), and, when seriously challenged, regularly erupted into rage-filled tirades. In terms of contact skills, Amy was more than capable of tolerating differences—*hers*, that is, and no one else's.

I ended up seeing Amy in an unusual set of circumstances. Her

parents were engaged in weekly family sessions at her brother's therapeutic school (sessions that Amy refused to attend), and she had
agreed to see me briefly as part of her plea bargaining for taking the
car: if she came to see me, her grounding (ineffective as her parents
were at enforcing it) would be lifted.

"No offense, Doc," she said to me at our first meeting (and insin-
cerely at that, because she certainly meant to offend), "but this is a
bunch of bullshit."

She might have a point, I conceded, but I had not made up my
mind yet. Amy was willing, with little encouragement, to talk ("rail"
would be more accurate) about her impossible little brother and her
hopelessly incompetent parents. And she did so at length, as long as
I was quiet and listened. When I gently challenged an assumption or
asked if there might be another side to the story, she flatly declared
"No," or "Absolutely not." She was not, to put it mildly, leaving
much room for differences of opinion.

But other aspects of Amy's presentation caught my attention. She
was bright, and in her diatribes against her parents she had hit more
than a few nails on their heads, especially where her parents' misman-
agement of their parental duties was concerned. I kept asking her why
was she so interested as to have subjected her family's process to such
rigorous analysis. This was where I issued my first real challenge.

"I don't think you're the family delinquent at all," I told her. (Her
parents had taken her to the police.) "I think people have got you all
wrong. I think you're the family *therapist.*"

"I don't think so," she replied sarcastically, disputing this observation on the grounds that it implied she *cared* about her family.

"We'll just have to disagree about this," I countered, letting our
disagreement hang in the air between us.

We continued this exchange, on and off, for several weeks. She
would rail against her parents, and I would bring up the issue of what
her role was, pointing out at times that she understood the broader
topic of family dynamics as well as some professionals did (which was
flattery but also truth). She would insist that she did not care about
the rest of them, and I would stubbornly insist that it did not matter;
after all, she talked and thought like a family therapist.

"And what if I am, as you put it, a 'family therapist'?" she asked
at the beginning of our fourth session.

"Well, I am, too," I said, "and I'd be happy to compare notes."

And so, without quite agreeing to do so, this is essentially what we did for the next several weeks. We talked, we debated, we shared observations and speculations, not just about her family but about families in general, about the do's and don'ts of parenting, about the strange forces that keep families together, about the growing-up needs of teenage children. And the significant thing here, the *therapeutic* aspect of our meeting, lay not in the content of our discussions or even in the feelings she shared about her family's craziness but rather in the *form* of our contact, in Amy's emerging capacity to tolerate (even enjoy) differences in a contact field with an adult.

Only a few weeks later, Amy announced summarily that she was through seeing me. Our talks were interesting, she conceded, but unnecessary—a waste of time. ("No offense," she added.) She also said, rather incidentally, that she had negotiated a truce with her parents the previous week, having come to the following conclusion: "The fighting isn't worth it. They're gonna do what they're gonna do, anyway. And I figured, why not make it easier on myself?"

My challenge to Amy had to do with the *meaning* of her behavior; it is more classic and conventional in adolescent therapy to challenge clients on the *wisdom* of their behavior. Decisions (or nondecisions) to act out anger, defiance, helplessness; experimentation with drugs, alcohol, sexuality, risk taking: these are the usual fare of therapeutic confrontation. Time and again these issues arise in the context of therapy, and when they do, the therapist's ability to challenge without polarizing the adolescent, keeping the field intact as a contact milieu, proves invaluable. On many occasions, I have persuaded clients to look more objectively at their behavior (for example, by assenting to an assessment for chemical dependency), having first established a therapeutic field where differences were tolerable and debate was experienced as a mode of contact.[1]

---

[1] It is important to recognize, however, that psychotherapy is not an effective primary intervention with serious acting out, especially drug abuse and dependency. Contextual interventions that have the necessary leverage to curtail the dangerous behavior are far preferable in these situations. Nonetheless, it is unavoidable that in the course of psychotherapy these sorts of issues are going to surface, and insofar as it is deemed clinically responsible to continue individual therapy (as opposed to, say, terminating therapy and initiating drug treatment), the maintenance of the contact field is essential.

Disembedding-Stage Therapeutics

Psychotherapeutic work has a characteristic style and feel. With adolescents whose relationships with adults are generally strained and awkward, the adolescent adopts a client posture in the interest of dialogue and self-discovery. This is more the objective than the starting point. In the course of this enterprise, there are therapeutic strategies that will help us realize this objective.

Structuring Initial Interviews

With disembedding-stage clients especially, it is generally helpful to provide some structure to the opening sessions. I usually begin the first individual session by asking how my client thinks the previous meetings (with the parents) have gone. Does he think they went well? Were they what he expected? Did he get a chance to say everything that was on his mind? I then bring up the referral issues (however much they were discussed previously with the parents present), and I ask to hear, or hear again, the adolescent's view of these matters.

Whoever has made the referral has defined "the problem" in a way that made sense to him or her: "He is depressed," "She is having serious mood swings," "His temper is getting him into trouble," "She is doing poorly in school." But "the problem," so defined, often does not quite fit the adolescent's experience of the situation, and my inquiries may be the initial window into this adolescent's world. In many cases, the therapist's management of this window can have a dramatic impact on the relationship that is beginning. The simple willingness to listen respectfully to the client's own views and feelings sends a powerful message about how this relationship might be different from existing relationships in the adolescent's life, implicitly confirming the adolescent's tentative self as real and substantial. The tactical decision to explore "the problem" (versus setting it aside) depends on the heuristic value of doing so. When pushing this discussion seems likely to polarize the budding relationship, entrenching the client in the role of child or delinquent, it may be best to let it go for the time being, in favor of content more supportive of rapport and connection.

Once the referral problem has been addressed, my interest shifts to the phenomenological understanding of this individual and his or her world. Friends, family process and background, hobbies, music, books, sports—anything that furnishes the adolescent's world—are all legitimate topics for dialogue. Therapists who are familiar only with adult therapy are sometimes disconcerted by this focus on external experience but with disembedding-stage adolescents in particular it is the price of admission.

Early in an evaluation, it is valuable to invite the adolescent to shift the focus away from other people and outer-world involvements and toward the interior of self experience. The client's response to these invitations gives an important first glance at his readiness to make this shift and helps us envision the nature of the therapy work that lies ahead. Some adolescents respond to these invitations uncomprehendingly; others, reticently or ambivalently. Still others make the shift readily, even eagerly. I usually issue some fairly blunt solicitation, as early as the opportunity presents itself. To a thirteen-year-old boy telling me about a recent family fight or some difficulty with a peer, I might say, "What about you? What goes on inside—you know, your personal feelings and thoughts—when all this stuff is going on outside you?" Whether he distinguishes a phenomenology of "outside" and "inside" or feels ready to share his private experience will often be apparent at this point and give me cues for the task ahead.

With disembedding-stage clients, it can be very helpful to use something that structures the dialogue in such a way that it becomes more focused on experience of self. Oaklander (1978) sometimes uses projective instruments or astrological "reports" to focus dialogue on the self, giving her client a chance to accept or reject the statements offered. As a psychologist by training, my bias is toward using psychological tests, provided that they are not experienced by the client as threatening or intrusive. I generally use the High School Personality Questionnaire (HSPQ) because it is nonpathologically oriented and can be easily and nonthreateningly presented to the client as a source of hypotheses about himself. Several years ago, I authored a computerized interpretation of the HSPQ results, a report written to the adolescent himself. If my client expresses some interest in this feedback, I provide this report, and we go over it together. The report serves implicitly as an interview structure, orienting our dialogue to the adolescent and his world. The advantage of such an approach, especially with a client who is not disposed or able to focus reflectively on himself, is that it does promote a reflective focus but without requiring me to challenge or confront the client prematurely.

I find several interview themes particularly worthwhile in the early stages. One is the theme of the adolescent's family. Some of the techniques originated by family therapy, such as genograms and family maps, can be helpful here. I sometimes give a client a large sheet of paper and ask him to diagram his family, helping him articulate the patterns he experiences: who allies with whom, where the power lies, what behaviors trigger other behaviors, and so on. With some clients, especially younger and more concrete youths, I may ask for floor plans of the house, learning as the clients draw them the location of bedrooms, finding out where people spend their time, exploring traffic patterns, and so on. These concrete issues lead quite naturally to interpersonal themes of family relatedness. For most adolescents, it is enormously helpful to begin seeing the families in perspective, and this can be for them a relatively unthreatening way of beginning to reveal their world.

Another thing I often try to do within the first several interviews is to explore the client's social network. Traditional sociometric diagrams suffice, helping the adolescent articulate the subtleties of his or her social landscape. An adolescent's response to inquiries about friends is often revealing, particularly because friends are invested with so much narcissism at this age. Some clients are evasive and vague. Others discuss their friends eagerly and are psychologically "touched" by my interest in their associates. Many adolescents have different types of friends, and the topography of these types is likely to be a map of the internal topography of self. Discussion about friends can reveal attitudes toward parts of the self, integration of or dissociation from various components of experience, conflicts, dilemmas, and so on.

Working Within the Projection

Regardless of how well we initiate the individual work with disembedding-stage clients, we will be required to contend with their characteristic unreadiness to identify and share their inner experience. In contrast to work with developmentally more mature clients, therapy at this stage takes the capacity to focus on the self as its *goal* rather than its starting point. With some clients, this capacity may develop gradually over the course of the therapy, ushering in a progression to the stages of interiority and integration. With other clients, the inability (or unwillingness) to dwell on experience of self will be a working parameter for the entire therapy. In either case, the therapist of adolescent clients must accommodate this state of affairs, this instinctive focusing of awareness away from the "I" boundary and toward the "out there" of the world and other people.

Much has been written, particularly from a psychoanalytic viewpoint, about the role of projection in psychopathology. But, as we have seen, to some extent projection serves to regulate the newly synthesized self's exposure to the potentially destructuring forces in its environment. Projection pushes the tension of self-awareness and contact away from the self's intrapsychic space and onto its boundary with the environment, reducing the experience of internal doubt and conflict that otherwise might occur. With many adolescent clients, the tendency to focus experience away from the self does not represent a specific defensive maneuver, in the psychoanalytic sense of obscuring some particular neurotic conflict. It has more the quality of a generalized *experiential style* whose purpose is to maintain the security and integrity of the fledgling adolescent self.

Working within the projection means accepting the premise of the adolescent's organization of awareness "out there." The adolescent finds it more natural to describe his or her friends, siblings, parents, guitar lessons, bedroom, school; and so on, than to speak in terms of feelings and reflections. This is not avoidance; it is revelation. As van den Berg (1972) writes, "If we want to gain insight into another person, his condition, nature, habits or disturbances, we should not inquire first about his introspectively accessible, subjective account of his observations. This account, although essentially possible, does not, as a rule, contain much information. We get an impression of a person's character, of his subjectivity, of his nature and his condition when we ask him to describe the objects which he calls his own" (p. 39). It is a self-defeating attitude to view the adolescent's outward focus as simply defensive, concealing intrapsychic reality, rather than as a window into the adolescent's world. The therapist who accepts the projective framework of the adolescent client's experience, and who then proceeds within that framework to build a working relationship, will find ample opportunity to do the rich work of psychotherapy.

Consider Jeremy, a fourteen-year-old struggling to disembed from a very disturbed and disturbing family field. Jeremy's family field included a younger brother, Adam, twelve; a mother he described as "too emotional" (an understatement, since she was given to loud eruptions and explosive retaliation whenever she felt "under attack," in her own words); a father who thought he was "perfect" (which may have been an overstatement, but not by much); and a three-year-old divorce that was as angry, crazy, and blaming as they come. Jeremy's functioning was below par in many ways. His emotional state found expression in a panoply of nervous twitches and facial tics (which surfaced like clockwork whenever the subject of his parents' relationship came up), and in periodic explosive rages, usually toward his younger brother.

But, for all this, Jeremy stated flatly that his parents' relationship (and their respective attempts to use the children as weaponry and ammunition) did not bother him at all ("I'm used to it," he said), nor was there any need for him to be in therapy, other than the minor benefit of getting his mother somewhat off his back. Jeremy clung tenaciously to these opinions, from start to finish.

In therapy, Jeremy was projectively riveted on his younger brother, whom he venomously denounced as the source of everything bad. He was wild, uncontrollable, and mean; he did nothing around the house but whine, provoke, and stir their mother into rages. *He* was responsible for their parents' breakup because he had been so unmanageable that they had fought about him constantly.

My early efforts—in fact, *all* my efforts—to shift the focus onto Jeremy himself (how he felt about the divorce, about his parents' endless childish feuding, about how angry *that* might have made him) proved frustratingly fruitless, as is so frequently the case with projecting, disembedding-stage clients. No, he insisted with maddening certainty, his brother was the problem, and that was that.

What can be done with such a client? Usually when a projective content becomes an unproductive preoccupation, I challenge it in a fashion commensurate with the strength of the relationship. I may simply change the topic, or ask if it is *really* helping to go on and on about this subject. Or, if we are solidly enough connected, I may admit that the topic is getting a bit boring and ask if we can find some problem that we can do something about. And all the while, I will continue poking around and nudging our focus back toward the client's "I" boundary, asking him from time to time how things make him *feel* and whether there may be something about *himself* that nags at him or makes him mad. But, since we are talking about projecting, disembedding-stage clients, the answer will always come back "No, I'm fine, thank you. It's just my damn brother that bothers me."

A strategy I considered with Jeremy was to bring his younger brother into a session, so that I could enter and share this dimension of his world with more contact and more realism, and less through the medium of his projection. But Jeremy would not have it: his brother would only embarrass him if he were brought into a session.

What I did with Jeremy, whose projection was nearly obsessional, was to announce that we would begin each session, for at least twenty minutes, with a report on his brother. I wanted to hear every gory detail about the most recent episode of this impossible brother's behavior. And, after twenty minutes or so, if Jeremy had not already dropped the subject spontaneously (which he began to do as soon as I joined him in his obsession), I would say, "Enough. Let's switch to something more interesting for both of us." And we would.

Thus with Jeremy, as with most projecting clients, my first task was to get the projective lens to dilate, so that we could begin to explore more corners of his world. And, over the course of several months, we did just that, talking about the mundane concerns of Jeremy's week-to-week life. He had joined a record club and was experimenting with his tastes in music. He was considering ways to earn money—perhaps caddying at a local golf club. He was losing interest in model cars, his avocation for several years, but was beginning to get interested in running and was considering trying out for the school's track team.

We talked a bit about his facial tics, when I brought them up, which I did casually and in moments that seemed opportune. He would roll his eyes to "press against a dead spot" because "it seemed to stretch something" and ease the tension he felt almost constantly in his head, but he would not discuss the meaning of his tics. Once, when we were talking about his parents, his twitching increased dramatically over the course of several minutes, leading him to acknowledge "butterflies" in his stomach. I wondered out loud what it was all about. "This damned puzzle," he said, holding in his hands a difficult wooden puzzle that he had been absentmindedly fiddling with as he spoke.

"No," I challenged. "You love puzzles."

"The yearbook," he then suggested. "I haven't figured out what to put under my picture, and it's been bothering me."

I let the topic change, and as it drifted away from his parents, he became noticeably more relaxed, and his twitching stopped. A few minutes later I pointed that out, and again I wondered out loud if the twitching might have had something to do with what we had been talking about. This time—and it was the closest he came in the entire course of therapy to reflecting on the emotional ground of his behavior—he said, "Maybe."

In retrospect, Jeremy's projective focus and the doggedness with which he clung to it made all the sense in the world to me. He lived in a family where *no one* owned or took responsibility for his or her own interiority, where no one acknowledged being mobilized by his or her *own* feelings, and where everyone was just reacting to everyone else. What seems so obvious to me now is how dangerous—indeed, how crazy-making—it would be in such a family to open up the vulnerable inner zone of the self. For children in families where interiority is not modeled, supported, or treated respectfully, its emergence (if it is to emerge at all) must await the successful disembedding of an adequately *bounded* self from the family field. Only then, when inside and outside can be choicefully segregated, is it safe to allow the aware emergence and growth of the self's interiority.

As I learned this lesson over again with Jeremy, I relaxed and journeyed with him through his ordinary world of music, caddying, and running. And each of these themes, once I sincerely joined him there, with no hidden psychotherapeutic agenda, began to loop back naturally toward concerns that were closer to the heart. The record club, it turned out, was a bit of a problem because his mother insisted on knowing about every penny he spent, and she used every conversation about money to discuss his father's stinginess and manipulation of child-support payments. Caddying was a tough decision for Jeremy, and he came to the conclusion that it was too much waiting around and not enough money for the time invested. But, in the end, he decided to do it anyway because his father did not want him to, and so if he decided *not* to do it, his mother would go on and on about how Jeremy was just letting his father make his decisions for him. Jeremy and I agreed how crazy it was when something as simple as a decision about whether to caddy or not could be made so infuriatingly complicated when parents could not let go of their hatred for each other.

So how was Jeremy managing to keep himself sane, I wondered with genuine amazement.

"Right now, it's running," he answered.

And since I knew all about that, having once myself survived a difficult stretch of life with the help of running, we shared in great detail our mutual experience of the goodness and satisfaction of running, and our ideas about training regimens, shoes, running injuries, competitive strategies, and the like. Running became important for Jeremy. He began to compete in local races, usually finishing near the lead for his age group. But, more important, he often got to the race site on his own, by bicycle, and reflected later that this had made him realize that he could really do things on his own. Indeed, what became clear was that Jeremy was beginning to do more and more things—simple, ordinary, day-to-day things—more under his own direction; that is, he was doing the work of disembedding. He no longer felt compelled to be confluent with his mother when she raged against his father. His disengagement from his parents' field became less the *posture* it had been when we first met and more a *reality* that supported the integrity of his experience of self. He stopped twitching. He fought less with his brother and more with his mother (but less explosively) about issues that were practical, real, and wholly appropriate for a boy almost fifteen years old.

And so, returning full circle to the question that led me to Jeremy in the first place, what can be done with a projectively focused disembedding-stage client that constitutes psychotherapy? Some of the more interesting possibilities will be discussed in the next chapter, where we will look at adolescents who are closer to the developmental cusp of interiority. Here, I want to belabor the obvious, since it is so fundamental and inelegant that we sometimes lose faith in its healing power: we have *conversations with the child about his world*. And these conversations reveal his world to him, and his role in it, in ways that are new, enlightening, and generally supportive of the developmental process of disembedding an authored self. As we do that, we are teaching the client a new form of contact with people outside the family, a way of engaging that nourishes and emboldens the self and that can be taken beyond therapy and used with other real-world adults. Two aspects of these therapeutic conversations are worth emphasizing. One has to do with the power of fantasy and role playing with these clients. The other has to do with a dimension of therapeutic conversation that I call ego tutoring.

Fantasy and Role Playing with the Projecting Adolescent

Even resistant adolescent clients often cooperate readily in constructing and playing out a fantasy scenario. Suppose a boy brings in the following vignette:

> My science teacher, Mr. Samson, comes up to me for no reason at all and starts ragging on me for not doing this stupid assignment that no one else in the class did, either. So I say, "No, I didn't do it," and he sends me out of the room for no fucking reason, because he's such a complete asshole. So I let him know what I think of him. I flipped him off.

Suppose further that he has been sent to the dean of discipline for his behavior, and he now relates the story from a very defensive and projective posture. Our conversation might go like this:

Therapist: So let's bring the dean of discipline into the room. Where would he sit?

Client: Anywhere.

T: What does the dean of discipline look like?

C: Bald dude.

T: If I asked him what his complaint about you is, how would he answer me?

C: He'd say, "This kid's a definite juvenile delinquent."

T: Seriously? If he did, I'd argue with him about that. What are his real complaints?

C: He'd say I'm cutting classes and mouthing off to teachers. But it's all bullshit, because (getting angry) they don't even know what Mr. Samson did to me.

T: Hold on. Slow down. So if I could get the dean to sit there and listen for five minutes, what would you say to him? Go ahead, tell him.

C: I'd tell it like it really happened. But he wouldn't listen, so this whole thing is bullshit. This is stupid.

T: Well, this is just fantasy, so go ahead and tell him.

C: (Looks down, shakes his head from side to side.)

T: Maybe you're right. Maybe you couldn't get him to listen. But is there anybody else who might be willing to listen? Which one of your teachers would be the most willing to hear your side of the story?

C: Mrs. Lockley.

T: So go ahead. Bring her into the room. Where does she sit? Tell her your side of the story.

C: (Recounts his version of the incident.)

T: What is it she would be able to understand that the other adults aren't listening to?

C: She'd listen, that's all. She doesn't jump to conclusions like asshole Samson.

T: What does she see about you that Samson doesn't?

C: She knows I'm not a delinquent.

T: How does she know that? I mean, what do you show her that you don't show Samson?

C: (Smiling) She thinks I'm funny.

T: So you show her your humor. And she likes that. So I'm wondering, if we were all sitting here and I asked Mrs. Lockley to tell the dean what you're *really* like, what would she say to him? Go ahead, say it like she would say it.

Therapy issues related to support and confrontation, and even the capacity to objectively describe one's own behavior, are often easier to engage with when we accommodate the adolescent's inclination to focus externally. The impromptu construction of such fantasy scenarios allows the adolescent to focus on an imagined external milieu rather than on an internal milieu and lets other people speak his experience for him. Furthermore, the therapist has an access to the fantasized characters that he or she may not have to the adolescent's "real self." The client may summarily dismiss the therapist's stated willingness to be objective and listen seriously. But the same client may accept this support indirectly as the therapist "interacts" with some character in the projected scenario.

Ego Tutoring

In the overall context of the emerging adolescent self's engagement with its environment, the term *ego functioning* refers to the self's capacity to choose actively and deliberately from the array of possibilities for awareness and action and, in so doing, to heighten its own sense of agency, identity, and purposefulness (Perls, Hefferline, and Goodman, 1951, pp. 378–379). In this mode of functioning, the self emerges from the thrall of the compelling field forces of its environment by identifying with or ruling out different possibilities, by selecting goals, and by identifying plans and means for achieving them. As Perls, Hefferline, and Goodman point out, this is not an interruption of the self's spontaneous functioning but rather a taking possession of it. In other words, the self's ego functioning generates the experiences of ownership and responsibility that are so central to adolescent development.

The term *ego tutoring* refers to the dimension of the therapeutic work that is perhaps most common to all approaches and methods of counseling and psychotherapy with teenagers. It is nothing dramatic or fancy. It is more like Socratic tutoring than like the provocative or creative interactions that we sometimes associate with psychotherapy. In ego tutoring, the therapist essentially, and in a variety of ways, prompts the client to stop his or her ongoing process and make more deliberate choices about it. This involves helping the client develop a repertoire of basic ego functions:

- Describing and labeling

  Are you saying that your parents are so caught up in

slamming each other that they don't notice how it affects you and your brother?

It strikes me that you have really studied your family very carefully. You've made yourself an expert on how things work in your family.

Are you saying you're the *family delinquent*?

Let's see: you can handle kids your own age, but not adults. You're never sure if they're going to blow you off or make you feel insignificant. Am I getting that right?

It sounds like riding your bike to these races really matters to you. What's different about that from the way things used to be? How do *you* feel different when you get yourself to the race by yourself?

- Anticipating

  What does your school do when kids cut classes?

  Make a prediction. What will your parents say when they find out?

  Imagine yourself a month from now. What could this lead to?

  Have you thought through the consequences of this choice?

- Testing reality

  How do you know your science teacher doesn't like you? What's your proof?

  So you run away, and you manage to get to Tennessee. Then what?

- Planning

  How are you going to get this band started? What are the different things you have to make happen? What's the first step?

- Weighing alternatives

What's the part of you that wants to break up with him saying? What's the part that wants to stay with him saying?

If you decide to talk to your father about his drinking, what outcomes can you imagine? If you don't talk to him, what's likely to happen? How will you feel in either case?

These are interventions of the simplest order, but they are powerful when the adolescent is receptive to being influenced. This sort of stopping and thinking may be what adults have been urging this particular adolescent to do all along, but without a ground of support and neutrality. Such exhortations are not likely to have had much impact.

These are skills that some adults are inclined to take for granted, forgetting that the adolescent self is only now developing its capacity to stand outside its embeddedness in immediate process, bracket its impulsive reactivity to the environment, and assume a more deliberate and self-possessed mode of engaging the world. In the context of a carefully crafted working relationship, this tutoring of ego functioning—stopping and thinking; reflecting on motives, intentions, and wants; looking ahead; anticipating consequences—sometimes has the most dramatic impact.

Conclusion

Most adolescents, I believe, size adults up quickly. In the opening moments of an initial interaction, they may carefully assay the safety, level of interest, rigidity or flexibility, disposition to judge, confidence or uncertainty, anxiety or comfort, and sincerity or phoniness of the adult whom they are encountering. Many such initial encounters are easy and natural, but many are not. There is something odd and unsettling about an arranged encounter between two persons years apart in age and experience, neither of whom has chosen the other. But this is the starting point of most psychotherapy with adolescents. It is fair to say that the adolescent therapist is tested, not just by his or her knowledge of individual development, adolescent culture, and family dynamics, but also by the elusive and unsung ability to have his or her prospective clients become, in fact, clients.

There is no one correct way to go about the business of building relationships with adolescent clients, and I certainly do not wish to prescribe any of the ideas and methods that I have described. What I do most of the time with adolescent clients is try to get to know them, and I have described some of the ways I have learned to do this over time. I have struggled with this challenge over the years of my professional practice, and I fully expect to continue struggling with it as long as I work with adolescents.

CHAPTER ELEVEN

The Inner World of the Adolescent: The Psychotherapy of Interiority and Integration

When disembedding from the family field goes well enough, adolescence involves the emergence and deepening of inner experience, a growing awareness of interiority. Supporting the transition from disembedding-stage boundary negotiations to interiority-stage awareness is a major dimension of much adolescent psychotherapy. Many of our clients are on the verge of this growth but need a sufficiently safe interpersonal context to support its emergence. Others have opened up their inner worlds in an oppressively private way and need the presence and witness of another person in order to integrate it. With many adolescents, the work of therapy is to help them discover their interiority, a sort of therapeutic involvement that requires high activity and creativity on the part of the therapist. With others, what is required is high receptivity, the simple but powerful offering of a safe environment for articulating, sharing, understanding, and integrating what is silently borne alone by the self.

We are touching here on an essential, core dimension of all psychotherapy: the creation of an interpersonal field where the interiority of the self can emerge, be fleshed out, and become whole. Wheeler (1994) has written about this aspect of Gestalt therapy with children, pointing out that the inner world of the self is inextricably a function of its interpersonal history and milieu:

> The articulation of this "inner" world, the world of feelings, desires, thoughts and fears, wishes, doubts, appetites and fantasies, is not an obvious thing we are born with, *but is itself a developmental achievement*, at least as much as knowledge and exploration of the "external" world is learned and achieved over time, and by dint of considerable active energy and work. And more than this, even the skills and structures involved

in getting to know one's internal, subjective world are themselves developmental achievements. That is, we aren't born
knowing ourselves, or knowing how to know ourselves. All
that too is learned, *and the process by which it is learned is an
intersubjective process.* We learn how to be curious about ourselves, *always and only* through the benevolent, stimulating,
empathic curiosity and interest of another person. [p. 17]

This, then, is the objective of interiority-stage work with adolescents: to make therapeutic conversation into personal, even intimate, conversation. But, as I have pointed out repeatedly, this does
not happen easily with a great percentage of the adolescents who
come for psychotherapy, and so the artistry of the work lies in making
just this sort of conversation possible.

To some extent, as we shall see, the adolescent's interiority
emerges naturally in a therapeutic field where matters of disembedding have been carefully attended to—where respect, confirmation,
and tolerance of difference have been cultivated. In many instances,
however, more is required; active solicitation and careful guidance
are necessary to establish the client's contact with the nascent interior world. The variations on this work are the subject of this chapter.

Interiority as a Natural Outgrowth of Disembedding

In some instances, the therapeutics of disembedding—of cultivating
a point of view and a voice, and of learning to be in the field as a
bounded, interacting self—lead rather spontaneously to awareness
and expression of interior experience. I am reminded of Dwayne, a
seventeen-year-old who felt that coming to therapy meant that he
might be "mentally ill." Much of Dwayne's meaning-making activity
was shaped by his incorporating the implicit and explicit views of his
large, enmeshed family. He was also exceptionally shy and nervous.
When I met him, he could speak of his family members only in terms
of how much he loved and appreciated them.

When we began our work together, Dwayne seemed committed
to giving me what I wanted; when he could not figure that out, he
seemed as frozen as a deer staring into a car's headlights. He had
hardly a clue about the relevance and value of his *own* experience.
Dwayne organized himself habitually around the introjects delivered

by significant adults in his environment, even when these were not useful. When his baseball coach told him to charge all ground balls, Dwayne did just that, charging balls indiscriminately and disregarding, in the moment, his own perceptual assessment of how to make the play. His fielding deteriorated immediately, and he was soon dropped back to the second team. Even so, he continued to charge ground balls in this fashion.

On the basis of an accumulated anthology of introjects, Dwayne blocked and buried much of what was native to his own experience. Around the age of fifteen, he had begun to synthesize a self-picture in relationship to his family, as most teens do, but he did it according to the introjected reality of his childhood. He began to "understand" himself and his role in the family, but his "understanding" was to "realize" that he was dumber and less adequate than his siblings, to "see clearly" his failure in school and at sports, and so on. His self had begun to organize experience, in other words, but *without* properly appropriating this function—that is, without taking *ownership* of such synthetic making of meaning *from a particular point of view.* Dwayne had begun to "see the larger picture"; unfortunately, it was not *his* picture.

For months, our work together had the unmistakable look and feel of disembedding-stage therapy. I made myself intensely interested in what *he* had to say, supporting him in carving out his own space, both in the family field and in his relationship with me.

"Finish that sentence," I would often encourage him when his soft utterances trailed off in mid-sentence.

"But I have no thought," he would protest. "My mind is just blank."

"Finish the sentence," I would insist gently, and to his surprise, he would do so, invariably revealing some blossom of self, some nascent if fragmentary point of view.

The shift that I wish to highlight here came only after Dwayne had begun to relax and find his voice in my presence. I had been teaching him how to complain, something he almost never allowed himself to do. I had given him the task of finding something to complain about in the therapy. After considerable hemming and hawing, he "complained" that therapy had not yet relieved him of the persistent pressure and pain that he felt in his chest (something he had never mentioned to me before).

This was wonderful! Finally, there was a symptom I could sink my therapeutic teeth into. I pushed Dwayne to attend to the pain and see what happened. Nothing happened. I urged him to visualize it: What might it look like? He was then able to imagine and draw the pain as a pile of bricks covered with tar. What would the image say if it had a voice? Dwayne hadn't a clue. What would it *do* if it were to reorganize itself in the shape of a human body? Dwayne made an abrupt shoving gesture in response to this question. "Do it again," I told him. Once he seemed to have assumed the gesture into his own body, I renewed my invitation: "*Say* it to me this time." He stopped abruptly and began to smile, as if he were literally hiding something inside his mouth. "Go ahead," I said. Then, in sharper, clearer tones than I ever would have expected, he blurted, "Shut up!"

I did, but not for long. He had often felt like saying this to me, he admitted, sometimes because he did not want to hear what I was saying, but mostly when I told him what to do, as I had been doing throughout the course of this experiment. He *didn't like* being told what to do, he said; it made him feel tense inside, *angry* (new territory for Dwayne), sometimes even like *slugging someone*. We dropped the experiment but proceeded, in that session and future sessions, to talk at great length about the anger and resentment he felt but had never before identified to himself. And here is what is important about this example: Dwayne's physical tension and interpersonal deference might well have been interpreted as anger by an astute observer, but the *interior* of his anger was hidden to him—or, more accurately, *undeveloped*— until he managed to disembed from our therapeutic field.

Cultivating Dilemmas

As we have seen, it is characteristic of disembedding-stage adolescents that conflict and tension emerge most often at the interpersonal boundary, organized within a projective framework of experience. As the self becomes secure within its various interpersonal fields, its dimensions of interiority begin to flower. This maturation, in its concreteness, shows up in the adolescent's shift from projected conflicts to experiences of internalized dilemma. Polar tensions that first show up at the interpersonal boundary migrate toward the intrapsychic boundary, broadening the adolescent's domain of awareness and heightening the ownership and centeredness of self.

Promoting and supporting this shift is one of the most important tasks for the therapist of adolescent clients.

Dilemmas are intrinsically painful experiences precisely because they are so unmistakably lodged within the self. Whenever I find myself in this state, there is an implied possibility of *choice* (even though I cannot make up my mind) and of personal *responsibility* for making that choice (which is precisely why it makes me uncomfortable). In terms of maintaining my comfort, I would much rather be righteously and singlemindedly battling with someone else than wrestling with a dilemma.

But the experience of a dilemma carries the self beyond the comfortable integrity of monadic singlemindedness. It stretches the self, requiring it to shuttle back and forth between, and eventually hold open simultaneously, alternative ways of organizing experience. A dilemma generates what Gestalt therapists call the experience of *impasse*, a state of energized, owned ambivalence that potentially yields to growth and integration. In the lifelong process of development, the experience of dilemma is a critical—in fact, an indispensable—ingredient, carrying within its folds the seeds of ownership, choice, and empowerment of the self.

The question, then, is how to foster developmentally useful dilemmas for our adolescent clients. Most often, it requires some form of experiment designed to creatively reorganize, at least for the moment, the client's experience of himself in some situation. The general form of the intervention is to ask and support the client to experimentally own some part of a budding polarity that is being carried by the environment. Role playing, an easy way of challenging the adolescent's experience, is one possibility. If a client is telling me about a conflict with her parents, I may ask her to imagine that she is grown and has a daughter the same age as herself, and then to imagine that she has come to consult me about some concern she has about her daughter. I will take up her daughter's cause, insisting that she stay in her "parent" role and do her best to represent the parent's point of view. Or I may ask her to play her own twenty-five-year-old self and to talk with me as I play the role of her in the present. The point is simply to find a way of introducing the projected pole of the conflict into her experience and to ask her to inhabit it, however briefly. It is not necessary to push the point or ask her to change her thinking; it is sufficient that she catch a glimmer of the experience of dilemma. Another comfortable way to generate dilemma experiences in therapy is to invite, in fantasy, "polarity friends" into the discussion: "What would your brainy friend Paul have to say about this?" This device shifts the point of view in a way that most clients find nonthreatening.

Very often, adolescents orchestrate the interpersonal environment in a fashion designed *precisely* to prevent a dilemma from erupting into awareness. At just the moment when they would begin to struggle with themselves over some personally important issue, they will bait someone (usually a parent) into taking up the struggle with them. Therapeutically, it is invaluable if the adult players in the drama can be coaxed into staying off the stage and allow the adolescent the opportunity to own both ends of the polarity. This can sometimes be achieved in fantasy within the framework of individual therapy. Sixteen-year-old Jim was just beginning to experiment with smoking marijuana and made a point of raising this issue with his parents, as a matter of "philosophical difference." I sensed that he was highly ambivalent about his marijuana use, since he had several acquaintances who had put themselves into real trouble with it:

> Jim, imagine that when you woke up tomorrow morning, your parents came to you and said something like "You win. We've decided to let you smoke marijuana. Use your own best judgement." My interest is this: With your parents no longer an issue, what questions would *you* raise for *yourself*? What would *you* see as the pros and cons of pot smoking if you didn't have this ongoing debate with your parents to distract you?

It has always amazed me how receptive most adolescents are to such invitations to ambivalence, provided that the therapeutic field remains neutral and the therapist remains invested in the *process* of the dilemma, rather than its content.

In the same spirit of fantasy, I sometimes introduce "science fiction" as a shorthand way of asking my clients to try on an experience that expands their boundaries of ownership with some issue. Fifteen-year-old David provides a good example. David reported to me one day that he had a new "girlfriend," a classmate with whom he regularly left school at lunchtime and went to the nearby home of a mutual friend for a fast sexual encounter before hurrying back for afternoon classes. While describing the story in tantalizing detail, David could own only half of his potential dilemma. Talking about these escapades with his friends, he undoubtedly would have owned his lust and excitement. With me, an adult, he would own only the restraint side of the issue: "I know this is wrong; I'm just using her. I'm telling you about this because I know I have to stop it."

This was classic. David's tone was shallow, and his distress was unconvincing. He was essentially asking me, as we spoke, to collude with him in allowing only half of the dilemma into awareness. And it was precisely this dissociation, this blunting of intrapsychic contact, that needed to be challenged. David had segregated the sides of this issue intrapsychically by segregating his awareness of it into separate interpersonal fields. He would own half of it with his friends, and the other half with me, but never would the twain meet. The net effect was to keep the two sides of David, out of contact with each other.

If I had responded simply by agreeing that this was not a good way to treat someone, and that he would be better off ending the relationship, he undoubtedly would have nodded his agreement, verbalized his guilt, and gone out to do the same thing the next day. But my objective was to generate for David an *experience* of dilemma: "Okay, David: science fiction. I've got this pill here, just invented. If you take it, it will magically take away your sexual feelings for this girl. Not for anyone else, just for her. Get it? This pill is the absolute, sure-fire solution to your problem. Take it, and poof! no more lunchtime snacks." (I took a piece of candy from my pocket, smiled, and placed it on the table between us.) "It's yours for the taking."

David looked at the candy, and then at me. Blushing, he allowed a broad smile to cross his face. "Oh, I don't know. When you put it *that* way . . . " He picked up the candy, smiled again, shook his head, and put it back down on the table.

"So maybe it's not just 'it's a bad thing'—maybe it's more like 'it's a bad thing and I want to do it anyway.'"

"Yeah, that's it."

There is a critical difference between *talking about* an issue *as if it were* a dilemma and actually *feeling* the opposing pulls of the issue, which is an immediate *experience* of the dilemma. The experience is fertile ground for integration and growth; conversation is just rumination.

David chewed on this dilemma for several days. In his next session he commented, as an insignificant aside, that he had lost interest in the relationship.

Most dilemma work in adolescent therapy is not nearly as neat and tidy as it was with David. Dilemmas most often rear their heads as projections and tales of polarized conflict with the environment. They often represent major issues of self-definition and character formation, played out across the interpersonal field. They do not, as a rule, yield to single-session experiments; they require a more protracted sort of therapeutic attention and nurturance.

Fifteen-year-old Scott presented me with this sort of challenge. As a preadolescent boy, in sixth and seventh grade, Scott had desperately wanted a sense of belonging to his peer group. He had always been a bit of an oddball—closely connected to his family, uncommonly articulate and abstract, never quite fitting in. In seventh grade, as he told the story, he had taken stock of his situation and consciously decided to find a way into the mainstream in-crowd. He became particular about the way he dressed, attended to his hairstyle, was calculating in what he talked about, and so on. He tried his hand at class clowning. But in the end, he had still felt the outsider, still felt shut out by the kids with social power, and now he remembered this chapter of his growing up with unmistakable, if unacknowledged, pain.

By the time I met Scott, he had adopted the opposite tack. He dressed in black—quite creatively, I might add—and he dyed his hair jet-black, sometimes wearing lipstick to match. He grew his fingernails to a striking length and generally cultivated a persona that was as outside the mainstream as he could get. As for the mainstream itself, he despised it. He could not say enough about how disgustingly conforming and mindless the majority of his peers were, how much they sacrificed themselves to the god of *belonging,* and how glad he was not to be one of them. *They* were the ones who placed belonging above all else; *he* was the one who had learned to value his individuality and personal uniqueness above the social field.

Belonging versus individuality, merging versus differentiating— for Scott this was not a dilemma of the self but a crusade against the environment. The therapeutic project invited by his growing capacity for interiority was one of promoting and supporting his ownership of *both* ends of the issue. It was easy enough for me to presume, especially in light of his history, that he was working out his own struggle with these apparent opposites—his wanting to belong, and his wanting to preserve and develop his uniqueness. I expected that somewhere in the course of therapy Scott would recover his projected need to feel connected and would begin to feel more fully the dilemma inherent in the emergent polarity. I also expected that this recovery and its aware experience would carry him past the apparent dichotomy and toward an integration of these possibilities. I had faith from the beginning that this would happen. But how?

My own dilemma was what to do, how to nurture Scott's awareness and ownership of this polarity issue. I considered the approach of simply bringing it up, pointing it out, offering an interpretation of what this antinomy revealed about himself. But I thought better of it, on account of the precarious integrity that Scott's views maintained for him; I feared that my interpretation might be experienced as a frontal assault on his best attempt to fashion a suitable face for his adolescent world, an invalidation of his adaptive adolescent-self gestalt. I wanted instead to raise the issue more respectfully and more slowly. Therefore, I became interested in what it meant to be such an outsider and a maverick, and I invited Scott to explore both the integrity of his persona and the *sacrifices* that it entailed.

I found myself paying careful attention to Scott's expression of self in the here and now—listening carefully to how he spoke about the issue, and looking for postures and gestures that might enact his divided wants right here in the room. When I saw these things—the exaggerated disdain, the flippant "I couldn't care less" manner in which he related his tale of seventh-grade pain—I called attention to them, introducing my observations into our conversation and asking him to describe his experience more fully. But it seemed important not to push these issues beyond his manifest interest in them, lest I mistakenly heighten his awareness beyond his capacity to bear it.

My preference for nurturing a dilemma-in-waiting is to do my provocative and supportive best to get my client interested in the buried and projected portion of his own experience of self.

"Why *so* disdainful of these kids?" I asked. "How come you're *so* cool and detached from the pain of seventh grade? Don't you think it's pretty interesting and amazing how you've learned to do that?"

Cultivating the client's interest often takes weeks or months, and so I have learned to work patiently at it. Still, I wanted to do everything I could to tickle Scott's awareness—an experiment, perhaps.

But I could think of nothing, at least nothing else in the office, but express my relentless and gentle curiosity about this whole business of belonging and standing apart.

What happened with Scott is what often happens with adolescent clients when I am wrestling, frustrated, with my insufficient therapeutic creativity: he came up with his own experiment, one that was skillful in its design and courageous in its execution. One day, he produced from his pocket a hacky-sack (a small beanbag that is played with usually in groups, the object being to keep it from hitting the ground, using only the feet). He casually told me about the group of kids who played regularly on the steps behind the school. He had ventured to join on the periphery of the gathering, where he stood around and watched the others play. After several days of this, he had accepted an invitation to join the game. This was a courageous thing for him to do, treading as it did on old and painful territory. He related these events with carefully wrought offhandedness, not wanting to admit to either himself or me that he *cared* about his inclusion in this group activity, or how satisfying the experience had been. I accepted the story just as it was offered, and I wheedled from him a brief tutorial in the impossible mechanics of hacky-sack, taking care not to push his awareness of the "belonging" dilemma beyond what his sense of adequacy and integrity could support.

If there was any method to my therapeutic intervention, it was this: to stay curious about and interested in his experience of belonging and not belonging, of individuality and isolation, but keeping a vigilant eye on the tentative integrity of his adolescent-self gestalt, allowing his awareness and ownership of the dilemma to develop at a tolerable pace.

And develop it did, spontaneously and in short order. Scott began to see his peers less as caricatures of conformity and more as interesting people, themselves often anxious and struggling for acceptance. He was able to retell his seventh-grade story with more heartfelt compassion for its desperation and pain, and he became interested in "philosophical" discussions of the complex interplay of belonging and individuality. Finally, he began to confide his dilemma, the one he had been living all along but only now was beginning to own as an interior experience, a problem of personal values and parts of self.

Therapy as Anthropology: Entering the Adolescent's World

When I try to describe the attitude and spirit in which an adult can approach an adolescent and be taken into his or her world, I am reminded of the manner in which field anthropologists approach the members of a different culture. This is more than an analogy, because adolescence is in many respects a subculture unto itself, a boundary that separates those who belong from those who do not. The therapist, as a new and unfamiliar adult, is most certainly an outsider. The demeanor of the adolescent therapist is one of respect and curiosity. He or she is interested in entering, in being taken in, but holds no illusions about becoming one of the natives. The meeting of therapist and client is precisely a contact boundary, a meeting that preserves differences, and not a confluence that pretends to dissolve them. This attitude of curiosity and interest is felt and appreciated by most adolescents because it is an inherently respectful approach.

Self Symbols

We have seen that the adolescent's new sense of self is not an encapsulated, intrapsychic phenomenon. The self *projects* itself, investing aspects of its environment as extensions of itself. This is no less true for adults than for adolescents. A man identifies with his business, or his salary. A woman identifies with her professional training, or her home. Parents identify with the accomplishments of their children. Phenomenologically, these things are extensions of the self. In therapy work, particularly with adolescents, such self symbols afford an avenue for contact and rapport and are often the most direct means of encountering and cultivating the adolescent's emergent interiority. Adolescents often reveal themselves in highly invested fragments: a type of music, a best friend, a favorite author, distinctive clothing, and so on. Seemingly incidental interests—skateboarding, Dungeons and Dragons, fashion design—may lead circuitously to the core of a youth's feelings about self, strengths and weaknesses, the world, the future, and so on. The projected theme, the self symbol, is the window through which entry is gained. In many cases, it is the most direct and effective means of joining the adolescent client at the heart of his experience.

For the adolescent, self-identifying symbols—someone's ring worn around one's neck, sunglasses worn as a trademark, symbols that announce one to be a vegetarian or an anarchist or a punk—held out to the world as lightning rods for testing the interpersonal atmosphere. Clothing, for some adolescents at least, is like the psyche turned inside out: it defines and advertises what has been owned and disowned in the menu of possibilities.

One client of mine had developed an elaborate color coding to reflect his undercurrents of mood, undercurrents that were complex and deeply rooted, and which he eventually explored in his therapy. Outwardly, and long before he could articulate these emotions, he would include some carefully selected item of a particular color, worn against a backdrop of black, as a privately coded semaphore flag, simultaneously announcing and concealing some deeply felt state to the outside world. For most individuals, self symbols are more straightforward—a letter jacket, a brand or style of shoe, a way of wearing clothing (shoe laces untied, pants slung low), or a certain stylistic look (grunge, prep, punk, and so on). Self symbols are also layered. Some represent loose, changeable identifications. Others represent more deeply personal expressions of self-identification and synthesis. A common adolescent self symbol like music may have different values for different individuals. For many, it is casual entertainment, but I have also known teenagers who felt virtually lost and formless without their music, as if the music, at least for a time, could give the self both voice and shape.

Music

George was a very depressed fifteen-year-old who had become almost completely uncommunicative with his family. He had begun to wear black and had adopted a quasi-punk appearance. Drug use was suspected but, in time, ruled out.

George was an extremely bright boy and in spite of his depression, he continued to do adequately at school. He was by temperament quiet and sensitive. He was slight in appearance and aesthetic in his tastes.

George had been adopted as an infant and, as fate would have it, was adopted into a family of smiling, warm, gregarious, handshaking, back-slapping, sports-loving extroverts. Understandably, and through no fault of his own or his family's, George felt vaguely cut off, out of step, odd, and defective.

Given this core of experience of self, George was not interested in opening up to me; he was certain this could only reinforce his deep sense of insufficiency. His parents had taken him to a therapist briefly when he was younger, and the therapist had tried to teach him to be more outgoing. George was certain that he could only disappoint me and was secretly sure that I had been hired only to "fix" him—that is, make him more like the other members of his family. But he knew that was a hopeless project: he himself had been trying to accomplish it for years.

George's depression served to numb him to his deeper sense of failure, both in his family and in life generally. He had begun to create around himself, as adolescents do, a sort of theater-in-the-round. He played the depressed aesthetic, as an artist might. He dressed the part, and he regularly retreated into his music, which was dark, atonal, harsh, dissonant, and, indeed, rather depressing.

For several sessions, he and I addressed his referral and his immediate situation. He was cooperative in the initial interviews, but he was clearly neither interested nor hopeful that therapy might lead to anything of value. He felt that he was doing as well as he could on his own, and the prospect of one more adult reminding him of his difficulties did not appeal to him.

After half a dozen or so visits of exploration and admittedly superficial rapport building, I asked George if he would bring some of his music to a therapy session. I initially approached this idea with a sort of open-ended curiosity, allowing myself to become interested in learning something about the music itself, rather than psychologizing or interpreting it. I learned that George's musical world, which initially sounded to me like fairly undifferentiated noise, in fact admitted of a variegated typology. There were traditional punk, New Wave punk, thrash, and industrial music, among other subtypes. I wanted to know what distinguished this music and what distinguished the people who preferred one type over another. Eventually, I got around to asking George about himself: What did different pieces mean to him? when did he listen to what? and so on.

As is true of many adolescents, music was a lexicon for George's nuances of emotional experience. He began to talk about the various states of mind and heart that called for one particular type of music over another, or one particular track of music. He unfolded his musical interests in the way that a more revealing and verbal client might have uncovered progressively deeper layers of affective experience. Early in this mutual exploration, we did not talk about George's private thoughts and feelings. We did not even talk about how the music made him feel. These themes would have been much too transparent for his comfort. We simply talked about music—not casually, but seriously, with him as the teacher and myself as the student. But we might as well have been talking about those "deeper," more personal themes, since my efforts to genuinely and respectfully understand his music, appreciate its identity and meaning, find aspects of it that made sense to me and that I could appreciate, were what gained me entry into George's personal world.

Later on, our conversation did begin to resemble what we tend to think of as psychotherapy, and we shifted our focus from the music itself to the emotional states and experiences that the music expressed for George. Like many adolescent clients, he had offered me a self symbol and watched carefully how I handled it, testing in a safe way the potential of our budding relationship.

Indeed, music is important to many adolescents. It helps demarcate the generations. It helps identify personal tastes and preferences, contributing to early, tentatively formed trial identities. It serves for many as an uncluttered language of affective experience. Perhaps because emotions so dramatically outrun verbal expressive abilities during adolescence, music becomes for many teenagers a ready and powerful means of identifying and expressing feelings. I commonly find that clients who seem unable to access feeling states, whose capacity to describe feelings is impoverished, undeveloped, or inhibited, are able to identify the music they listen to when they are sad, angry, lonely, "psyched up," and so on.

I keep a tape and compact disc player in my office and invite clients who seem interested to bring their music in to share and instruct me. Teenagers often bring music at first that they think will shock me (if I am going to hate their music, they want to find out right away), or something that is emblematic of identity. From whatever starting point they choose, it is easy to ask about different feeling states: "What do you play when you've been fighting with your parents?" Surprisingly, youths who in words may reveal only that they are angry at such times often introduce music with much deeper and more complex dimensions of feeling: anguish, turmoil, yearning, and so forth.

As therapists, we can utilize a piece of music much as we use a drawing. In fact, asking our clients to produce lines, colors, or images that are congruent with a piece of music is an effective and straight-forward way of finding words for, and generating a sense of ownership of, unarticulated feeling states.

An adolescent's musical tastes often tell a great deal about what he or she may do to avoid feelings that seem overwhelming, and for which he or she has not yet discovered words. I have some clients who opt for loud, driving, angry music whenever *any* strong emotion is evoked, since anger may be experienced as the only safe emotion during moments of emotional vulnerability. Even this kind of desen-sitization and avoidance can sometimes be identified and coaxed into awareness more readily through music than in any other way.

Literature

Drizzt Do'Urden was a drow elf, the second son of House Do'Ur-den, or "Daermon N'a'shezbaernon," as the Ninth House of Men-zoberranzan was called in the ancient tongue of their race. Menzoberranzan was Drizzt's homeland, a cavern-city deep beneath the earth's surface in some ancient, mythic time, in the world of the Underdark. Like all drow elvan children, Drizzt was strictly indoctri-nated for the early years of his life into the diabolical ways of drowian society—ways so sinister that loyalty and goodness were despised as weaknesses, and treachery and assassination vaunted as the keys to survival and success. During this time of indoctrination and training, Drizzt was trained in the arts of combat and distinguished himself as unparalleled among his peers for his sheer skill and resourcefulness.

But Drizzt was not like other drow elves, and managed during these formative years not to give into the "chaos and vileness that rule the dark elves' hearts." This was due in part to the subtle and surreptitious mentoring of Zaknafein, the Weaponmaster who super-vised Drizzt's childhood training, and who himself had never re-nounced his true nature, his humanness (or elveness, we should say) and integrity, to the evil drow culture. And so it was Drizzt's fate to struggle against these forces, both in his homeland and in himself, and because of this to incur the collective wrath of House Do'Urden and the other ruling houses of Menzoberranzan. To save his life and his soul, he exiled himself to the netherlands of the Underdark, and in time made his escape to the surface. There, Drizzt found himself as much an outsider as ever, perhaps more so, because he couldn't speak the languages and because he was a drow, a dark elf, and dark elves were universally feared for their savagery and wickedness.

Drizzt's tale, told in *The Dark Elf Trilogy* by R. L. Salvatore (1990), is probably typical of the adventure-fantasy literature that has captivated many readers, especially adolescent readers, since J. R. R. Tolkien's (1965) publication, *The Lord of the Rings*, defined the genre some thirty years ago. It is a story in the tradition of the hero-myth, with many of the elements thereof—leaving home, the journey, being tested, discovering and transcending the father, the struggle of good and evil, establishing one's true self, and so on.

This particular story became central to my therapy work with thirteen-year-old Jack, who was enduring his own epic struggle with good and evil in the form of his emergent sexuality. Jack's older sister had graduated from college a year earlier, and, after doing a year of volunteer work, she had returned home to live with the family. She was nine years older than Jack, and they had never been close. Jack's mother called me when she discovered that he was hoarding some of his sister's clothing, mostly underwear, that she suspected he used for "sexual purposes." This coincided with a dramatic change in Jack's demeanor and behavior over a recent stretch of several months. Always a wide-eyed, energetic, optimistic boy, Jack had begun to show unmistakable signs of withdrawal and depression, retreating from the family and appearing apathetic periodically. He was in eighth grade and was, for the first time, having difficulty keeping up with his schoolwork.

Jack's mother was beside herself and requested a consultation. At my suggestion, she brought Jack along. In my experience, adolescent boys who are found engaging in some form of sexual indiscretion respond first with ironclad denial and, if confronted with certain evidence of their behavior, typically crumble under the weight of overwhelming shame. Jack's mother didn't know whether this situation was something she should be concerned about, but she wanted to be sure. They had talked about the situation at home but, in her words, had "gotten nowhere." In my office, I could see what she meant: Jack's style of conversation—and this was particularly striking when we discussed the evidence of the hoarded clothes—was remarkably deflective and superficial. He conceded most factual matters immediately and moved the conversation skillfully and almost invisibly toward peripheral and tangential topics. No, he didn't remember taking the blue dress; was that the one she wore at Christmas? And yes, he had found the clothing exciting, but that was just a phase that he had now passed.

Following this meeting with Jack and his mother, I met with him alone. I asked him how he felt the first meeting went, suspecting that it had been excruciatingly difficult for him. He looked at me quizzically and asked, "What part?" revealing only a sketchy memory for the session. What he recalled was fine, he said casually, but also very sincerely, and I began to appreciate the extent to which Jack was capable of compartmentalizing and dissociating his experiences. In spite of my best efforts to be direct, clear, supportive, and confrontive, this style of interaction characterized our early conversations. Jack's contact style was so casual and devoid of emotion that an outside observer who could not hear our conversation would have thought we were talking about the weather.

And this was how our interactions remained, until Jack introduced me to Drizzt Do'Urden, second son of Daermon N'a'shezbaernon. He had mentioned his interest in reading before, when I first asked about his hobbies, but I hadn't detected how important it was to him. Then he mentioned in passing one day that he had read this particular series of books *three or four times*, which caused me to sit up and take note. No one reads anything three or four times, certainly not a whole series of books, unless it touches deeply some resonant chord in one's interior being. And so I came to hear the tale of Drizzt's struggles and journey and, in the process, encountered a different Jack, a boy much more interested in and attentive to the depths of things—to the conflicts and dilemmas of development, the passions that move men (and elves) to reflection and action. At first, the stories provided a strictly projective focus for our conversation, a self-symbol that mediated the building of rapport and the formation of a therapeutic relational field. We focused on the story's events and characters, exploring their inner experience—Drizzt's disgust as he gradually learned, as a warrior apprentice, the true nature of the culture into which he was born, his shame as he learned of his own family's ignoble past, his deep affection for Guenhwyvar, the astral-plane panther who became his loyal companion on his journey. This was a private world that Jack was sure no adult would have time for, and his attitude toward our sessions together changed noticeably as he began to feel my acceptance and implicit confirmation.

The exploration of self-symbols, particularly in literature, often provides therapy with much more than rapport and an opportunity for confirmation. It also has the potential of providing language and metaphors for extracting the meaning of the client's own inarticulate experience. This was to happen many times in the course of my work with Jack. It became clear that he had begun to develop an interest in inner-life issues; he had just kept this interest compartmentalized and dissociated, like everything in his world, such that the richness of his developing awareness self-function remained unavailable to his reflective experience of himself.

Jack's family history, which shed considerable light on his dissociative style, only came to light late in therapy, when I relied on his mother to bring me out of the dark. Jack's family, though enlightened and open by all appearances, held (like Drizzt's family) its own dark history, much of which related to dissociated sexuality. His older sister, it turned out, had been molested by a friend of the family many years before—a divinity student who lived for a year in their home while attending the university. In her first year of college (when Jack was nine), she had become pregnant and had been sent away to have the baby. Not a word was spoken within the family of this shameful occurrence. In the best sexually repressive tradition of religious neo-Victorianism, Jack's family was a burial ground of undisclosed sexual secrets. His parents apparently communicated very little about their daughter's pregnancy, and I suspected (or at least imagined) that there were unresolved sexual incompatibilities that kept them alienated from one another.

There was also the matter of his father's possible sexual liaisons. When I finally cornered Jack's mother about the vagueness of the family background and history, she confided in me the unhappy history of their marriage and the salient inattention of her husband. I began to wonder if he might have had affairs, and I asked her whether she had ever wondered about this. She acknowledged that, yes, she had often thought about it. But she had never *said* anything about it, or really tried to investigate the possibility because there was nothing she could do about it. This was a family field where sexuality had a dank, ominous, almost haunting presence that was systematically kept away from figural awareness. It was no wonder that Jack was secretly captivated and mystified by his own budding sexuality, but was resigned to exploring it (with considerable shame and guilt) in the Underdark of his own interior world.

In the end, therapy accomplished something simple and straightforward: Jack and I talked about sex. We talked about girls, masturbation, his suspicions concerning family secrets, women's underwear, the Victoria's Secret catalog that mysteriously arrived at his house every so often, feeling excited, and so on. But in truth, conversations with thirteen-year-old boys about sex are not all that simple. Such conversations *should* occur because boys that age benefit from getting their feelings, fantasies, and questions expressed in words, in the presence of someone who is familiar and comfortable with sexuality (adolescent sexuality, in particular) to make such a conversation possible. Unfortunately, these conversations don't often take place in the lives of boys, and they certainly don't often take place in the lives of boys who are discovering their sexuality under the darkness of shame and guilt. But Jack and I had this conversation in manageable bits and pieces, over the course of about a month. He clearly felt relieved by our talks, and he "got better," pulling out of his withdrawn depression and developing age-appropriate interests in girls and dating.

None of this would have happened, I am quite convinced, without the help of Drizzt Do'Urden and his compatriots. The trail that led us to talk so frankly about what was on Jack's mind began, as well as I can reconstruct it, with my asking him about his relationship with his father. Jack didn't have much of a relationship with his father, as far as I could tell, yet whenever he spoke of his father, he tended to do so in idealized terms. Now I was pressing him a little. My hypothesis is that a boy who is haunted and confused by his sexuality often feels disconnected to the male role models in his life.

"It's good—great, in fact," Jack said of his relationship with his father.

"How would it compare to Drizzt's relationship to Zaknafein (the Weaponmaster who tutored Drizzt in the arts of elvan manhood and who, later in the story, is discovered to be Drizzt's true father)?" I asked, pushing the issue further.

This twist to my curiosity about Jack's own experience made it tougher for him to avoid (or perhaps easier to grasp) the concrete reality of his experience. Zaknafein alone among the drow adults had preserved some sense of decency and valor, and he had risked (and, in the end, sacrificed) everything to ensure that Drizzt absorbed his values. That was how Jack liked to think of his own father, but he had to admit that his dad was no Zaknafein. He was clearly troubled as he said this, becoming, perhaps for the first time, silent and reflective.

Then Jack related a portion of the story that matched his own experience—a portion incidental to Drizzt's story but central to his own. There is a point when Drizzt's older brother, a drow captain, reveals to Drizzt that Zaknafein years before had taken part in House Do'Urden's murderous overthrow of another ranking family. Drizzt, upon hearing this tale of his mentor's complicity, is crestfallen and disillusioned. Jack had never liked that part of the story, he said, and now he knew why—this was how he had slowly began to feel about his own father, a man who talked about being a good father, but who was rarely there for Jack.

This was a crushing admission for Jack to make, and this sharing of genuine perceptions and feelings marked a turning point in our work together. It initiated a new relationship with his largely word-less interior world and defined our relationship as a place where this sort of self-exploration was possible. What is central in this example is the fact that this development was mediated through his literature. The story of Drizzt had allowed me to ask questions in a way that he understood, and made the images and words he needed to grasp and articulate his experience available to him. We came back to this theme many times in the ensuing weeks, more frontally and themati-cally, as he began to look at his father less through the myth of child-hood hero and more through the medium of his own experience. The work was difficult for Jack, but grounding at the same time.

Drizzt also played an instrumental role in helping Jack learn the therapeutic *form* of reflecting on himself. It was clear that Jack iden-tified with his elvan hero, and he readily accepted my suggestion to describe Drizzt's adventures and experiences in the first person. Jack identified with the action scenes, and he could describe specific bat-tle episodes in minute visual detail from the vantage point of Drizzt himself. From this starting point, I pushed him to expand his perspec-tive: How did you feel when you saw your dearest companion (a pug-nacious dwarf) taken down by the red dragon, and you believed him dead? How did you feel when you finally met up with him after his escape, in the moment you realized he was alive? What was it like when you wandered alone for all those years on the surface, isolated because no one spoke your language, spurned and rejected by everyone you met because of your race? Did you ever cry? Didn't you ever *feel* like crying? And how did you feel when you finally met the old, blind Ranger, and the two of you communicated by speaking the Goblin tongue, after all those months of isolation? And what about all the *guilt* Drizzt carried with him throughout the three volumes of the tale—a deep and vaguely specified guilt, a sense that he was responsible for every evil he had failed to prevent? What is it, Drizzt, that you feel guilty about, *really?* This exercise was useful because Jack found it interesting and challenging rather than frightening and shameful. And though Drizzt Do'Urden was not the most emotionally complex character in literary history, Jack began to get the idea that there was another dimension to any story, a dimension of interiority, which fills out and broadens the meaning of the action.

What Jack seemed to admire most about Drizzt was his incredible sense of inner virtue and goodness—against all odds, he was able to rise above the amorality around him and stay on moral course. Jack's deepening understanding of his hero supported our shift of focus to his own internal sense of virtue and goodness. How did Jack fare by these measures, I asked out loud. He readily told me about his values and ideals, especially where they applied to competition and sports. When I shifted the focus and asked him about his values concerning sex, he accepted the invitation, telling me about how one should behave (and not behave) in this arena. Sex was for grownups, he said flatly—married couples in particular—and he recited for me a coda of sexual mores from the 1950s that he had absorbed from his family field.

In a sense, Jack was like Drizzt, I pointed out, except that he was not as able to stick to the purity of his ideals, which Jack conceded uncomfortably. His contact with himself clearly expanded from the earlier dissociation and deflection when sexual issues were raised. Then we talked about sex—about feelings, urges, fantasies, and guilt—in the manner described earlier, as genuine interest and concern that came from the heart. Jack revealed that he had been preoccupied with "weird" thoughts, curiosities, and feelings related to his older sister for a long time. He had begun by *wondering* about her. He watched her develop as an adolescent, spied on her occasionally as she dressed and undressed, and was mesmerized and awed and confused by her body and by the feelings that were stirred in him. He had imagined her "doing it" with her boyfriend and had found these fantasies both horrible and exciting. And all of this had reawakened with a vengeance when she returned home after college to live again with her family.

Our conversations were simple, but real, and their power lay in releasing Jack from his isolation, his wandering (like Drizzt in his first months in the surface world). The tale gave us—as the Goblin tongue had given Drizzt and the Ranger—a common language. And for Jack, as it had for Drizzt, language provided the turning point, the beginning of a real escape from the Underdark of his own interior world.

Artifacts of Personal Life

I am forever asking my clients to bring small pieces of their lives into the therapy hour, and the value of their doing so is immediately clear in the level of disclosure and connectedness that is yielded. I ask to see yearbooks, pictures of friends, articles about sports teams, letters, awards, inventions, and so on. One boy brought in an assemblage of electronic gadgetry that he used to "burglar alarm" his room, and he demonstrated its workings with glee. Physical, tangible sharing is generally much more evocative for adolescent clients, and much more fertile ground for meaningful exploration and discovery, than is merely verbal and symbolic sharing.

A therapist acquaintance of mine, Kay Glor, has described the following instructive piece of work. She had met half a dozen times with Louise, a difficult thirteen-year-old whose background included sexual abuse and a dysfunctional, largely alcoholic family. After finding Louise resistant to various efforts to engage her around personal and meaningful themes, Kay asked Louise to bring in two things that were personally important to her. Louise brought a photograph of herself and her best friend, and a necklace that had belonged to her grandmother.

She began by talking about her best friend, describing the things about her that she liked, their activities together, and so on. As the conversation continued, Louise confided that her best friend had been sexually abused (something that she had also acknowledged about herself but refused to talk about). Kay stayed with this theme, and together they discussed the friend's experience and how it had affected her life. Finally, Louise's focus shifted naturally onto herself, and for the first time she began to share her own experience of abuse.

Later in the same session, Louise turned her attention to her grandmother's necklace. She revealed that this grandmother, now deceased, was the only person in her family with whom she had felt known and cared about, her own parents being preoccupied with their chemical use and related problems. The necklace had been given to her by her grandmother shortly before her death, and Louise now treasured it as a reminder of this most positive part of her history.

Ideally, therapy would not be confined to an office apart from the existential reality of the adolescent's day-to-day life. Too often, however, it is so confined, but this need not prevent our clients from bringing their lives to us. There is hardly a more powerful way for this to happen than for them to bring in the artifacts of their concrete existence. Sometimes I ask a client to "bring something important," and sometimes just the opposite: "Bring something from your bedroom that you're sure has no special meaning." Sometimes I ask clients to dig through the buried ruins of childhood: "Bring something buried in a closet or a drawer, something you put away long ago." I might ask them to represent separated portions of their lives: "Bring something that your parents are quite proud of, and also bring something that only your friends would appreciate." The variations are endless and bounded only by the limits of a therapist's curiosity.

For Kay Glor, in her work with Louise, the impact of the time spent sharing these two artifacts of Louise's life was immediate and unmistakable. The sense of connectedness and, accordingly, the working relationship deepened considerably and allowed them to address the hitherto unspeakable aspects of Louise's life.

Hobbies also constitute a sort of artifact and played an important part in my work with Todd, the sixteen-year-old described earlier with an overbounded style. Todd, we recall, was less than interested in coming to see a therapist. Even when he and I had settled into a working relationship, he was not disposed to reflect on and cultivate awareness of his inner life.

But Todd kept exotic fish, and this was an enthusiasm he shared readily, especially his affinity for African cichlids. In our second or third session, Todd told me about this hobby, describing at length the mechanics of keeping an aquarium, maintaining an aquatic habitat, and mixing types of fish. He spoke of sitting for long periods staring into his fish tank; this fascination, to his mind, bested anything television had to offer. I suppose that this early discussion fell into the category of rapport building. For an hour or so, we touched on an area of his life that afforded me the opportunity to become interested in him and his world. And Todd seemed to appreciate the interest.

What often happens in adolescent therapy is that this sort of early "anthropological" exploration pays dividends later on, often by providing a context or a metaphor for mutual exploration of some lesser known part of the adolescent's interior world, some portion without language or a map. One day, several months into therapy, Todd was wondering about his future, speculating about what he could do that would sustain him in the adult world. He imagined himself becoming a wildlife biologist, building his own home and living alone in some remote corner of the American wilderness. He talked about this fantasy with relish.

"Describe the house you'd like to build," I said.

He described his delicious fantasy of a lone house nestled on a wooded hill. And inside, if he could have it just as he wanted it, he would build a fish tank that covered an entire wall. He had imagined this many times before, he told me, even working out in his mind the complexities of the tank's construction. And inside the tank would be cichlids, of course, the most incredible assortment of cichlids he could imagine. With enough of them in the tank, he said, the display of color would be breathtaking.

Only now did I glean a hint of how deeply Todd was taken with these particular fish, and so I pushed the issue.

"Why cichlids?" I asked. "There are many other types of exotic fish, many more beautiful and unusual. But you go for cichlids. Why?"

"I don't know."

"You must know."

He thought for a minute, smiled, and began to describe for me how cichlids do battle, how they are highly territorial and protect their territory from other fish, even fish much larger and more dangerous than themselves.

"They flare their gills and puff themselves up to almost twice their normal size," he said, "and they get really aggressive. I've had African cichlids devour South American oscars, which are a lot bigger and more predatory."

Todd had already described his own aggressive style of protecting himself from peers and adults who threatened him. But he had supplied that description as "information," conveyed with little emotion and in the guise of a "practical strategy" for managing people. I was struck now by how differently he spoke about his cichlids—with feeling and appreciation, *caring* what I thought, *wanting* me also to appreciate these creatures who meant so much to him. He was more open, less defended, more invested in the contact process between himself and me. And when he had finished his enthusiastic reflection on cichlid behavior, and I had asked all the questions I had to ask, we both sat in silence for a while. In those moments, I found myself looking at Todd and smiling to myself. He smiled, too, a comfortable and knowing smile.

"I think I understand you better now," I said, and he nodded, unmistakably conveying that he understood himself better, too. The power of such moments in the therapy of an adolescent client can hardly be overstated. They are moments of simultaneously being known to oneself and being discovered by another, moments of transformation in the client's field structures of relatedness, moments when the interior of experience and the contact boundary between self and other reorganize themselves in a more comprehensive and integrated fashion.

Therapy as Evocation: Inviting the Inner Self into the Room

With the publication of *Windows to Our Children* (1978), Violet Oaklander extended the power and richness of Gestalt therapy to work with younger children. There are clear differences between working with preadolescent and adolescent populations, but a great deal of what Oaklander does with younger children can be adapted to work with adolescents.

Oaklander believes that the small child's native capacity for sensory experience and physical and intellectual expression form the underlying base of the child's sense of self: "A strong sense of self makes for good contact with one's environment and people in the environment" (p. 57). Oaklander rightly equates sense of self and self-esteem with the child's contact functions—looking, talking, touching, listening, moving, smelling, tasting—and notes, diagnostically, that "children in trouble are unable to make good use of one or more of their contact functions in relating to the adults in their lives, to other children, or to their environment in general" (p. 57).

Working with art materials and encouraging the use of fantasy, Oaklander creates a therapeutic milieu where the child's limitations and potential for experiencing and expressing become accessible to the therapeutic process. For Oaklander, fantasy is the "royal road to the self." She cultivates her clients' capacity for sensory awareness by encouraging children to attend to and describe their immediate experience as they engage in expressive activity. "What did it feel like as you drew this?" she might inquire. She asks her clients to describe their productions, and then to explore and elaborate them as they do so. After having a child do a drawing, she might have the child "become the picture," describing himself in the first person or identifying with some particular part of the picture and talking with other parts. She often supports the children in elaborating on fragments, building these into rich fantasies or stories. She also invites children to bridge the gap between their fantasy work and their more reality-based experiences, asking if there are parts of their pictures or stories that they can own: "Do you ever feel that way yourself?" "Does that fit in with your life in any way?" The impact of Oaklander's style of doing therapy with children is a heightening and integrating of their sensory experience, their inner worlds of fantasy and feeling, and the solidity and acceptability of their sense of self.

Using Art Materials with Adolescent Clients

The use of art materials with adolescents works well when it flows naturally and congruently from the person of the therapist and from the interactive field of therapist and client. I know some therapists who rely almost exclusively on art therapy as a medium for working with adolescent clients, and they seem very much at home doing so. Other therapists, equally effective, are less familiar or at home with art materials, and so they do not include these in their therapy work at all. I am somewhere in between, keeping certain materials—newsprint, pencils, colored markers and crayons—at hand for use in impromptu exercises and experiments. I tend to call them into play whenever I feel that we are venturing into something important, where words seem too flimsy to carry the weight of the work.

Let me describe a session I had recently with a seventeen-year-old boy where drawing, although used in a very simple manner, served to infuse energy and feeling into what otherwise had become a deadened, defended, and too-much-talked-about theme in my client's life. Brandon was referred for an evaluation by his school and his parents because he was dropping out from mainstream adolescent life—avoiding schoolwork (although he was bright and had been a good student), and alienating himself from his parents. He was ambivalent about the consultation but readily conceded that his life was going poorly and that he had been feeling depressed. He acknowledged but minimized his marijuana smoking, even though it was strongly suspected as the root of his difficulties. In our second session, I had told Brandon what I know about marijuana's probable effects on the brain's physiological development, but I also had let him know that I was not interested in rehashing this issue and joining the conflict with the other adults in his life. In the session described here, our fourth, I offered Brandon newsprint, colored pencils, and crayons at a point in our dialogue when it occurred to me, without forethought, that art materials might put Brandon more in touch with his words.

I had begun the session by asking Brandon what he had been doing on the current Christmas vacation.

"Nothing productive," he replied, but then, after a few moments, he smiled slowly and added that he was looking forward to a New Year's eve concert featuring a rock band. After inquiring about the concert and the band, I asked him what he meant by the word *productive*. He answered that he was thinking about his college applications, something he "had to do" over vacation, and he added that he was agonizing over them, finding it nearly impossible to mobilize himself.

In these few moments of casual conversation, Brandon had sketched the major themes of his current developmental struggle. He was pulled between his wants and his "shoulds." The wants had plenty of his native energy and interest, but the "shoulds" were carried only by the pressure put on Brandon (and provoked by him) by his parents and teachers. Brandon's wants, fully owned, represented freedom and pleasure; his "shoulds," mostly disowned and projected, represented responsibility, planning, and fitting into society. This was a classic developmental struggle between the newly identified wants of adolescent experience and the imposed introjects of an earlier version of self. For Brandon, these two seemed to pose irreconcilable differences. The closest he had come to working out this conflict was to settle on a neo-hippie resolution: to finish the school year and then spend a year following the Grateful Dead as the band toured across the country.

As we talked about these two areas of his life—the upcoming New Year's concert and the "productive" activity of completing college applications—I asked him to represent each one with a single colored line on paper. He willingly undertook this task, proceeding very slowly and thoughtfully. First he drew a single heavy dark blue line across the top of the paper, to represent the "productive" dimension. Then he took a pinkish-red crayon and drew a meandering, looping line underneath; this, he said, was his playful and creative side.

I asked Brandon to supply several adjectives for each line. For the blue, he noted *bland, heavy,* and *boring.* For the red, he offered *unpredictable, fluid,* and *carefree.* I asked, "What part of all this belongs to you?" He readily accepted the red line as his. He was not so sure about the blue line, stating that it felt alien and imposed, but he added that he was not completely sure about this, conceding some ambiguity about whether the blue belonged to him or to the adults in his environment.

Next I asked him about the relationship between the two lines on the page. After a long pause, in which he seemed entranced with the drawing, he said, "The blue one takes precedence." This was an interesting conclusion, one in perfect contradiction to the message transmitted by Brandon's outward behavior. I studied the drawing myself and said that it looked to me as if the blue line were suppressing the red line underneath. "Yes," he replied.

After a few more minutes of silence, I asked Brandon to draw a third line, one that could represent the feelings produced in him by the conflict between the blue line and the red. He immediately picked up a bright red crayon and quickly drew a sharp, jagged line across the bottom of the page.

"Can you give it some adjectives?" I asked.

"Uncertainty," he said.

"How about anger?" I asked, and he immediately agreed.

We talked for a while about his confusion, frustration, and diffuse anger over how his life was going and his inability to feel completely himself either as an "establishment type" or as a neo-hippie. Again we sat for several minutes in silence, Brandon riveted on the drawing in front of him. Finally, I asked if he thought he could turn the lines into some sort of picture that would include them all. He puzzled over this for a while, and then he picked up the bright red crayon and drew more jagged lines, proliferating the anger and conflict represented on the paper. Then he sat silently once more. I noticed that he had begun to look sad, his face drawn and his shoulders slumped. I commented on this. In response, he picked up the blue crayon and, above the first heavy line, he drew another and then another. He said, "After this line, there's just going to be another, and another after that. There will always be something productive that I'm supposed to be doing, no matter how old I get."

We sat quietly now for quite a while, both of us transfixed by this simple yet remarkable rendering of Brandon's life as he experienced it. I was silently caught up in the truth of his dilemma, remembering similar struggles from my own development, but also remembering how I had managed to work them through eventually. Without saying any of this to Brandon, I picked up the blue crayon and asked if I could add to the drawing. He nodded. "I imagine a different future from the one you have just imagined for yourself," I said, and I added a series of outlining blue strokes to his playful red loops, with the blue conforming to and supporting the red design, rather than the other way around, as he had envisioned.

Brandon stared for a while, and then he smiled, with a pleased but puzzled expression on his face.

"It can work this way," I said. "Trust me on this one thing, and we can work together. You don't have to sell out to make it in the world. You hold your ground, and I'll help you figure out how to make it work."

Brandon smiled again and nodded. "Okay," he said.

The simple use of drawing changed what might have been a superficial interchange about the ups and downs of Brandon's Christmas vacation into a moving reflection on the core dilemma of his life. Colors and lines gave access to feelings of frustration and confusion that Brandon was accustomed to projecting or denying when he was operating within the familiar modality of words and ideas.

As Oaklander demonstrates so thoroughly, drawing serves to anchor and focus the therapeutic field. For adolescents especially, it removes some of the self-conscious pressure to "say something"; and, as the session with Brandon illustrates, it turns silences from awkward gaps into pregnant moments for dwelling and reflection. Brandon's few simple lines served to hold our field and keep it on target for a full fifty minutes, giving us both a comfortable and concrete focus for our time together.

By the beginning of our next session, Brandon was clearly changed, noticeably more relaxed in my presence, feeling more known and accepted by me and more in contact with his underlying emotion and with the organizing themes of his experience. Within several more sessions, we got around to the topic of his marijuana use, and he discussed it with more frankness and openess than before. He agreed to meet with a chemical dependency expert to assess more objectively whether his marijuana use was part of his problem. Our time together had helped to soften his defensiveness and support the emergence of his honest, reflective self-awareness.

Storytelling

Storytelling is generally thought of as a therapeutic method for younger children, but I have found that it can sometimes be used productively with adolescents. I discovered this initially when using the Thematic Apperception Test (TAT), a projective instrument that requires the client to elaborate a story in response to a "neutral" stimulus card depicting people in ambiguous circumstances. The TAT is not designed as an interactive instrument, but it can be used that way. One boy, Marty, a thirteen-year-old who was explosive, combative, and rather uncommunicative with his parents, told the following remarkable story to a card showing a lone figure, silhouetted against the light of an open window:

> He's been sent to his room, and he's afraid of the dark. The room is all dark, so he's standing by the window because he wants to get into the light. So what he does is, he jumps out of the window into the light. Then, when he hits the ground, he bounces off of it, right back up into the room where he started. That really surprised him. So then he tried again, and he bounced back into the room again, and he was really frustrated, and finally he tried one more time, and this time he made it, and he stayed outside in the light. ["What did he do then?" I asked.] He stayed outside as long as he could, until they made him come back in again.

I worked with Marty after the fashion in which Violet Oaklander works with children. First I asked him if he would be willing to become the boy in the story and let me do a sort of "postgame interview" with him. This appealed to the sports fan in him. I asked what it had felt like to keep jumping out the window and bouncing right back into the room.

"*Really* frustrating," he said.

"How did you know it would eventually work?" I asked.

"I didn't," he answered, "but I didn't know what else to try."

"I understand that you're afraid of the dark," I commented offhandedly.

Marty squirmed a bit: this struck closer to home than he was comfortable with, but he stayed in his role.

"Yeah, but it's no big deal."

"Must be a big deal," I suggested, "or why else would you be willing to risk life and limb jumping out of that window?" Before he could formulate an answer, I went on. "What's it *feel* like being up there in the dark?"

"It's really alone," he answered thoughtfully.

"So you know what it's like to feel really alone," I said. "How about in your real life. Do you know that feeling in your real life?"

What followed was a dialogue in which Marty described being in his family at this particular time in his life, with a clarity of description and understanding that I had not thought him capable of. He talked about feeling alone, especially when his parents "ganged up on" him. And he talked about how awful and ashamed he felt whenever he really lost it, and how helpless he felt that his anger was sometimes too big for him to control.

Predictably, his ability to control his anger began to increase, although Marty himself was at a loss to explain why. But it was not mysterious to me. Marty had discovered a way to talk about his feelings, and that is always a good bet to deepen both the interiority and the choicefulness that goes with it.

I suspect that before the storytelling, Marty had not been quite capable of talking and reflecting about his personal experience. The story, it turned out, was itself a window for Marty to jump through, allowing us to shed light together on his world and his experience in the context of the story.

Enactment

Pounding pillows and swinging bats has gone mostly out of style in psychotherapy, and adolescents, at least in one-to-one therapy, often find such florid enactments awkward and uncomfortable. But plastic-tipped darts are another matter. I have a game, or exercise, that I use with clients who are particularly out of touch with their anger. In my office I have a plastic dartboard, and the darts are the kind that make a nice, crisp thud when they hit the board (and they do not pierce walls and doors when thrown errantly). I ask my client to stand and throw the darts one at a time, letting his muscles do the work with as little cognitive calculation as possible. Then I identify and describe various situations from his life and suggest that he let his throw express the amount of frustration or anger connected to those situations. I describe a catalogue of situations: "Your younger sister takes something from your room without asking." "Your mother lectures you about your schoolwork." "Your girlfriend flirts with your best friend." "Your father refuses to believe that you really tried to get home on time." With each scenario, he lets fly a dart—no words or explanations, just the physical act of throwing.

Anger is carried much more purely in the body than it is in words and ideas, and a simple exercise like this one makes feelings of frustration and anger much more readily accessible to adolescents who tend to suppress and deny these feelings. Once expressed in this way, these feelings are undeniable. They are acknowledged and shared through their enactment, through something as simple as pitching a plastic dart with a momentary explosion of energy.

Enactments, with adolescent boys in particular, do not generally need to be planned or designed; they simply occur in the course of things. I keep a nerf basketball hoop in my office (as much for my own amusement as for my clients), and one fourteen-year-old, Phillip, did little else but play with it while in my office. I was his third "shrink," he had told me, and he made a special show of disregarding what he saw as the conventional forms of therapy. "You want to hear about my *feelings*, Doc?" he would ask sarcastically as we began a session.

Phillip was extremely bright, and he flaunted it. He was highly verbal and physically huge—more than six feet tall and about 230 pounds. He took after his family in this respect. His father in particular presented an intimidating presence.

Though he came to my office willingly enough (at least when he had nothing better to do), Phillip was not interested, so he said, in therapy. But shooting hoops was another matter. This he loved, and he readily collaborated in designing contests of one sort or another. His favorite was a game we called "shot blocking." In shot blocking, I would sit in my chair in one corner of the office while Phillip stood underneath the basket, which was mounted on the opposite wall. At some point, he would come out from underneath he basket to "guard" me, and I would launch a high arching outside shot toward the basket. It was a game of very small tolerances. He, on the one hand, could jump within six inches or so of the ceiling, leaving very little room for the ball to pass over his outstretched arms. If I waited even a moment too long before releasing my shot, he would be right in front of me in all his height and breadth, making any attempt of mine futile. I, on the other hand, have been shooting at this same hoop for many years, and am, by my own modest appraisal, a deadly shot.

We were matched pretty fairly, with Phillip blocking and my making about an equal number of shots. But it was clear that this was not satisfying for him. He began bending the rules. When I called him on it, he lobbied for changes in the rules. He wanted, he eventually conceded, to block *every* shot. He wanted to be a supreme shot blocker, as good as Shaquille O'Neal. He wanted every play to be an exercise in intimidation. He wanted to see me helplessly hurling the ball toward the hoop, and he wanted to rub my face in my helplessness. It was critical, I learned later, that we had played the game as we did, with me seated while he stood towering over me. I was the small man; he was the supreme shot blocker.

I pushed Phillip to talk about these themes in a more personal vein—about his experience at home, his fearfulness, his failed competition with his father and his feeling of being completely overwhelmed in that relationship. We had these discussions for several sessions before Phillip lost interest in therapy and began to find after-school activities that made attending sessions difficult. Summer vacation came quickly, and he faded away with the work of therapy unfinished, in my opinion. I am convinced that I lost him because I lost my nerve, my faith in enactment, in basketball as therapy. And having done so, I pushed him into the conventional therapeutic forms that he had already told me he was unable or unwilling to tolerate.

Fantasy and Role Playing

Even very self-conscious adolescents will often engage in fantasy role playing, provided that these are introduced incidentally, without too much setup or fanfare. I most often initiate them with a casual suggestion: "If your friend were here right now, sitting over there, what would you want to say to him?" I often conduct elaborate family therapy sessions with just the adolescent in the room: "Let's bring your family in. Where would your parents sit? What are their expressions? their postures? Who would speak first? How would you react when she said that?" With a little urging, most clients will enter such fantasy constructions with some degree of interest, and they will often produce feelings and reactions that would not likely emerge in straightforward dialogue with the client alone.

I often construct questions that utilize imaginary circumstances, as a way of teasing sub-figural thoughts and feelings out into awareness. I usually ask such questions when I am after something, trying to create an opportunity to focus on some particular feeling, conflict, or relationship. I often ask clients to imagine various circumstances involving their parents: illness, death, divorce, remarriage, change of heart, and so on. I particularly like to ask "miracle questions" (see DeShazer, 1988): "What if a miracle happened to your father that mysteriously made him open and uncritical for exactly ten minutes, and you had this one chance to tell him something important about yourself? What would you tell him?" "If somehow, miraculously, your parents were to resolve their differences and get remarried, how do you imagine your life would change?" Adolescents by and large enjoy hypothetical scenarios that allow them to utilize their expanding capacity for cognitive abstraction. I am continually amazed at how effectively such exercises generate real feelings and awareness.

Joint Sessions

Joint sessions, where other family members are actually included, are even more effective at bringing the adolescent client's emotional self into the therapy room. With some adolescents, it is a good idea to set up therapy from the very beginning so that every third or fourth session there will be other family members (most often parents) in the room. Apart from the more obvious and common objective of working through family dynamics, these sessions have the added benefit of eliciting the client's more authentic, feeling-filled, everyday self. Some clients are simply unable to bring this dimension of their psychic functioning into a one-to-one therapy session. These are the clients who tell us week after week, "Things are okay," or "Nothing much is happening" because they have flushed their day-to-day misery from their awareness and have neither the motivation nor the insight to reactivate it. Periodic joint sessions change this situation quickly and make these dimensions of the client's existence a shared reality for mutual curiosity and exploration.

Journals and Reports

Journals have been demonstrated to be an effective adjunct therapy tool for different age groups. Many adolescents keep journals spontaneously, as an outgrowth and expression of their deepening inner experience. I recommend journal keeping to many of my adolescent clients, and some clients ask me to read them, which I always agree to do. It is not necessary, however, for the client to bring the journal directly into the therapy relationship. For many, this feels too risky, especially early in the work. But the very act of private journal keeping affects the therapy work. It directs the adolescent to the opening world of feelings and insight and cultivates awareness of the experience of self. The writing serves to fix and hold otherwise fleeting experience, to make it more real and substantial. Clients who are keeping journals, whether or not they bring their writings to share with the therapist, bring their heightened awareness of self to the therapy hour.

A variation on journal keeping is one I have borrowed from Csikszentmihalyi and Larson (1984), who report their quasi-anthropological research on adolescence in a wonderful book called *Being Adolescent.* They equipped their subjects with electronic pagers and asked them to record their thoughts, feelings, and activities at various times during the day when they were signaled to do so. In this way, they collected random samplings of their subjects' hour-to-hour, day-to-day experience—events, feelings, thoughts, and so on. I borrowed from this method with one boy who seemed unable to recall and articulate his mundane daily experience during the therapy hour. I was trying to understand what he experienced in the late afternoons at home after school. According to his parents, he wandered about the house in a depressive funk, but he was unable to confirm or describe this when I asked him about it. His reports were classically impoverished adolescent reporting: "I don't know," "Not much," "Nothing."

I gave him my old alarm wristwatch and a hand-held tape recorder that I sometimes use for dictating letters. I set the watch for 4:15 P.M. and elicited his agreement to record whatever was on his mind when the alarm went off each day for a week. The results were dramatic. When we played the tape together at the next session, it was all right there. He was preoccupied with minor events that had occurred during the school day, particularly with several boys who mocked him and generally made his school day miserable. He was annoyed with his younger brother, whose acting out kept his mother constantly tense and angry. He would think about peers he wanted to telephone, but he never quite got the courage to do so. In short, this simple arrangement produced, in short order, a wealth of issues, dilemmas, and feelings for us to explore together.

Conclusion

It would be a mistake to assume that interior-stage work must always be a challenge, or that it always involves a supreme effort of creativity or cleverness on the part of the therapist. Because of the times we live in, increasing numbers of adolescents view psychotherapy as a viable option for working through their developmental and emotional difficulties, welcoming the mutual exploration of private experience with an interested adult. Most therapists would agree that work with a motivated, insightful adolescent can be both inspiring and enlivening. But such a client may continue to be the exception for most of us who work with adolescents.

Our work with other clients—the ones who might not have chosen therapy initially on their own, who seem like outsiders to the culture of psychotherapy, and who make this special field of work so discouraging for so many therapists—is possible, and just as inspiring and enlivening, if we are committed to meeting them on their own phenomenological turf. Therapy is the careful, heartfelt, spontaneous management of contact process with someone who requires that contact in order to further her or his development and growth. We must commit ourselves to finding the path to meet our client, the path where we can become the witness whose "benevolent, stimulating, empathic curiosity and interest" (Wheeler, 1991) bring the adolescent into contact with the self and confirm that self through its participation in the interpersonal world.

What about *integration*, the part of the work that most completely overlaps with adult psychotherapy? We encounter it regularly in the seventeen-year-old who is struggling to decide what to do after graduation, or in the thirteen-year-old who is choosing which parent to live with, or whether to have a steady boyfriend. These are the moments when, whatever the individual's status in the embedding family milieu and whatever the degree of achieved awareness of inner self, these accomplishments become the given background for a figural process of actualization, life choices, and commitment.

This, of course, is just as true for the forty-five-year-old client who is struggling to put his life (or some corner of it) into order. And it should come as no surprise to us that our adult clients must often go through the same developmental cycle as our adolescent clients do, working back through issues of disembedding and interiority. This developmental structure is *recursive*. As such, it describes *any* process of change and growth. (And our change and growth, as we all know, is never completed.)

This fact—that *all* therapy work admits to some degree of this developmental structure—points back to adolescence as a special and critical time in development, a time when the authored patterns of being in the world are laid down, and when the timeless themes of philosophical existentialism—the search for meaning, aloneness and connection, choice, responsibility and commitment—become palpable, lived realities. For the therapist whose primary focus is not adolescents but adults or children, this is why work with adolescents is so instructive and enriching: it teaches something essential about this universal process of growth. And, for therapists who have made adolescent psychotherapy our life's work, this underscores the tremendous importance of what we do. Our work is to tend to the *hinge on which adult life swings*, to shepherd the passage from childhood into the world, a passage that, in one way or another, changes our clients forever.

Therapy with adolescents, distilled to its skeletal structure, is nothing more and nothing less than the art of promoting this developmental process in individuals and families who have become stuck or derailed along the way. The constituent tasks and projects, in their concreteness, are as varied as the clients we treat, and our therapeutic repertoires are as idiosyncratic as we ourselves are. But, however differently we may engage our clients and go about the concrete business of therapy—building rapport, evoking the deeper structures of affect and meaning, and so on—there is something elemental to the work. There is an ordinariness to the relationship, the dialogue, the learning, that conceals the power of the enterprise. When we look back over our own developmental journeys through adolescence and identify what we received from the adult world that helped us get through (or what was missing that would have made a difference), we nearly always discover something simple and largely unintentional, but, by the same token, something profoundly human and reassuring. Some senior member of the tribe stopped and took us in, got *interested* in us, and thereby got us *interested in ourselves*, in ways we had not quite expected. Someone sought us out, found us wandering and alone, took us by the hand (however momentarily), and led us to the light.

References

Ackerman, N. *The Psychodynamics of Family Life*. New York: Basic Books, 1958.

Arieti, S. *Interpretation of Schizophrenia*. New York: Basic Books, 1974.

Bateson, G., Jackson, D. D., Haley, J., and Weakland, J. "Toward a Theory of Schizophrenia." *Behavioral Science*, 1956, *1*, 251–264.

Blos, P. *The Adolescent Passage*. New York: International Universities Press, 1979.

Bowen, M. *Family Therapy in Clinical Practice*. New York: Aronson, 1978.

Crocker, S. "Boundary Processes, States, and the Self." *The Gestalt Journal*, *11* (2), 1988, 81–124.

Csikszentmihalyi, M., and Larson, R. *Being Adolescent*. New York: Basic Books, 1984.

DeShazer, S. *Clues: Investigation Solutions in Brief Therapy*. New York: W.W. Norton, 1988.

Dillard, A. *Pilgrim at Tinker Creek*. New York: Harper's Magazine Press, 1974.

Erikson, E. "Identity and the Life Cycle: Selected Papers by Erik H. Erikson." *Psychological Issues*, 1959, *1*(1), entire issue.

Fishman, H. C. *Treating Troubled Adolescents: A Family Therapy Approach*. New York: Basic Books, 1988.

Fromm-Reichman, F. "Notes on the Development of Treatment of Schizophrenics by Psychoanalytic Psychotherapy." *Psychiatry*, 1948, *11*, 263–273.

Gilligan, C. *In a Different Voice: Psychological Theory and Women's Development*. Cambridge, Mass.: Harvard University Press, 1982.

Gilligan, C., Lyons, N. P., and Hanmer, T. J. (eds.). *Making Connections: The Relational Worlds of Adolescent Girls at Emma Willard School*. Cambridge, Mass.: Harvard University Press, 1990.

Giorgi, A. *Psychology as a Human Science*. New York: HarperCollins, 1970.

Glasser, W. *Reality Therapy*. New York: HarperCollins, 1965.

Gurwitsch, A. *The Field of Consciousness*. Pittsburgh, Pa.: Duquesne University Press, 1964.

Haley, J. *Uncommon Therapy: The Psychiatric Techniques of Milton H. Erickson, M.D*. New York: W.W. Norton, 1973.

Hawley, R. *Boys Will Be Men: Masculinity in Troubled Times*. Middlebury, Vt.: Paul S. Eriksson, 1993.

Jackson, D. D. "The Question of Family Homeostasis." *Psychiatric Quarterly*, 1957, *31*, 79–90.

Jones, E. *The Life and Work of Sigmund Freud*. New York: Basic Books, 1961.

Kaplan, M., and Kaplan, N. "Individual and Family Growth." *Family Process*, 1978, *17*, 195–205.

Kempler, W. *Principles of Gestalt Family Therapy*. Costa Mesa, Calif.: Kempler Institute, 1974.

Kepner, J. I. *Body Process: A Gestalt Approach to Working with the Body in Psychotherapy*. Cleveland, Ohio: Gestalt Institute of Cleveland Press, 1987.

Koffka, K. *Principles of Gestalt Psychology*. Orlando, Fla.: Harcourt Brace Jovanovich, 1935.

Kuhn, T. *The Structure of Scientific Revolutions*. Chicago: University of Chicago Press, 1970.

Lidz, T. "The Intrafamilial Environment of the Schizophrenic Patient: II. Marital Schism and Marital Skew." *American Journal of Psychiatry*, 1957, *114*, 241–248.

McLeod, L. "The Self in Gestalt Therapy." *British Gestalt Journal*, 1993, *2* (1), 25–40.

McGoldrick, M., Pearce, J. K., and Giordano, J. (eds.). *Ethnicity and Family Therapy*. New York: Guilford Press, 1982.

Mahler, M. S. "Thought About Development and Individuation." *Psychoanalytic Study of the Child*. New York: International Universities Press, 1963.

Meeks, J. *The Fragile Alliance*. Baltimore, Md.: Williams & Wilkins, 1971.

Merleau-Ponty, M. *The Phenomenology of Perception*. New York: Humanities Press, 1962.

Merleau-Ponty, M. *The Structure of Behavior*. Boston, Mass.: Beacon Press, 1963.

Millon, T. *Disorders of Personality*. New York: Wiley, 1981.

Minuchin, S. *Families and Family Therapy*. Cambridge, Mass.: Harvard University Press, 1974.

Oaklander, V. *Windows to Our Children*. Moab, Utah: Real People Press, 1978.

Papernow, P. *Becoming a Stepfamily*. Cleveland, Ohio: Gestalt Institute of Cleveland Press, 1993.

Perls, F. *Ego, Hunger and Aggression*. New York: Vintage Books, 1969.

Perls, F., Hefferline, R., and Goodman, P. *Gestalt Therapy: Excitement and Growth in the Human Personality*. New York: Dell, 1951.

Polster, E., and Polster, M. *Gestalt Therapy Integrated*. New York: Vintage Books, 1973.

Rich, S. "Daughters' Views of Their Relationships with Their Mothers." In C. Gilligan, N. P. Lyons, and T. J. Hanmer (eds.), *Making Connections: The Relational Worlds of Adolescent Girls at Emma Willard School*. Cambridge, Mass.: Harvard University Press, 1990.

Salinger, J. D. *The Catcher in the Rye*. London: Hamish Hamilton, 1951.

Salvatore, R. *Homeland*. Lake Geneva, Wis.: TSR, Inc., 1990.

Salvatore, R. *Sojourn*. Lake Geneva, Wis.: TSR, Inc., 1991.

Satir, V. *Conjoint Family Therapy*. Palo Alto, Calif.: Science and Behavior Books, 1967.

Schachtel, E. *Metamorphosis*. New York: Basic Books, 1959.

Singer, M. T. and Wynne, L. C. "Thought Disorder and Family Relations of Schizophrenics, III." *Archives of General Psychiatry*, 1965, *12*, 205–220.

Stierlin, H. *Separating Adolescents and Parents*. New York: Aronson, 1981.

Straus, E. *The Primary World of Senses*. New York: Free Press, 1963.

Sullivan, H. S. *The Interpersonal Theory of Psychiatry*. New York: W.W. Norton, 1953.

Tolkein, J.R.R. *The Fellowship of the Ring*. New York: Ballantine Books, 1965.

van den Berg, J. H. *A Different Existence*. Pittsburgh, Pa.: Duquesne University Press, 1972.

Wertheimer, M. "Principles of Perceptual Organization." In D. C. Beardslee and M. Wertheimer (eds.), *Readings in Perception*. New York: Van Nostrand Reinhold, 1958.

Wheeler, G. *Gestalt Reconsidered: A New Approach to Contact and Resistance*. New York: Gardner Press, 1991.

Wheeler, G. "Compulsion and Curiosity: A Gestalt Approach to O.C.D." *British Gestalt Journal*, 1994, 3(1), 15–21.

Whorf, B. L. *Language, Thought and Reality*. Cambridge, Mass.: MIT Press, 1956.

Wynne, L., Rycoff, I. M., Day, J., and Hirsch, S. I. "Pseudo-Mutuality in the Family Relations of Schizophrenics." *Psychiatry*, 1958, *21*, 205–220.

Wynne, L., and Singer, M. "Thought Disorder and Family Relations of Schizophrenics, I. A Research Strategy. II. A Classification of Forms of Thinking." *Archives of General Psychiatry*, 1963, 9, 191–206.

Yontef, G. *Awareness, Dialog and Process: Essays on Gestalt Therapy*. Highland, New York: Gestalt Journal Press, 1993.

Zinker, J. *Creative Process in Gestalt Therapy*. New York: Vintage Books, 1977.

Zinker, J., and Nevis, S. "The Gestalt Theory of Couple and Family Interaction." Working paper, Center for the Study of Intimate Systems, Gestalt Institute of Cleveland, 1981.

Index